The Folklore of the British Isles
General Editor: Venetia J. Newall

The Folklore of Hertfordshire

*For Budge
and
Robert Edward St Clair*

Other books in the series:

General Editor: Venetia Newall

Jacqueline Simpson *The Folklore of Sussex* (1973)
Enid Porter *The Folklore of East Anglia* (1974)
Sean O'Sullivan *The Folklore of Ireland* (1974)
Katharine Briggs *The Folklore of the Cotswolds* (1974)
Ernest Marwick *The Folklore of Orkney and Shetland* (1975)
Tony Deane & Tony Shaw *The Folklore of Cornwall* (1975)
Margaret Killip *The Folklore of the Isle of Man* (1975)
Ralph Whitlock *The Folklore of Wiltshire* (1976)
Wendy Boase *The Folklore of Hampshire & the Isle of Wight* (1976)
Ray Palmer *The Folklore of Warwickshire* (1976)
Kingsley Palmer *The Folklore of Somerset* (1976)
Anne Ross *The Folklore of the Highlands* (1976)
Jacqueline Simpson *The Folklore of the Welsh Border* (1976)
Marjorie Rowling *The Folklore of the Lake District* (1976)

The Folklore of Hertfordshire

DORIS JONES-BAKER

St Alban and the Miraculous Spring, graffito, St Albans Abbey

B. T. BATSFORD LTD
LONDON

First published 1977

© Doris Jones-Baker 1977

ISBN 0 7134 3266 7

Printed and made in Great Britain by
Billing & Sons Limited
London, Guildford and Worcester
for the Publishers
B. T. Batsford Ltd, 4 Fitzhardinge Street
London W1H 0AH

Contents

Map of Hertfordshire	6
Foreword by Venetia Newall	8
Introduction	13
1 Churches and Bells	21
2 Treasures and Tunnels	31
3 Giants and Bogeymen	46
4 Dragons and Monsters	54
5 From the Cradle to the Grave	62
6 Graves and Ghosts	77
7 Cures, Charms and Healers	91
8 The Devil	104
9 Witches and Wizards	110
10 The Turning Year	119
11 Local Humour	180
Notes	197
Museums	228
Select Bibliography	229
Index of Tale Types	232
Motif Index	232
General Index	236

HERTFORDSHIRE

Foreword

Modern times have subsequently seen a reversal of the trend, but there was in the nineteenth century a strong reaction against an earlier tendency to idealise the Noble Savage. A product of the dilettante's wishful thinking rather than actual reality, the direct interest of this figure to the folklorist is marginal – a different matter, of course, from the notions inspiring its invention. The same is true of the converse. Napoleon, for instance, declared his disillusion with Rousseau's ideas: having seen the terrible poverty in Egypt during his campaign there, he was moved to comment *'l'homme sauvage est un chien'*. Thomas Malthus, whose father was a friend of Rousseau's, took a more balanced view. He considered that deprived societies produce the behaviour patterns best suited to their practical requirements, and in this way a basis for interplay between custom and daily necessity is evolved. This was a shrewd observation, which need not be limited to the customary behaviour of underprivileged peoples.

During Malthus' last two years at the East India College in

Hertfordshire, Bartle Frere was among the students, and it was his daughter, Mary Frere, who became the doyenne of Anglo-Indian folklore writers. Her *Old Deccan Days* (1868), prepared during travels with her distinguished father, who wrote the foreword, led up to a new pattern of thinking which culminated thirty-two years later in Hartland's presidential address to the Folk-Lore Society: 'No ruler who does not understand his subjects can govern them for the best advantage, either theirs or his.... With the new century let us turn over a new leaf in the history of our dealings with savage and half-civilised nations....' Professor Dorson neatly categorises these views as the 'empire theory' of applied folklore.

It was at this time that Hatfield House became the venue for 'great official garden parties' given by the Marquess of Salisbury, 'with their strange congeries of Eastern statesmen, Indian chiefs and Negro kings ...'. This was how *The Times* described in 1903 a scene surprisingly cosmopolitan and exotic for rural Hertfordshire. But even in Malthus' day the College at Haileybury had a sprinkling of eastern teachers; six Indian languages, as well as Arabic and Persian, were part of the syllabus. Harriet Martineau, who visited Malthus there in 1833, mentions 'the curious politeness of the Persian professor'.

She leaves an attractive, nostalgic picture of Haileybury in the year before Malthus' death. What delighted her was 'the well-planted county of Herts. Almost daily we went forth when work was done – a pleasant riding party of five or six, and explored all the green lanes, and enjoyed all the fine views in the neighbourhood. The families of the professors made up a very pleasant society – to say nothing of the interest of seeing in the students the future administrators of India. The subdued jests and external homage and occasional insurrections of the young men; the archery of the young ladies; ... the fine learning and eager scholarship of the Principal Le Bas, and the somewhat old fashioned courtesies of the summer evening parties are all over now.'

Malthus was Professor of Political Economy at Haileybury during the major part of his working life, the first man in Britain to occupy a chair in the discipline. Here he elaborated many of his economic theories, and also carried on the exchange with David Ricardo, which Keynes described as 'the most important literary correspondence in the whole development of political economy'. A saying derived from Tusser and popular in Hertfordshire states that 'God never sends mouths but he sends meat', a belief entirely at odds with the views of Malthus. In fact his arguments, superficially at least, still help to explain the troubles of non-industrial nations, just as Marx's later diagnosis, removed from its intended context, has an identical application.

Marx and Engels both felt a deep hostility towards clergymen, and Malthus, an ordained priest, was unkindly dismissed by Marx as a 'reverend scribbler'. He would have liked the phrase coined by William Cowper, an earlier Hertfordshire writer, when he describes a priest as 'a piece of mere church furniture at best'. The anti-clericalism of the two old socialists was, in part at least, a facet of their selective anti-intellectualism. A by-product of this widespread attitude is often a nonsensical interpretation of folk culture, regarding folklore in its various aspects as in some special way natural, and thus superior to so-called intellectual culture. This outlook remained particularly fashionable in Germany until the end of the Third Reich. It is peculiar to find Engels, in his diatribe against Dühring, a nineteenth-century forerunner of National Socialism, apparently assenting to his criticism of Malthus and the 'defects peculiar to his parsonical views'. Elsewhere he refers to Dühring as 'the Richard Wagner of philosophy, but without Wagner's talents'.

Bonar, Malthus' biographer, quotes Marx's critique at some length, but unfortunately stops short at a section which he considered 'neither decent nor true'. This is a pity, since the missing passage has Marx, or Old Nick, as he liked to be called, quaintly interpreting Genesis 3.17-24 in economic terms: 'It is characteristic that the economic fall of man, the Adam's apple, the urgent appetite, "the checks which tend to blunt the shafts of Cupid" ... that this delicate question was and is monopolised by the Reverends of Protestant Theology....' Wagner, a contemporary of Marx, saw the expulsion from Eden as punishment for Adam's vegetarian tastes.

It was Wagner's great operas which for the first time sought deliberately to implant a political ideology by manipulating folklore and traditional belief, coupling this with a specially orientated musical language. Perhaps this dates from early in his life when, for example, he saw enshrined in the first eight notes of *Rule Britannia* the whole character of the British nation. His own political ideas were not far removed from those of Dühring, while his operatic stock-in-trade consisted of a brilliant misuse of legend, coupled with his own musical genius and curious linguistic theories. Nineteen years after his death, Ludwig Woltmann, inspired by similar racialist and anti-urban opinions, established the *Politisch-Anthropologische Revue* and brought scientific anthropology into the service of political decadence.

The history of our own discipline in this country during the same period should not permit us to feel complacent. Hartland's desire to harness folklore in the service of colonialism was endorsed by Brabrook, his successor as President of the Folk-Lore Society, and a memorandum on the subject was even sent to the Colonial Secretary. If Wagner felt that his ideals could be furthered by an appeal to certain innate cultural instincts, the motives of contemporary British folklorists were not much different. While advocating more sympathetic government of dependent peoples, they saw in their method little beyond tradition in the service of efficiency, and hence a new and effective prop in the imperial structure. Cecil Rhodes was even more directly Wagnerian in outlook. A Hertfordshire man, he had made a will some two decades earlier, leaving his fortune – at that point in time still to be made – specifically to extend the bounds of Empire, regain the United States and generally consolidate British imperialism. Just as Wagner held that the Aryans, the Teutonic master beings, had sprung from the ancient gods themselves, so Rhodes believed that the Anglo-Saxon race was the summit of human genius. This resulted from a divine plan, of which he himself was to be an agent.

Shaw, who made Hertfordshire his home during the second half of his life, thought Wagnerianism progressive. In an article about Oscar Wilde, whom he referred to as 'an old-fashioned Irish gentleman', he said: 'it is difficult to believe that the author of *An Ideal Husband* was a contemporary of Ibsen, Strindberg, Wagner, Tolstoi or myself.' He argued cogently that *The Ring* expresses socialist principles, failing to recognise the decadence of Wagnerian socialism. Where, in Wagner, are the humanitarianism and benevolence which provide socialism's overriding justification?

Of course, Shaw himself seldom allowed sentiment to be any part of his public image. Here he is replying to the suggestion that he might like to be buried in his native land: 'I know too much about earth burial to contemplate such a horror. It should be made a 'criminal offence.' And of his adopted homeland: 'I can hardly grudge it the handful of clean, harmless cinders which will be all that will remain....' For Shaw, this last remark seems almost emotional, a mood inspired, maybe, by the charm of his Hertfordshire home, where he was being interviewed at the time.

Like Shaw and Malthus, Doris Jones-Baker did not originate in Hertfordshire, but she has made the county her home for the last fifteen years. Her distinguished professional and academic background made her a welcome newcomer to the intellectual life of her adopted county. She was soon appointed editor of the local parish magazine, and this work inspired a continuing interest in local history and folklore. *Old Hertfordshire Calendar,* published two years ago, is her first book on the county – a wealth of information from oral or unobtainable sources, to which she brings an attractive literary style, combined with scrupulous erudition.

Her love of Hertfordshire has been sharpened by early family ties. A favourite ancestor, Nathaniel Ward, was Rector of Walkern, when he saw *The Simple Cobler of Aggawam* through the press, the book which brought him lasting fame. This was some 130 years before the American Revolution, and just after his return from Massachusetts, where Doris Jones-Baker herself was educated. Sir Richard Saltonstall, another forebear, who was contemporary with Ward, owned property in Hertfordshire, and his portrait was painted by Rembrandt, a fitting ancestor for so distinguished an author.

London University
June 1976

Venetia Newall

Matthew Paris (d.1259) historian of St Albans Abbey, an early collector of Hertfordshire folklore, self-portrait from his Chronica Majora

Introduction

> Some will wonder how this Shire, lying so near London, the staple of English civility, should be guilty of so much rusticalness. But the finest Cloth must have a list, and the pure peasants are of as coarse a thread in this County as in any other place. . . .
>
> Thomas Fuller, *The Worthies of England,* 1662

THE WONDER is in the truth of this today, more than three centuries after Thomas Fuller, who was for some years curate at Waltham Abbey across the River Lea in Essex, wrote, and that Hertfordshire, one of the smallest English counties scarcely one day's journey on foot or a short ride from London and separated from it only by Middlesex, evolved and preserved its own customs and traditions. In large part this has been due to the long continuance of Hertfordshire as a place of agriculture and rural if not primeval landscape broken only by villages and market towns, which remained its character essentially until the latter half of the twentieth century. If the export trade to London in hay, grain, and provisions well profited Hertfordshire farmers, the convenience of Hertfordshire for the country estates of successful City men of business was a powerful factor in the exclusion of industry until very recent years.

If much of Hertfordshire's wealth has derived from London, its historic and cultural ties have been strongest with its neighbours to the east and north, Essex and East Anglia (with the exception to some degree of the westward 'finger' of the County and the Chiltern parishes which centre upon the ancient market town of Tring). The Chiltern Hills formed a barrier and a boundary to the west as did in early times the large tracts of waste and woodlands by Middlesex. The origin and shape of folk custom and traditions owes much to the fact that at Domesday and well into Medieval times the centre of population was in the north and east – adjacent to the influences of peoples living in Essex and Cambridge and the reverse of what it is today. Here are now (possibly excepting Chiltern parishes) the most rural parts of Hertfordshire, the villages with the longest social continuity, and dotted through the farmlands and woods most of Hertfordshire's deserted Medieval villages, ruined churches, 'lost' castles, and moated farms – whose remains have kept alive so much of County folk memory and bred folk legends and tales without number.

Political ties to the east and north in the formative times of local custom and tradition are still apparent in Hertfordshire folklore, particularly in its stories of ghosts, giants, and dragons. Under the Saxon Heptarchy Hertfordshire was divided between the Kingdoms of Mercia and Essex along the ancient trackway of Ermine Street (which runs from Waltham north and west to Ware, Wadesmill, Braughing and Buntingford to Royston and the Cambridge border). Before the Norman Conquest Hertfordshire north of the River Lea was, like its neighbours Essex and Cambridge, within the Danelaw. Hertfordshire itself was not mentioned by name until the eleventh century, and under the Normans was administered with Essex – reflecting to a degree the contiguity of population – which continued until the sixteenth century when, under Elizabeth, the first Sheriff of Hertfordshire was appointed, Sir John Brockett of Hatfield in 1566. Less than a century later Hertfordshire became the western outpost of the First Eastern Association (with Essex, Cambridgeshire, Norfolk and Suffolk) formed in the winter of 1642-3.

In the migration of its folklore beyond the significant purview of London – as carried 'up' by its people on business or settlement or by the groups of Morris Men and others who took holidays there and paid their way by giving street performances – as taken overseas and to the colonies – Hertfordshire largely followed the pattern of its Essex and Cambridge neighbours, during the time of the 'Great Migration' to New England of 1630-1640, and later. Hertfordshire folklore thus transported was kept in mind – as other relics of identity are so often far from their origins – and made its contribution to colonial cultures – a subject beyond the scope of this book; but collected in Canada, Australia, New Zealand, as well as the United States and other places and, brought back to Hertfordshire, this 'travelled folklore' has added much to knowledge of ancient ways here forgotten.

In the last quarter of the twentieth century one may fairly say that Hertfordshire folklore, like its native dialect, has survived among its people however much below the surface and shrunken in number. It has even resisted the Cockney invasion so apparent in the far south, in suburbanized parishes threaded to London by commuter railways and motorways such as Harpenden, and the London 'overspill' in the New Towns of Stevenage, Letchworth, Hatfield and Welwyn Garden City. There is evidence, moreover, that the newcomers and civic and other groups in the New Towns have valued their local heritage and done much to make known and to promote interest in the old customs and traditions.

The stronghold of living folklore, however, remains in the rural areas predominating in the east and north, and the 'remote' parishes along the western curve of the Chiltern Hills. While this book includes much oral material collected in many parts of the County over the past fifteen years, it draws as well upon manuscript and printed sources, the oldest of which belong to Saxon times.

If in Hertfordshire the collection of folklore as such did not begin until the twentieth century, a long succession of writers with a taste for antiquities and a wish, as Tom Fuller said, 'to entertain the reader with delight' included 'folk' material in their works of local history and topography. Perhaps the earliest written reference to folklore in Hertfordshire appears in the Anglo-Saxon Chronicle where it mentions the miraculous cure of Uther Pendragon at the St Albans well. The first collectors of tales in Hertfordshire, however, were the chroniclers in the scriptorium of the great Benedictine Abbey at St Albans. Most eminent of these was Matthew Paris (d.1259) who included local legends and tales apart from those of the Hertfordshire saints Alban and Amphibalus – such as the Dragon of Wormenhert – in the *Gesta Abbatum Monasterii Sancti Albani*, which relates the history of the Abbey under its first 23 abbots.

John Norden's *Survey of Hertfordshire,* published by order of Queen Elizabeth in 1598, and John Weever's *Ancient Funerall Monuments* of 1621 include folk material, the latter the first known version of the legend of Piers Shonks, the giant of Brent Pelham. The earliest parish and town histories – like many later ones – are useful folk sources. The manuscript 'History' by Francis Taverner (d.1657) of his manor of Hexton (British Museum ADD. MSS. 6223) has the earliest description of Hock-tide celebrations in the County, while John Shrimpton's (d.1636) 'Antiquities of Verulam and St Albans' (MSS. copy at H.C.R.O.) includes traditions in this first history of a Hertfordshire town.

Of the four great County histories, the first, published in 1700, *The Historical Antiquities of Hertfordshire*, so admirable for its lively style as for its scholarship, is a disappointment to the folklorist, giving little beyond the dates of fairs and civic festivals. Its author, Sir Henry Chauncy (1632-1719), Recorder of Hertford, of a family long seated at Ardeley Bury, was a great-nephew of the Rev. Charles Chauncy (1592-1671), Vicar of Ware in Hertfordshire and later second President of Harvard College. Sir Henry, however, pointed to a great problem shared by historian and folklorist when, commenting upon the fabulous *Travels* (1366) of Sir John de Mandeville of St Albans, he wrote:

> ... The variety of Wonders caused some Suspition of the Truth of his Relations; but all things that seem improbable are not impossible, and the Ignorance of the Reader does oftentimes weaken the Truth of the Author....

Folklorists in Hertfordshire, however, will be forever in the debt of the second County historian, the Rev. Nathaniel Salmon, for some years curate at Westmill, whose comparatively short *History of*

Hertfordshire appeared in 1729. Salmon is the first historian in Hertfordshire (and one of the first in England) to use oral tradition and legend as source material and as an integral part of what we now call social history. Salmon's work has many descriptions of folk customs and accounts of ancient legends whose origin may never be found, often, in modern fashion, describing the old farmer or village character who gave him the information. Hertfordshire scholarship was not to see his like again – alas – for a century and a half. His successor as County historian Robert Clutterbuck, whose three volume *History of Hertfordshire* appeared between 1815 and 1827, condemned Salmon, moreover, for 'the frequent digressions of its author into matter foreign from the subject of a Provincial History ...'.

Another important early source of Hertfordshire folklore is the work of another eighteenth-century writer who, like Salmon, was branded as frivolous for his untoward digressions: William Ellis, of Church Farm, Little Gaddesden, author of *The Practical Farmer, or the Hertfordshire Husbandman*, first published in 1732, and a number of other books on the new 'scientific agriculture'. Ellis could never resist a good folk tale or country cure, and he recorded folklore which now can be found nowhere else.

Salmon's 'successor' was John Cussans, last of the County historians, whose *History of Hertfordshire* appeared between 1870 and 1881. Cussans collected traditions and old customs as part of his searches for historic material, driving himself through the ever-winding Hertfordshire lanes in a pony cart and interviewing all and sundry. More than this, he made bold to tell his readers: 'Local traditions and unpolished verses, when coming from local lips, should never be despised. They frequently contain germs of interesting matter. I am not ashamed to confess that I have picked up many valuable suggestions in the taprooms of village alehouses ...'. Cussans' post-publication notes and manuscripts mounted in the grangerized copy of his *History* at the H.C.R.O. form one of the best collections ever made of Hertfordshire folklore.

The great mystery relating to the sources of Hertfordshire folklore is the extent to which such material was collected in the County and used by the noted antiquarian and engraver Joseph Strutt in his *Sports and Pastimes of the People of England* (1801) and later in his medieval romance *Queen Hoo Hall* designed to illustrate medieval customs. For several years in the 1790s Strutt and his apprentices boarded with a Hertfordshire farmer, John Carrington of Bacon's Farm, Bramfield, and the name *Queen Hoo Hall* was taken from a small Tudor mansion house (still standing) nearby. Strutt died before *Queen Hoo Hall* was finished, and the last chapter was written by Sir Walter Scott who saw it through the press in 1808. Scott himself must be numbered among the collectors of Hertfordshire folklore, stopping off on his way to and from London, as was his habit, to visit places of antiquarian interest. The story of the haunted castle of the so-called 'wicked' de Mandeville Earls of Hertfordshire and Essex at South Mymms that appears in *The Fortunes of Nigel* is but one of a number of instances where Scott made use of Hertfordshire folk material.

Some of the earliest published articles on Hertfordshire folk customs were contributed – mostly anonymously – to William Hone's *Every-Day Books* of 1826 and 1827, *Table Book*, and *Year Book* (1832). Notable among these were descriptions of May-Day customs at Hitchin and Baldock, a drawing by Sears of chimney-sweeps dancing on May-Day by Hitchin Church, and the earliest known printed version of the Hitchin Mayers' Song.

Although the Folk-Lore Society was founded in 1878, it was not until the 1890s that much material on Hertfordshire folklore came to be published. Outstanding among the early articles were two that appeared in 1894 in the short-lived *Hertfordshire Illustrated Review* (1894-5): Edith Rinder's 'Twilight in Hertfordshire. Some Gleanings of Folk-Lore', the first attempt recorded to introduce this seemingly 'new' subject to anything like a 'popular' reader in this County, including a variety of local traditions, rhymes and fables, and Ellen Pollard's article 'Some Points of Interest in and Around Hitchin', which gives the legend of the Devil and the building of Pirton church. Later, as Lady Robertson Nicoll, she published *Bells of Memory* (1934), a source book of Hertfordshire in the late nineteenth century. Another early article of great importance was 'Folk-Lore in Essex and Herts', by U. B. Chisenhale-Marsh, which appeared in *The Essex Review* in 1896, the first survey of folklore on both sides of the boundary Stort and Lea Rivers.

Folk material as well as local history appeared in *Middlesex and Hertfordshire Notes and Queries*, published in four volumes between 1895 and 1898, edited by the archivist William Page. Both the St Albans and East Hertfordshire Archaeological Societies sponsored monthly columns of *Notes and Queries*, again including references to folk material in the *Hertfordshire Advertiser* (1909-11) and *Hertfordshire Mercury* in the dozen years before the outbreak of the First World War. The series of *Transactions* of the East Hertfordshire and St Albans Societies have also printed folk material, notably also in the volumes which appeared before the First World War.

The volume *Highways and Byways in Hertfordshire*, which appeared in 1902, is one of the most valuable in this excellent series of topographical books for its collection of folklore which was made at first hand by the author, Herbert Tompkins, who spent much of his boyhood in Whitwell where his father was a Nonconformist Minister. The illustrator, Frederick Griggs, was a Hitchin baker's son.

Significant contributions to the recording of Hertfordshire folklore after the First World War were made by Lady Mary Carbery – daughter of J. H. Toulmin of Childwickbury and a Treasurer of the St Albans Society – in her memoirs, *Happy World* (1941), and as joint author with Edwin Grey of *Hertfordshire Heritage* (1948), a vocabulary of Hertfordshire dialect which contains a wealth of folk material. Edwin Grey's own *Cottage Life in a Hertfordshire Village* (1935) gives a unique account of folk customs and beliefs in the neighbourhood of Harpenden in the 1860s and 1870s.

In more recent years the county magazine *Hertfordshire Countryside*, which began as a quarterly in 1948, has printed a number of authoritative articles on Hertfordshire folklore, and for the period of its publication is an irreplaceable record of all manner of folk beliefs still current as well as remembered, particularly its column of letters to the editor. Doris Jones-Baker's *Old Hertfordshire Calendar* (1974) was the first general survey of Calendar customs to be made for the County.

Of the manuscript collections drawn upon for this book notable are those of R. T. Andrews at Hertford Museum, which relates particularly to East Hertfordshire, the manuscripts of John Cussans at H.C.R.O. mentioned above, and most extensive of all, the collections of William Blyth Gerish at the H.C.R.O. and the St Albans library. Although Gerish wrote a series of pamphlets on Hertfordshire folklore: 'A Hertfordshire St George', 'The Wicked Lady Ferrers' and more than a dozen others, as well as the longer 'Tour through Hertfordshire recording its Legends, Traditions and Ghostly Tales' printed at Bishop's Stortford in 1914, his reputation as an Hertfordshire folklorist rests today upon his monumental work as a folklore collector, and editor of the two series of *Notes and Queries*, which appeared in the *Hertfordshire Mercury* and the *Watford Observer*.

It is the object of this book not to be a comprehensive study but to survey and introduce the major aspects of folklore both living and historic in Hertfordshire. Included therefore are a variety of local legends, traditional beliefs and magical practices, major events in the cycle of life and the folklore of calendar customs, giants and dragons, devils and witches, and most Hertfordshire of things, humour and hoaxes. Because in Hertfordshire music was an integral expression as well as a vehicle for so many of the Calendar Customs, tunes have been given for two of the folk carols (Christmas and May-tide) and two of the seasonal begging chants (Valentine's Day and the Boxing Day Wassail). The many variants of Hertfordshire folk songs would make a book in themselves.

Finally, as the writer, I would like to suggest that this book, if it becomes a stepping-stone to interest in the folklore of Hertfordshire and to works that follow after it, will have fulfilled its hope. I would be most grateful, moreover, to hear from any who would add folk tales, traditions and customs – or new versions of them – to those which appear, or offer additions or corrections.

I wish to express my thanks to the many people who in past years so kindly shared with me their knowledge of Hertfordshire folklore, and especially to the Hertfordshire County Archivist Peter Walne, to Mrs Shelagh Head, County Local History Librarian, to Sheila Richards of Tring, and to Venetia Newall for her help and encouragement.

St Paul's Walden Parish, 1976   Doris Jones-Baker

Tewin Church and Lady Anne Grimston's Tomb, 1976

1   Churches and Bells

ACCORDING TO TRADITION churches and religious houses in Hertfordshire were built at places sanctified by Christian miracles – or, in the case of most parish churches whose origin is touched upon by local tale or history, where the old gods, popularly referred to as the Devil, not being powerful enough to repel the Christian forces altogether, decreed they should be built.

The great Benedictine Abbey of St Albans stands today on the hilltop overlooking the River Ver where the English martyr met his death early in the fourth century. Alban, according to the Venerable Bede (673-735), was born in Verulam in the third century, and for some time served abroad as a Roman soldier. After returning to Verulam in the year 303 Alban gave shelter to a Christian priest, Amphibalus, who was hiding from the authorities and their persecution of Christians being carried out by order of the Emperor Diocletian. Amphibalus converted Alban to Christianity, and when soldiers came to search for the priest Alban sent him secretly away and disguised himself in his clothes. Alban was taken into custody, and refused an order to worship Roman deities. For these things he was condemned as a Christian, tortured, and led to the hill of his execution by way of the ford at St Michael's.

Here began the miracles of Alban's Martyrdom: the waters of the River Ver parted at his command so that Alban and the multitude that had come to witness his execution crossed on dry land; a spring gushed forth from the ground at the top of the hill when Alban prayed for water to quench his thirst; and the executioner was stricken blind on the spot. 'Thereafter', wrote Bede,

> 'Nigh unto the city called Verulamium (which is now of the English called Verlamcaester) where after the settled calm of Christian times returned, there was a church builded of a marvelous rich work and worthy of such a martyrdom, in the which truly even unto this day are sick persons cured and doing of manifold mighty works ceaseth not to be openly wrought.'

Nothing remains of the church and hospice of St Mary de Pré, founded as a refuge for leprous women by Warren de Cambridge, twentieth Abbot of St Albans, at the place of the martyrdom of Alban's teacher, Amphibalus, near Redbourn. According to the legend set down by the Abbey chroniclers, Amphibalus was captured by the Romans in Wales, and about 800 years after he had been put to death at Redbourn appeared in a dream to a man of Walden. Announcing that the place where his bones rested was sacred, Amphibalus said that the man was chosen to tell the Abbot that it should be venerated. The Abbot heard the man of Walden's story, and learned afterward that St Alban himself had appeared in a vision to another layman, and revealed the spot where the bones of St Amphibalus lay. The relics, he said, had been taken from thence to St Albans, and many were the signs and wonders of their removal. The shrine of St Alban had been carried out to escort the remains of Amphibalus, and had become miraculously light to aid the monks in their journey, while a great drought which had blighted the district came suddenly to an end with a great shower of rain, which fell upon the golden hoods and rich feather-work of the monks without wetting them.

The founding legends of parish churches which have survived, however, show the odds in the struggle of Christianity to establish itself over the older pagan beliefs more evenly balanced.

It is said that the church of All Saints at St Paul's Walden, where the Queen Mother – who was born in this parish – was baptized by the Vicar, the Rev. Henry Tristram Valentine, should have been built near the manor house – these are called Burys in Hertfordshire – in a field still known as Dove House Close. The old road to the market town of Hitchin ran through this field, and in ancient days there may have been a hamlet here built near the fortified Bury for protection against marauders. According to the legend the people of Walden began to build their church – only to have the stones and other materials transported by magic in the night through the air across a little valley and up the hill about half a mile away.

At St Paul's Walden it is no longer remembered which supernatural agency moved the stones of the church. The people of Kensworth on the Bedfordshire border have a similar legend about the mysterious removal of the parish church from Kensworth Common about a mile away to the present site near Bury Hill.

A more elaborate version of this legend has survived at Stanstead Abbots, on the River Lea. Here it was proposed to build the ancient church of St James in the town – a borough of some importance with seven burgesses at the time of the Domesday Survey – instead of where it now is, above a mile away. Each night, however, saw all the labour of the day undone. The building materials were miraculously carried up the hill above the town and re-erected on a place belonging to the Abbey of Waltham, which was the lord of Stanstead before the Reformation. Some say that it was the monks of Waltham Abbey who moved the church. Others that it was the work of the Devil.

Tradition is in no doubt that it was the Devil who chose the sites for the parish churches of Pirton and Walkern.

The Devil is supposed to have been particularly annoyed because the people of Pirton were building a cruciform church – one of only three medieval parish churches of this type in Hertfordshire, the other two being Anstey and Wheathampstead. The foundations were laid for the Pirton church of St Mary at the top of Toot Hill, the large mound adjoining the south-west boundary of the present churchyard. The origin of the mound has been lost, but at the time of Domesday it was part of a castle held by Ralph de Limesy and surrounded by a moat which enclosed the Toot Hill mound, the church, and Bury field.

When the building began the Devil lost no time taking a hand in the work. During the first night he removed each stone to the bottom of the hill, but his powers were not absolute, and he had to place the stones just as they had been laid on top of the hill: in the form of a cross. Next day the workmen moved the stones back to their position at the top of the hill, only to discover next morning that the Devil had again been at work and that they had been taken back again to the field below. The builders made yet another attempt to remove the stones to the top of the hill, but, finding that the Devil had once more taken them down, they gave in and completed the church where the Devil had decreed, in the field below the mound, in the form of a cross. The transepts have been demolished for several centuries.

It was the Devil, too, who chose the site of Walkern parish church, across the River Beane from the village street. It was decided, so the story goes, to build a church at Boxbury - now a deserted medieval village - in what was to be later known as Chapel Field. No sooner were the foundations laid and the building begun, however, than the stones were miraculously transported through the air to the present site of St Mary's church at Walkern. They say, too, that as the Devil moved the stones he was heard to cry out: 'Walk-on! Walk-on!' - thus giving his own name to the village.

The fairies - who were not active in Hertfordshire as compared to other counties - chose to put the church of St Bartholomew on a hillside in the now deserted medieval village of Layston. Layston had already become a ruin when Sir Henry Chauncy wrote his *Historical Antiquities of Hertfordshire,* published in 1700: 'The Saxons in old time erected this Vill in the fields, above a mile distant from Aspenden towards the East, where nothing now remains than the church.' Deserted and left to decay, the old church at Layston has given rise to many a folk tale.

If, in legend, the sites of Hertfordshire churches were thus chosen by supernatural means, good and bad, they were all made to face the east and the sunrise, traditionally the compass point where the sun rose on the feast day of the patron saint. Where the chancel was inclined from the nave toward the north - as at Brent Pelham - this was supposed to represent the inclination of Our Saviour's head upon the Cross. Where churches were built near places formerly used for pagan worship - a number of these churches are already known, and archaeological research is expected to identify more – care was taken to locate them just to the south: hence the belief that the north door of a church was the 'Devil's door', and the north part of the churchyard, necessarily with least sun, was a place to be shunned.

There are stories as well of the materials used in building: Anstey church is supposed to have been made with stones from the castle of a wicked Norman baron which stood on the high, tree-crested mound nearby. Architects have said that the castle of Anstey was not finally destroyed until the time of Henry III and that the greater part of the church dates from before that period, but there is evidence from the graffiti in the church – one of the best and oldest collections in Hertfordshire – which supports the truth of the tradition.

Hertfordshire parish churches traditionally have no steeples because, it is said, the Devil would not allow them. Most parish churches have only the stunted 'Hertfordshire Spike', and the saying is, around Hemel Hempstead, that people here kept the Devil at bay – and natural disasters – while they put up the great spire – over 200 feet – of the Norman church of St Mary. At Graveley they were not so fortunate: when the people set up a steeple on the church tower the Devil, who was digging several miles away by the Great North Road, saw it and threw a great shovelful of earth which knocked off the steeple and fell to the ground as a small but steep hill just outside the churchyard.

One Hertfordshire church tower made the fortune of a family of squires. Edward III, so the story goes, was hunting at Watton in Hertfordshire when his wife, Philippa of Hainault, gave birth to a son – the Black Prince – at Woodstock in Oxfordshire. Word was sent to the King by a messenger named Thomas Priour, a Burgess for Hertford in the Parliament of 1313, who rode at full speed with the good news. Edward III, as a token of gratitude, told Priour to climb the tower of Baldock church and claim for his own all the lands that he could see. Thus began the long history of the Pryors of Baldock, maltsters and brewers, and squires of Weston.

It was from another Hertfordshire church tower, St Peter's, St Albans, that the terrible famine of 1258 was foretold. Matthew Paris, the Chronicler of St Albans Abbey, wrote in the *Gesta Abbatum Monasterrii Sancti Albani:*

In the time of this John (23rd Abbot, 1235-1260) a very holy anchoress at St Peter's in the town of St Albans, who used to have not dreams, but prophecies from heaven, saw, among other things, a venerable figure, by his beard an old man, severe, stand before her in her cell, then leave impatiently and climb the church tower and with his face turned to the town thunder in a stern and menacing tone, saying – 'Woe! Woe! Woe! to all inhabiting the earth'. And when he had repeated this several times he departed. And soon, in that very year, the crops failed and the cattle declined and such a famine took place that in the city of London fifteen thousand people died of hunger. Indeed the dying writhed with all kinds of contortions as they piteously yielded up their spirits, whose number was so great that the grave-diggers, tired out, would throw several bodies together in a single grave.

No church in Hertfordshire was left for long without a bell, or ring of bells, for all in the parish to hear, the protectors of man and beast and drivers-away of evil of all kinds: famine, pestilence, lightning and storms, earthquakes, fires, and the Devil himself. Care was taken, as parish records show, to have the bells rung on All Hallows Eve, at Midsummer, and at other times when evil spirits were thought to be abroad and especially powerful.

Inscriptions stamped upon church bells were thought to give them double force. A medieval bell at Albury was inscribed:

HOC SIGNUM SERVA XPI MARIA THOMA
(St Mary, St Thomas, protect this sign of Christ)

The fifth bell of the peal of eight at St Mary's, Hitchin proclaims:

LAUDO DEUM VERUM	I praise the true God
PLEBEM VOCO	I summon the common people
CONGREGO CLERUM	I assemble the clergy
DEFUNCTOS PLORO	I lament the dead
PESTEM FUGO	I drive out pestilence
FESTA DECORO 1762	I celebrate the feasts

When the bellcot at Stocking Pelham Church was struck by lightning about 1836, two of the three bells were sold to pay for the necessary repairs. The third, a pre-Reformation bell, was re-cast, and, as the inscription on it says, care was taken by the churchwardens to give this remaining bell in the church the greatest powers to drive away evil:

VINCENCIUS REBOAT UT CUNCTA NOXIA TOLLAT

Many a folk rhyme was made from the stories and traditions of Hertfordshire churches and bells.

> Harpenden, proud people
> New church
> Old steeple

was a saying of Wheathampstead children (in a neighbouring parish) for generations. In 1861, in spite of protests, the Norman church at Harpenden was pulled down and rebuilt – all but the tower.

> Oh, the foolish Welwyn people,
> Sold their bells to buy a steeple.

This rhyme recalls the tragedy which befell the parish in 1663 when a violent storm did such damage to Welwyn church that the tower fell, carrying with it part of the north wall and vestry. The cost of repairs was very large, some £2,000, and the Rector of Welwyn, the Rev. Gabriel Towerson, appealed throughout the County for aid, describing his parishioners as 'numerous and very poor'. It was not until 1747 that a bell rang again at Welwyn church, in a turret erected above the west end of the nave, and nearly another century passed before this bell turret was replaced by a red brick tower (in 1834).

> Parson Davis and Farmer Lock
> Sold their bell to buy a clock.

This saying is still remembered at Hoddesdon, and the parish records of Broxbourne tell the story: 'At a Vestry held in Broxbourne Church on October 7th, 1700, it is agreed by the inhabitants of Hoddesdon that ye Churchwardens do sell on of Ye Bells in Hoddesdon chappell to by a new clock for ye said chappel.' The clock was put up in 1705.

In any case, the sale of church bells – like that of other assets –

was thought a sign of ill-luck or hard times for the seller. The parish of Sundon, on the Bedfordshire border, has a tradition that four of their ring of five bells were sold to Toddington – then in Hertfordshire. Since that time, it is said, Sundon has never prospered, and indeed Sundon remains a small village.

Church bells lost, carried away, or stolen have left tales behind them. At Hexton, in the folds of the Chiltern Hills, there is a legend that once, during repairs to St. Faith's church, the bells were sent away to be recast – never to return. They were 'taken away', so it is said, to St Albans Abbey – patron of the living before the Dissolution – and are hanging and ringing there still.

One of the medieval ring of bells at the parish church of All Saints, St Paul's Walden, was 'carried off' to the neighbouring parish of Knebworth. No one any longer knows why, or by whom.

There are several legends of the lost bell of Albury, on the Essex border, where there was once a peal of four bells, three dating from before the Reformation. About the year 1800, so it is said, one of the bells fell to the bottom of the church tower where it lay for some time before it 'disappeared'. Some supposed that the bell had been stolen for its valuable metal, and believed that when the thieves discovered they were being pursued – and to enable them to escape – they got rid of their heavy booty by dropping the bell into Halls Garden Pond, not far from Albury church.

Now, as far back as anyone could remember this pond was a place of magic. Some people said it was as deep as the tower of Albury Church was high. Others that Halls Garden Pond had no bottom at all: which was why the Devil – who was really the one who stole the lost bell of Albury – chose it for his hiding place.

If, according to Hertfordshire legend, village ponds were favoured hiding places for bells as well as other treasures, the truth of such tales was sometimes proved. In the parish of South Mimms the story was that an ancient bell had been lowered into the pond at Dyrham Park, near Dancer's Hill, to escape confiscation by Cromwell's Roundheads on their march through Hertfordshire to occupy London. At the end of the eighteenth century the pond was dragged, and a large sixteenth-century bell of Flemish make was found, inscribed:

MARC LE SER HEFT MEI GHEGOTEN MV^{c}LXXIIII

Church bells noted for the sweetness of their tone are thought to have been made partly of silver. There is a story in Great Hormead that when the tenor bell was being cast 'a lady emptied her lap which was full of silver into the mould'.

The bells of Bushey, however, could only make a dull sound, and this gave rise to the old saying, 'Worse and worse, like the parson of Bushey'. Once Bushey church had but one bell, which sounded 'tom-tom-tom', much to the dismay of a parson of Bushey, who added a second bell. But the people declared that the bells were shaming him, for they called out 'tom-fool, tom-fool'. Once more the parson added a bell, but this made matters worse, for the three bells now seemed to say 'tom-fool-still', and have said so ever since.

Some church bells in Hertfordshire, as in other counties, are supposed to sing a verse. (If one listens to call-change ringers who ring in the same order for a time, the bells soon start to make a jumble of words, which one forgets usually as soon as they make the next change.) In some places the words the bells have made have been preserved. At Ware they told a variation of the old custom among the poor of selling a wife:

> Lend me your wife today,
> I'll lend you mine tomorrow.
> No, I'll be like the chimes of Ware,
> I'll neither lend nor borrow.

There are tales of lost bells that still ring over their parishes as in earlier times, and of bell-ropes that are pulled by unseen hands. It is said that the three lost medieval bells of Minsden, a chapel-of-ease to Hitchin, standing now in a lonely hill-top wood and a ruin since the eighteenth century, still may be heard in the hours of darkness when the wind is high, summoning the people of the deserted village to their Holy Day oblations.

Similar legends hang about other deserted medieval villages in Hertfordshire where in most cases, as at Minsden, all that remains is the overgrown ruin of a church or chapel. On high ground, about half a mile from the busy market town of Buntingford, the medieval church of St Bartholomew which served the lost village of Layston still stands, a place of awe and mystery to those who know its story. Many a time, particularly on dark winter nights, its bells are heard to sound. Once in the last century, when the ringers at Buntingford heard the bells of St Bartholomew's ringing for evensong, they found the courage to investigate. When they came within view the bells were sounding from the tower and the ruined church was brightly lighted. The moment the ringers entered the church, however, the ringing stopped and the church was plunged into darkness.

Was it the Devil in the guise of a giant, or some witch or cunning man – who were noted for travelling through the air – that inspired this variant of one of the best known west Hertfordshire folk rhymes:

> Tring, Wing, and Ivinghoe,
> Three churches in a row.
> Take your shoes and stockings off
> And jump over them.

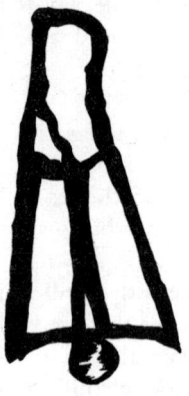

Medieval bell, graffito, Graveley Church

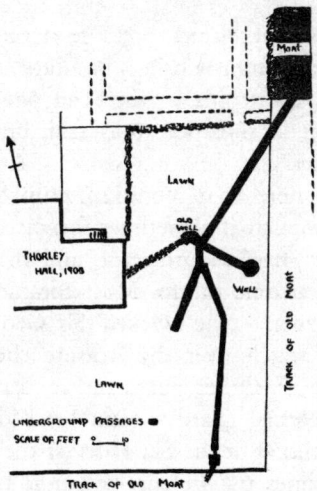

Underground passages at Thorley Hall, plan by R. T. Andrews, 1903

2 Treasures and Tunnels

In this year (418) the Romans collected all the treasures that were in Britain, and hid some in the earth that no man might afterwards find them, and conveyed some with them into Gaul.

Anglo-Saxon Chronicle

THERE ARE as many lost treasures in Hertfordshire, so the saying is, as pebbles in the miraculous Hertfordshire plum-pudding stone. Overlaid with legend, they are relics from every age and creation of man. There are tales of treasure hidden in prehistoric barrows and other monuments, churches, castles, and monastic buildings, on the sites of medieval crosses and deserted villages, in the mud of village ponds and old wells, under loose bricks and in hollowed-out beams in old cottages and farm houses – and as many more as the ingenuity of man can devise. Few towns and villages in Hertfordshire are without their share of old treasure stories which, like the tales of ghosts and hauntings, reach far back through local memory.

The belief persists that 'found' treasure never profits the finder, and that trying to gain from it brings bad luck. Even in the chance picking up of small lost coins in the road one runs a risk: these should never be kept, or hoarded, it is said, but quickly spent, or better still given away.

There was more here than condign punishment for gain at another's expense. Implicit if sometimes forgotten was the idea that every treasure had a guardian protector, and that these were often demons and other fearsome things. Most common in Hertfordshire are the ghosts of owners – the 'wicked' Sir Geoffrey de Mandeville is still supposed to watch over the treasure chest at his medieval castle of South Mimms. Other guardians are servants or dogs who are loyal, set upon eternal guard – giant black dogs with fiery eyes haunt the neighbourhood of the Six Hills by the Great North Road at Stevenage. Sometimes the treasure-keeper is the Devil himself – who in any case, tradition says, is certain to claim the thieving soul of a robber.

At the hamlet of Frithsden, in Berkhamsted, on the border of Ashridge Park, there once lived an elderly man named Rose, who dreamed that a chest of gold lay buried at the bottom of a pit, and that it would be his if he could reach it without speaking a word to break the spell. He took a young neighbour into his confidence, and, after hours of digging, their spades struck a metallic object. So excited was the younger man that he swore. At this invitation the Devil pushed in the sides of the pit, and the treasure diggers were almost buried alive. Nor has anyone else succeeded in outwitting the guardian of the Frithsden pit.

A darker tale is the legend of the lost treasure of Camlet Moat, by South Mimms Castle, which, it is said, had gates so large that they could be heard to shut as far away as Winchmore Hill – a distance of nearly three miles. By the time of topographer William Camden (*Britannia,* 1586) only the 'ruins and rubbish of an ancient house' could be seen on the mound, all that remained of the castle of the De Mandevilles, Earls of Essex, who had followed William the Conqueror to England and at the height of their power held some nineteen lordships in Hertfordshire, including much of the vast wilderness of Enfield Chase, which ran from Waltham Cross south and west over large parts of the parishes of Enfield, Edmonton, Monken Hadley, and South Mimms.

In the north-east corner of Camlet Moat, so the legend goes, there is a deep well, paved at the bottom, in which an iron chest full of treasure is hidden, the lost treasure of the De Mandeville's. Many have sought to raise it, but the treasure can be got up only so far and then it drops back and disappears.

This is the work of Sir Geoffrey De Mandeville, the wickedest of all the family, reclaiming his own. It is said that Sir Geoffrey was at last found guilty of a high crime, but when he hid in a hollow tree it sank into the well of his castle at South Mimms, and he perished miserably. The ghost of Sir Geoffrey De Mandeville, dressed in full armour, is still seen in the neighbourhood.

In Hertfordshire, as in other places, not all hiders of treasure relied upon the forces of evil to protect what was theirs. Some put their faith in Christianity with its terrible sanction of Purgatory for the wicked – and hid their treasure in churches or churchyards, under the protection of wayside and market crosses, and after the Reformation even at crossroads where these crosses had usually stood. That crossroads, and especially those a little way removed from villages or towns as at Codicote and Bishop's Stortford, were also favoured places for the parish gibbet and thus for a good share of the parish ghosts, was but an added security against molestation. If Hertfordshire crossroads had their local tales of buried treasure, a number of these are known to have been recovered over the centuries. One was at Great Offley at the turn of this century where the fabled £500 'Tit-Bit' treasure was found – as tradition proclaimed – at Offley Cross, a triangular bit of waste ground on the parish boundary.

A number of place names in the County seem to refer to lost treasure: Fortune Common, Fortune Gate, and Money Hill, in the parish of Rickmansworth; Money Hill at Oxhey in Watford. All have treasure legends attached to them. Some local tales of this kind are renewed – as legends often are – by an overlay of later happenings which draw upon the same folk theme or source. People still remember the story of how Moneybury Hill (Money Barr Hill in 1672) at Aldbury was said to have got its name. In the last century Lady Brownlow (of Ashridge) took the parish children on a Sunday School outing to the hill, and for a treat set them looking for hidden pennies. When none could be found Lady Brownlow hid her brooch, of pearls and precious stones, down among the leaves, but when the children searched the brooch could not be found either.

Among the earliest legends in Hertfordshire are those of pre-Christian treasures. A number of these are associated with wells, ponds, streams, and the springs that fed them. The well at Orwell Bury, in Kelshall, is thought to derive its name from the Old English *hord-weill*, meaning treasure spring, a place where articles of value were thrown. The 'lost' spring at Hexton, in Christian times sanctified to St Faith and whose offerings made by the pious supported the parish church before the Reformation, was another such ancient holy well.

In local legend most village ponds number among their secrets lost treasure waiting to be found beneath the reeds in murky waters. At Pirton the pond stands near the parish church and in the shadow of a great mound which is all that remains of a half-legendary 'baron's castle'. The village children still say:

> In Pirton Pond
> There lies untold
> Sacks of treasure,
> Pots of Gold.

Barrows and tumuli, most numerous in the north and west of Hertfordshire near the Icknield Way and other ancient tracks, are all supposed to contain hidden treasure. At Knocking Knoll, to the west of Pirton by the branch of the Icknield Way that rejoins the main track along the Chilterns at Pegsdon Hill, a British Chieftain is said to lie buried with his treasure chest. From time to time he can be heard to tap three times upon the chest to make certain it is still there. Some people still refer to this hill as 'Money Knoll' from the treasure thought to be hidden there.

The centuries-long Roman occupation left many visible remains in Hertfordshire of a lost civilization: a network of roads including the great Watling Street, Ermine Street, Akeman Street, and Stane Street; Verulamium and lesser towns; scattered villas and farm-houses without name and without number; artifacts of all kinds turned up by spade and plough. The sprinkling of Roman coins over the County, picked up and still carried 'for luck' by so many farm labourers and others, was enough in itself to encourage popular speculation.

There are many legends of a lost treasure city half way from

London to St Albans along Watling Street in the parishes of Elstree, Aldenham and Shenley near the old Hertfordshire border with Middlesex. A number of valuable finds of coins and other Roman relics made in the area from time to time, moreover, has – as elsewhere – given new lustre to tradition. In 1781 labourers digging near Bentley Priory on the boundary of the park came upon a hoard of gold coins, a golden bracelet, two gold rings, and other treasure. Drawings of two antique bronzes, one a small lion and the other a head of Apollo, found in the neighbourhood of Watling Street, were part of Horace Walpole's collection of antiquities at Strawberry Hill, Twickenham.

Two companion folk rhymes, each pointing to great treasure yet to be found on its side of the County boundary, are recited in Hertfordshire and Middlesex.

In Hertfordshire:

> No heart can think,
> No tongue can tell·
> What lies between Brockley Hill
> And Penny Well.

And in Middlesex:

> No heart can think
> Nor tongue can tell
> What lies between Brockley Hill
> And Perivale.

As so often happens local tales of long pedigree give a remarkably accurate account of ancient occurrences when considered with historical and other evidence. Legend fixed the site of the 'Roman Treasure City' at the strategic place of Brockley Hill, and named 'Caesar's Fort' (an ancient barrow) and 'Caesar's Pond' nearby. The *Antonine Itinerary*, a road-book of the Roman Empire, marked a station called Sulloniacae on Watling Street – just half way between Verulamium (St Albans) and London near enough by present reckoning to Brockley Hill. According to the Hertfordshire historian Rev. Nathaniel Salmon (*History of Hertfordshire,* 1728) the name of the parish of Shenley, part of it a narrow strip of ground lying between Barnet Common and London Colney, was derived from the Roman Sulloniacae. It was also called Salenae, which Ptolemy, the second century geographer and astronomer, named with Verulamium as the two cities of the Belgic tribe inhabiting the district, the Catuvellauni.

Never lost to view was the greatest of the Roman settlements in Hertfordshire, at Verulamium, now the town of St Albans. Here again local history was fitted neatly into a rhyme:

> When Verulam stood
> Saint Albans was a wood;
> But now Verulam's down
> Saint Albans is become a town.

Legends of the fabulous lost treasures of Verulamium rival any of their kind to be found in England. William Camden, the sixteenth-century historian and antiquary who so carefully gathered local tales to entertain the readers of his survey of the British Isles, *Britannia* (first printed in 1586), spared no wonder at the riches of Verulamium. 'Were I to relate', says Camden, 'what common report affirms of the many Roman coins, statues of gold and silver, vessels, marble pillars, cornices, and wonderful monuments of ancient art, dug up here, I should scarcely be believed.' According to Matthew Paris, of St Albans Abbey, the thirteenth-century historian, the legendary treasure was real enough: he describes how the early Abbots, particularly Ealdred and Eadmer, the eighth and ninth Abbots, pillaged the ruins of the Roman city of Verulamium for treasure and for bricks and other materials from which to build and enlarge the Abbey and its monastic buildings.

One of the oldest known of Hertfordshire's proverbs relates to the treasure of a supposedly lost city:

> Ware and Wadesmill
> Are worth all London.

This folk tradition of East Hertfordshire has continued – as such things usually do – in spite of literal-minded antiquarians who dismiss the rhyme as a local boast. Even the usually perceptive Thomas Fuller, 1608-1661, who wrote about Hertfordshire from first-hand acquaintance – he was for some years curate at Waltham Abbey on the River Lea – included the rhyme reluctantly in *The Worthies of England* (1662) among Hertfordshire's proverbs:

> Ware and Wade's Mill are worth all London. This, I assure you, is a master-piece of the vulgar wits in this county, wherewith they endeavour to amuse travellers, as if Ware, a thoroughfare market, and Wade's Mill (part of a village lying two miles north thereof) were so prodigiously rich as to countervail the wealth of London. The fallacy lieth in the homonymy of Ware, here not taken for that town so named, but appellatively for all vendible commodities. We will not discompose the writ of this proverb, by cavilling that Weare is the proper name of that town (so called anciently from the stoppages which there obstruct the river) but leave it as we found it....

It may be, however, that the folk rhyme is indeed good history: that Ware and Wadesmill were early settlements of great importance remembered by the inhabitants as part of their tradition for a thousand years and more. Richard Carew included a very similar rhyme in his *Survey of Cornwall* (1602) relating to Hingston Down near Launceston:

> Hengsten downe, well ywrought,
> Is worth London deare ybought.

Kit Hill, on the western end of Hingston Down, is the traditional site of the camp of the Danish King, Hengist, and of the battle in 837 between Hengist's army and Egbert, King of the West Saxons.

As for the Hertfordshire rhyme, recent archaeological research has confirmed the existence of a Roman settlement at Ware and the Roman bridge there of great strategic importance as the first crossing place of the River Lea north of London. It is not yet known when the Roman bridge at Ware was destroyed, thus diverting traffic to the Hart-ford or by Watton to Ermine Street, and with it, no doubt, the early prosperity of Ware. The *Anglo-Saxon Chronicle* does record that in 895 King Alfred built two forts by the River Lea twenty miles to the north of its junction with the Thames, and contrived to 'block' the river against enemy vessels. Recent excavation near

Wadesmill has revealed the site of a large Roman settlement at Puckeridge – the Goblin's Ridge – a place of many folk legends.

Among the best-known legends of medieval treasure in Hertfordshire are those associated with the Knights Templar, whose alleged wickedness caused Edward II to suppress the order in 1312 and take possession of their lands. If contemporary tales of the Templars as ogres who ate babies and were guilty of other evil deeds have faded, the stories of their lost treasures are still told, especially around places where the Templars were once lords, as at Temple Dinsley. In 1308, by Royal order, the six Knights Templar at the Temple Dinsley Perceptory, near Hitchin, were arrested: two were sent to the Tower of London and the remaining four to Hertford Castle. If the Templars were tortured in an attempt to discover their treasure, their captors were thwarted. Neither the King, nor the money-lending Jew, Geoffrey de la Lee, to whom the Templars' lands were assigned in Hertfordshire, was to lay hands upon the great hoard of gold, silver and precious jewels in the iron casket said to be buried at Temple Dinsley.

A Royal Commission, set up in 1309, 'to inquire touching concealed goods of the Templars in the County of Hertfordshire', found nothing, nor did the two men granted a patent to dig for treasure at Temple Dinsley by Edward III – on condition that the Crown took half the spoil. Centuries have passed since the Perceptory was demolished, but the lost treasure of the Templars has never been recovered. It is still believed in the neighbourhood that an ancient oak to the east of a pool, long ago filled in, is a clue to the resting place of fabulous treasure.

The Reformation brought many treasure legends, as well as riches taken into the Royal coffers, and these centered upon the largest foundation, St Albans Abbey. In the reign of James I the St Albans scrivener John Shrimpton wrote in his *Antiquities of Verulam and St Albans* (about 1631): 'At the suppression of it [the Abbey] much treasure as plate and monys was by the monks for spite buryed in the ground or conveyed away, some part thereof hath been since, by the report of some secretly found....'

So persistent were the stories of 'certeyn Treasure – Trove supposed to be found in or about certeyn of the late Abbies or Monasteries within our Realme of England ...' that James I issued a licence dated 29 April 1617 to 'our Wellbeloved Subject Mary

Midlemore, one of the Maydes of Honor to our deerest Consort Queen Anne ...' to search for buried treasure. By this grant Mistress Midlemore and her 'Executors, Administrators, Deputies, Servants, Workmen or Agents' were given 'Liscence, Liberty, Power and Authority ... during the term of five Yeares next ensuing the Date hereof, to enter into all every and any of the said Abbies of Saint Albones, Glassenbury, Saint Edmonds-Bury and Ramsey and into all lands, houses and places within a mile, belonging to said Abbies, there to dig and search after treasure, supposed to be hidden in such places. Two-thirds of 'all manner of Treasure-Trove, Bookes and other things whatsoever' found were to become the property of the grantee, Mistress Midlemore, while the other third was to go to the Crown.

The source of information for the St Albans and other Abbey legends may have been the notorious treasure hunter, Davey Ramsey, the famous clock-maker who was Page of the Bedchamber and later Groom of the Privy Chamber to King James. James's Court was often in residence in Hertfordshire, at Theobalds (which had been exchanged with Cecil for the Royal manor of Hatfield) and at the Royal hunting lodge at Royston.

There is no record that Mary Midlemore or her agents ever discovered any treasure: she died about nine months after the license was issued. None who knew the power of the so-called monk's curses upon those who would steal their hidden treasure would have doubted the cause: fear which grew from local tales of this kind hung about the vicinity of many a ruined monastic house and must have protected many hoards. One finds records of Royal Patents being issued to treasure-seekers – as again in the reign of James I, on 19 November 1617, to Thomas Atkinson '... to practice his best arte, endeavours, labour and industrie in digging for treasure trove supposed to be hid or laide at St Hippolitus near Hitchin ...' the site of a rich medieval shrine and church dedicated to St Hippolitus, patron of sick horses. But the records are silent in the way of finds being made – and the legends of monkish treasure remain.

Later, in coaching times, Hertfordshire being on the route of several of the most important thoroughfares to London, including the Great North Road and the Holyhead road through St Albans, there were many stories of highwaymen and their loot which was hidden for safekeeping and often never recovered.

Best known today of all Hertfordshire tales of lost treasure is one of these, supposed to have been buried near the twelfth-century Priory of St-Trinity-in-the-Wood, which stood west of St Albans on the way to Dunstable and was rebuilt by Humphrey Bourchier, son of the translator of Froissart's *Chronicles* and Chancellor of the Exchequer. The old rhyme is still well-known in the district:

> Near the Cell there is a Well.
> Near the Well there is a Tree.
> And under the Tree the Treasure be.

An older legend – that the treasure belonged to the Nuns of St Trinity who buried it at the Reformation – has been supplanted by the many tales of a folk-figure called the Wicked Lady Ferrers, who was Lord of Markyate. Dressed as a man, and masked, she was by night a highwayman who rode a black horse with white forefeet that could gallop like the wind, and was the terror of travellers, particularly on the busy Holyhead Road. Shot, finally, and mortally wounded, she made her way back to Markyate Cell – only to die outside by the entrance to a secret door. The ghost of the Wicked Lady Ferrers is still said to haunt the roads and lanes from St Albans north as far as Gustard Wood, in Kimpton parish, and westward from Markyate along the Holyhead Road nearly to Dunstable, in Bedfordshire, where it merges with the local legend of Dun the Robber, the founder of the town.

In Hertfordshire tradition caves – often isolated and disused chalk pits – were favoured places for the hiding of treasure, notably ill-gotten treasure. In Regency times the Parish Clerk of Welwyn, William Nobbs, made reference to these – and much other folklore of the district – in his rhymed directions for beating the parish bounds:

> ... By Pullen's Lane, then Lumbiss' you take,
> And onwards to Cave Wood your way you stake,
> Where Stevenage Robbers often did conceal,
> What to the World they never dare reveal.
>
> So up a Ditch, the Great Wood is your Way:
> Here Turpin, Whitney, Redbeard known afar,

More dread to Constables than peace or war,
Long play'd their Pranks, hid in the thickest Shade,
And from their Oaks the Northern Road invade;
Those Oaks, now down, there's not a trace remains,
Where those fam'd Robbers hid their lawless Gains ...

It was the hope of finding treasure that led to the exploration of the Royston Cave, said to have been a medieval oratory, which was discovered in August 1742, by workmen putting down a post in the Cheese and Butter Market. Bell-shaped and more than 30 feet high, it was cut out of the chalk below the ancient position of Royses Cross, from which the town now standing on the Cambridgeshire border takes its name.

Underground passages connecting ancient landmarks – usually parish churches, monasteries, nunneries and priories, manor houses, castles and inns – are among the most curious of Hertfordshire folk traditions. Many of these secret tunnels as they are called, have tales attached to them, some undoubtedly very old. Certainly in number the tunnels rival ghosts and lost treasures – with which they are often associated – in folk legend. Even today in an age of non-belief the idea of secret underground passages has a wide appeal to the popular imagination, and the parish without a tale or two of this sort is thought poor in marvels indeed.

Best known in the north of Hertfordshire is the story of the 'Lost Fiddler of Anstey', and the underground passage which, according to legend, runs from Cave Gate in the village nearly a mile to the medieval Anstey Castle, which stood on a mound close by the parish church. Once, it happened that George, the blind fiddler of Anstey, agreed for a pot-wager to explore the depths of the passage where no man had dared to venture for fear, some said, of the Devil himself. George accordingly set out with his dog from Cave Gate, playing his fiddle as he walked along the passage so that the village people might follow his progress from above. Suddenly the scrape of the fiddle ceased, there was a loud shriek, and then only silence. The people rushed back to the tunnel entrance at Cave Gate in time to see George's dog run out – frenzied, tail-less, and with all his hair singed off.

Blind George was never seen again. Various accounts of his fate were told in the neighbourhood over the years, nor has anyone been known to succeed in following through the underground passage. To this day, however, old inhabitants say that whenever snow falls on the hillside by the cave entrance a line of snow will melt before the rest along the traditional route of the tunnel, pointing toward Anstey Castle.

If it was the Devil who claimed Blind George, he was not waiting in all Hertfordshire's legendary tunnels. At Hemel Hempstead a narrow flight of steps in the old kitchen garden at the Bury was supposed to lead down to an underground passage that connected with an opening into the crypt of St Mary's parish church and proceeded westward beneath the meadows and the River Gade to the cellars of the mansion house of Lockers. A sailor home on leave and filled with Dutch courage after drinking at the local inn, once decided, for a bet, to put the old tale of the underground passage to the test. He went down the steps in the garden at Hemel Hempstead Bury, made his way along the tunnel and arrived safely in the crypt of St Mary's church – where he hammered for all to hear, on a blocked door. But the tale does not say how the sailor got out.

The oldest accounts of mysterious underground passages in Hertfordshire relate to the ancient and ruined Roman town of Verulamium. The tunnels of Verulamium, according to Matthew Paris, the thirteenth-century chronicler of St Albans, were destroyed by Ealdred, the eighth Abbot:

> Ealdred ransacking the ancient cavities of the old city, which was called Werlamcestre, overturned, and filled up all. The rough broken places, and the streets, with the passages running under ground, and covered over with solid arches, some of which passed under the water of the Werlam river, which was once very large, and flowed about the city, he pulled down, filled up, or stopped; because they were the lurking holes of thieves, night walkers and whores; but the fosses of the city, and certain caverns, to which felons and fugitives repaired as places of shelter, from the thick wood around, he levelled as much as ever he could.

Most numerous, no doubt, of all Hertfordshire tunnel tales are those associated with medieval religious foundations, and popularly known as 'Monks' Holes'. The Reformation and the passing of monastic property into secular hands, as might be expected, encouraged anti-clerical stories. So one still hears of the monks revelling in these underground passages, of their visits to neighbouring nunneries through secret tunnels, and of other illicit, nefarious activities which gave rise to gossip.

At Ware they still describe the secret tunnel that leads from St Mary's church to the priory – the Friary, now Council offices – across the road. The religious house of Ashridge was founded in 1296 by Richard, Earl of Cornwall, to keep holy relics entrusted to the care of a college of the Augustinian order of Bonhommes. The tale persists that the friars had a secret tunnel that went from Ashridge to the nunnery at St Margaret's. Another passage, it is said, runs from the cellars of the thirteenth century priory at Little Wymondley, near Hitchin, to Delamere House at Great Wymondley, visited by Henry VIII and once occupied by Cardinal Wolsey. This tunnel, according to an old inhabitant of the parish, was still open and a terror to small boys at the beginning of the last century.

Although they attracted many stories, the system of tunnels connected with St Albans Abbey which it is thought served as bolt-holes in times of civil disorder and as drains, were real enough. They were an object of curiosity even to the learned. Dr Joshua Webster, who practised medicine for many years at St Albans, explored the Monks' Holes, as he wrote:

> In the year 1746, the third of July, I entered one of these passages, with a light. I was obliged to creep upon my belly for six or seven yards as the stones and rubbish have nearly filled up the passage so far; at last with much difficulty and labour I came to a good bottom. It is five feet wide and near seven feet high, built of good masoned stone-work – and seemed to be rather winding, but finding it damp and my candle burning weakly, I retreated safe and well.

Popular fancy extended the Monks' Holes of St Albans Abbey in every direction for miles around. They were said to run from the Abbey to the Dominican Friary at King's Langley, and to Gorhambury House, seat of Sir Francis Bacon, popularly regarded as a wizard. 'It is an article of faith in Markyate Street', wrote a correspondent of a Hertfordshire newspaper in 1892, 'that a subterranean passage connects the Cell [markyate Cell] with St Albans Abbey, some four miles distant, and that in this underground retreat the restless spirits of departed monks patter their "aves" in the dead of night.'

'The belief in such underground passages still exists in St Albans,' wrote the Rev. H. R. Wilton Hall in his paper on the nunnery of Sopwell (*Memorials of Old Hertfordshire*, 1904),

> for less than a century ago one was known to exist between St Albans monastery and the River Ver. As the Ver flows between the sites of the monastery and the nunnery, sewers will account for the passages, and well-known scandals in both houses, coupled with a love of the marvelous, sufficiently account for the legend that St Albans monastery and Sopwell nunnery, some three-quarters of a mile apart, were connected by an underground passage which must of necessity have passed under the bed of the River Ver!

Farther away still is the parish of Shenley where the handsome red-brick Tudor mansion of Salisbury Hall, visited by Charles II and Nell Gwynn, with its many secret passages and hiding places that were havens for recusants and Jacobites, still stands surrounded by gardens and its water-filled moat. Down by the moat-side, facing toward the town of St Albans – which can be seen clearly on a fine day – is the circular, bricked-up opening of the underground passage, nearly five feet high, which still connects Salisbury Hall with St Albans Abbey.

There are few manor houses in Hertfordshire of any age without a legend of an underground passage. One of the longest in the County goes from Hatfield, the home of the Cecils, to Queen Hoo Hall in the parish of Bramfield which appealed to the antiquarian Joseph Strutt as the setting for his romance of England in the Middle Ages, completed after Strutt's death by Sir Walter Scott. At Widford there is a story of the subterranean way from the manor house to Blakesware, beloved of Charles Lamb, which runs under the River Ash. Other great houses with traditions of underground tunnels include the Rye House at Hoddesdon, noted for its connection with the Plot of that name (1683), which leads to Nether Hall, ancestral home of the Coltes, on the Essex bank of the River Stort; Cheshunt

House, said to have been built by Cardinal Wolsey, had a passage which led under the road to a moated house now demolished.

The palace of the Bishops of London at Much Hadham – birthplace of Edmund of Hadham, father of Henry VII – had an underground passage which went up-hill to the Red Lion Inn. This tunnel is said to have connected to a winding staircase which ran through the walls of the Inn – recently closed – to an exit behind the panelling of the dining room by the fireplace. The Bull Inn at Whitwell, which until recent years had a gallows sign spanning the road and whose cellars are medieval, according to local tradition has a vaulted underground passage that goes under the former stable yard down to the River Mimram. From there, and this tradition persists, the tunnel runs up Bury Hill, where it joins another from St Paul's Walden Bury, and ends at the parish church of All Saints nearly a mile away.

The Wallington Giant, graffito, Wallington Church

3 Giants and Bogeymen

GIANTS WERE the first inhabitants of Hertfordshire. Matthew Paris, the thirteenth-century chronicler of St Albans Abbey, re-told the story of Geoffrey of Monmouth (d.1154) in *Historia Britonum* that, when the Trojan immigrants and their leader Brutus (Britain) reached the island called Albion, they found it inhabited by none but a few giants, whom 'passing through all the provinces', they 'forced to fly into the caves of the mountains . . .'.

The chalk ridges of the Chiltern Hills to the west and north of the County, and along the prehistoric Icknield Way, would appear to have offered favourable conditions for cutting giants and other figures of folk tradition. If any of these was ever made, none has survived in Hertfordshire, even in legend.

It may be, however, that the large graffito figure of a man, deeply cut on the tower arch of St Mary's church at Wallington, was an attempt to depict a local hill-figure of a giant, or a giant legend. The church stands in the centre of Wallington, a small village east of Baldock in the chalk downs, and at the top of a hill which overlooks the countryside for miles around. Wallington is said to be named for 'Waendel's people' – the Wandels who gave their name to the great iron age fort of Wandlebury, not far distant in the Gogmagog Hills over the Cambridgeshire border, and near to which, according to legend, a golden chariot and two giant gods lie buried.

The giant god of the Hiccas – Iceni – called Hiccafrith by the Saxons, was noted for his supernatural feats of strength, which, however, have come down in Hertfordshire folklore as works of the Devil. The Hiccas once held large territories in what is now Hertfordshire, leaving their names at such places as Hitchin, Hitch Wood and the River Hiz.

Hiccafrith, armed with an axle-tree and a wagon wheel, is said among other things to have fought with another giant, and to have been especially fond of throwing missiles at churches. The story is still well known today of how the Devil dug with a great spade at Stevenage to make the Six Hills tumuli near Whomerley Wood by the Great North Road – and missed with the seventh spadefull, which knocked the spire from the tower of Graveley Church several miles away, and landed as a small but steep hill just beyond the churchyard.

Later, in the Middle Ages, Hiccafrith became a Robin Hood figure in Hertfordshire as elsewhere, defending settlements against marauding Danes, and the like. There are characteristics of Hiccafrith's exploits in the legend of the best loved of all Hertfordshire's folk heroes, Jack O'Legs, the Weston giant.

The earliest known version of the tale was written by the Rev. Nathaniel Salmon in his *History of Hertfordshire,* published in 1728:

> There once was a giant called Jack of Legs who lived in a wood in the parish of Weston. He was a great robber but a generous one, for he plundered the rich to feed the poor. He took bread from the Baldock Bakers frequently, who taking him at an advantage, put out his eyes, and after hanged him upon a Knoll in Baldock Field. He made them at his Exit but one single request, which they granted: That he might have his Bow put into his Hand, and where ever his Arrow fell he should be buried, which happened to be in Weston Church Yard.

Later generations have embellished the story of Jack O'Legs, and attributed to him the half-remembered deeds of other local and legendary figures. A hill on the Great North Road near Graveley is known as 'Jack's Hill' and said to be the vantage point from which he spied out rich travellers, while a cave not far away – filled in last century – called 'Jack's Cave' is the place where he is supposed to have hidden his booty. Some say that before hanging the giant the bakers of Baldock put out his eyes with a baker's peel. Others make Jack the founder of Weston church with the story that not only did Jack ask to be buried where his arrow fell, but that he begged all who had accepted his bounty to build there a chapel for the benefit of his soul.

Salmon, who valued legend for its relevance to history, wrote finally about Jack O'Legs in 1728:

> To follow such a story is almost as wise as to confute it: Yet considering how prettily these Relations are brought into the World, and how carefully nurtured up to gigantick Prodigies, one may believe the Pedigree of this to be from the famed Richard Strongbow, whose feats had been told by Nursery Fires, till they were thus happily improved.

Salmon was probably right in ascribing part of Jack the giant's legend to the very real and spectacular feats of arms which won Richard de Clare, Earl of Pembroke, the name of 'Strongbow'. There can be no doubt of his connection with the district as Lord of Weston, or that Weston was deprived of its Lord – and protector – when Strongbow was banished to Ireland for aiding King Stephen in his struggle with Matilda for the throne. The family did regain their lands under her son, Henry II.

Another version of Jack's legend, which may well have a basis in fact, portrays the giant as a leprous – and therefore outcast – member of the order of Knights Templar to whom Weston Church and its lands as well as the town of Baldock had been given by Strongbow's father, Gilbert de Clare, also Lord of Weston and Earl of Pembroke.

Whoever he was, the people of Weston – so it is said – buried Jack O'Legs beside what is now a path in the churchyard with one stone at his head, and another at his feet – fourteen feet apart. Two weather-worn stones still mark the giant's grave.

Jack's grave became a place of pilgrimage: all told his story. Enterprising Weston parish clerks kept what they called Jack's great thigh bone 'for a shew' in the parish chest which could be viewed for a 'consideration'. Among the visitors to the giant's grave was the noted antiquary John Tradescant, the younger, who was gardener at Hatfield to the first Earl of Salisbury from 1609 to 1614. According to Salmon, the historian, Tradescant bought Jack's thigh bone from the Clerk at Weston and added it to his famous 'Closet of Rarities' which, after his death in 1662, became the nucleus of the Ashmolean Museum at Oxford.

Apart from Jack O'Legs, two other Hertfordshire giants are known. Both are associated in legend with the eastern part of the County: Cadmus, the giant of Barkway, and Piers Shonks – Peter Longlegs – of the nearby parish of Brent Pelham.

Piers Shonks, lord of the manor called Shonks – later known as Beeches – is said to have lived about a mile to the south east of Brent Pelham Church, in a fortified house on one of two islands surrounded by a deep moat. It survived the Middle Ages. Writing in 1621 Weever (*Ancient Funerall Monuments*) described 'an old decayed house well moated ... called O Piers Shonks'. In 1743 an old moated barn known as Shonks Barn still stood near the manor house, but 'in a very tottering condition', and a nearby wood was called Shonks Wood.

The story of where the Barkway giant, Cadmus, lived has been lost. It was probably a stronghold similar to that of Shonks, a moated and fortified house so characteristic of the medieval Burys in the parishes that run along the Icknield Way and the chalk hills of north and east Hertfordshire. The most likely place was high up on Periwinkle Hill, opposite Rokey Wood and about half a mile from Barkway village, where there are still the remains of a small mount-and-bailey castle and the moat which surrounded it.

Folk legend, like history, takes more notice of those who are successful, and the story of Cadmus has come down only in the legend of his rival, Piers Shonks. The Rev. Nathaniel Salmon, who was for some years curate at Westmill, wrote the story of the two giants in 1728 as

> the Relation given me by an old Farmer in the Parish [of Brent Pelham] who valued himself for being born in the air that Shonk

breathed ... He saith, Shonk was a Giant that dwelt in this Parish, who fought with a Giant of Barkway, named Cadmus, and worsted him; upon which Barkway hath paid a Quit-Rent to Pelham ever since.

The story of quit-rent, or tribute, is at least in part historical. In the fourteenth century – and perhaps earlier – a family named Shank is known to have held lands not only in the parish of Brent Pelham but in Barkway as well, the manor of Berwick in Nuthampstead. Richard FitzAlan, Earl of Arundel, had granted 'the manor of Berwick' for life to Peter Shank, who also held Shonks and Beeches manors in Brent Pelham. The lords of Nuthampstead had the right to hold view of frankpledge in Barkway, although in 1347 the common fine was paid to the lord of Nuthampstead, and the lord of the manor of Rokey in Barkway received the amercements or fines.

The story of the fight between the giants of Brent Pelham and Barkway has been lost, possibly because, as often happens, it was overshadowed by a more unusual and spectacular tale associated with the same folk hero – in this case Piers Shonks' great victory over the fearsome Pelham dragon.

If in Hertfordshire legend giants were not impressive because of their size, and are remembered as benevolent figures, or for defending the parish against danger, bogeys or bogeymen did fearful things to ordinary people, and particularly children.

Harassed mothers with the many children to care for that were the family of past generations, teachers in Dame schools, and nannies in homes of the well-to-do, among others, told children stories of witches, ghosts and bogeymen to enforce discipline and keep them away from dangerous places such as disused chalk pits.

Bogeys assumed the character of threatened dangers to the community, particularly fears of war and invasion, and internal strife. Both Cavaliers and Roundheads spread stories of their opponents eating captives, and although comparatively little fighting in the Civil War took place in Hertfordshire, naughty children were still threatened with 'Old Noll' – Cromwell – within living memory. The repeated threats of invasion by Napoleon brought out the Hertfordshire militia; children played with sticks at drill and staged mock battles against the bogey that was Boney who would 'come and get them'. More recent were the 'Russian scare' of Crimean War days and in this century the Kaiser and Hitler. While the Empire lasted, and particularly in the years before conscription in the First World War, the threat to children that 'Father would go for a soldier' had still-remembered terror and the certainty of poverty for the family left at home.

The oldest known of Hertfordshire's bogeymen is a mysterious folk-figure called Miles's Boy, who would come and bundle naughty children into his big black sack and carry them off, no one said where.

Two bogeymen were associated with sabbath-breaking, long a civil as well as a religious offence. The Man-in-the-Moon would come down, it was said within living memory, and catch anyone wicked enough to 'go a-woodin' on a Sunday. It was the Devil, however, who would help the miscreant to evil by holding down the branches for those who would go nutting on the Lord's Day.

A 'Winter scare' around Bushey and other places in Hertfordshire was 'Spring-heeled Jack', a mischievous phantom with springs on his heels who would bound out suddenly from over fences and hedges and terrify people. A resident of Bushey in the 1840s recalled: 'At times I have seen a noisy crowd of youths armed with sticks shouting for hours for Spring-heeled Jack to appear, sometimes in Old Bushey, sometimes on the [Bushey] Heath, but the elusive gentleman never appeared.'

'Jack' seems to have had a curious attraction for hoaxers, and impersonators of ghosts were common enough in Hertfordshire. He was perhaps never better portrayed, however, than at Hitchin in the winter of 1835-6 by a bored young law student with an addiction to pranks and a taste for theatricals who would later rise to be Sir Henry Hawkins, High Court Judge, and Baron Brampton, (1817-1907). Reginald Hine tells the story in *Hitchin Worthies:*

> ... Walking across to the window, Henry leant out and looked up the narrow lane ... Was there nothing to be done in this prim and Quakerly place? These clients of his father, when they did come, how heavily they sat upon his spirit!
>
> Thanks to himself there had been just a little fun. A smile flickered over his pale and rather treacherous face as he thought of his exploits. The tying together of those knockers in Cock Street, for example. Rather obvious, but very gratifying. Still more

successful those snares of almost invisible string which he had fixed low down across the doorways in Bancroft. They had proved all the more deadly because most of the swell houses there had two or three steps descending to the street. If a rich and portly tradesman was taken by the ankles, then great was the fall thereof.

The smile broadened. He was thinking of those pleasant Sunday evenings the winter before, when he had played the ghost and spring-heeled Jack in one along the fence of the [Hitchin] Priory Park. Those springs on his shoes had worked remarkably well. What glorious sport it had been jumping over the fence, first one side, then the other! And, thanks to his father's night cap and shirt, and to his own under-sheet and gloves, what a marvellous ghost he had made! Who was it, he wondered, had set that snarling mastiff upon him? It was foolish to have kicked at the beast, and still more foolish to have cursed it. It was not in order for ghosts to kick and swear. It gave the show away. As it was some sneaking fellow had suggested to his father that, though the hand was the hand of a ghost, the voice of the swearer was suspiciously like the voice of Henry Hawkins. Old John had said nothing, but he had not been quite the same since then.

Some bogeymen were ghosts or spirits of people who had lived in a parish and held positions of authority, most often officious parish clerks or unpopular squires. The hamlet of Bendish in St Paul's Walden parish is haunted to this day by the farmer Bob Archer, who, riding his big black horse, still chases boys 'scrumping' apples from an orchard long ago cut down.

Near Tring the bogeyman is called Simon Harcourt – no one remembers why. A connection of the Harcourts of Stanton Harcourt (Oxon), a barrister of the Inner Temple and lord of Pendley Manor, (1694-1724), he is still a terror in the neighbourhood. 'Simon Harcourt'll get you – rattling his chains' was sufficient warning for any wayward child. And even, it seems, for grown men. One day men working for the Grand Union Canal Company, returning to Bulbourne from Dudswell on a regular trip, stopped for drinks at the Cow Roast. One of them, called 'Happy', was in a great fright later on Pendley beeches because of a grey figure ahead on the road. 'It's Simon Harcourt come to get me!' he said as the others hung back.

Luckily it turned out to be only Harry Osborne's donkey from Wigginton.

Jack o'Lanterns, usually called Will-o'-th'-wisps in the south and west parts of Hertfordshire, were said to hang in the hedgerows in marshy places and along river valleys, waiting for unwary travellers whom, bobbing along, they would lure from the roads into bogs or lose in the mists. At Bushey in the 1840s they told the story of how 'two men got drunk and saw a dancing light on Harroweald Common. They followed. It disappeared, then appeared. They followed this Will-o'-th'-wisp all night. When it finally disappeared they came home frightened but sober. The son of one of the men told me that he had been to the Common and saw the tracks made. They would have been clever to have caught the dancing light.'

The Man in the Moon, graffito, Codicote church tower

The Pelham Dragon, tomb of Piers Shonks, Brent Pelham Church, 1976

4 Dragons and Monsters

LEGENDS ABOUT dragons and monsters are among the oldest to be found in Hertfordshire. A legacy of pre-Christian tradition and medieval mysticism, they are still a part of the living – and oral – tradition of the county, particularly in the rural eastern hundreds of Odsey, Edwinstree, and Braughing, where Piers Shonks, the slayer of the Pelham dragon, still flourishes as a popular folk-hero.

Hertfordshire would have had no dragons, snakes, or thunderstorms at all, it is said, if St Paul had not confined his visit to Berkhamsted, from which he drove these scourges forever!

The attribution of this miracle to St Paul may be a folk-memory of a now-forgotten double dedication of the parish church of St Peter at Berkhamsted, and an example of the once popular belief that it was the function of the patron saint of the parish to protect the inhabitants from the forces of evil and their great weapon, the disasters of nature. To some extent at least this legend of St Paul appears to be grounded in fact: while a Victorian rector of

Berkhamsted, the Rev. John Cobb, in a lecture about the parish given in January 1855, noted that in his experience thunderstorms did occur there from time to time, the modern historian of Berkhamsted, Percy Birtchnell, maintains that 'the sight of a snake in the district is certainly rare'.

Snakes, including besides the adder the benign grass snake and the slow worm, are still to be found in other parts of Hertfordshire, notably in the many country parishes where their natural habitat survives. According to local tradition the village of Aspenden, lying in a small valley on a tributary of the river Rib, was named for the asps said once to have bred there in astonishing numbers.

In Hertfordshire as in other places all snakes, cursed of God, have been shunned by man. By some they were invested with mysterious and magical powers – they were thought never to die before sunset – and their dried skins were used as charms to ward off disease.

Dragon legends are to be found in the oldest collections of folklore made in the county, the series of chronicles written by the Benedictine monks of St Albans Abbey. The greatest of these chroniclers, Matthew Paris (*c*. 1200-59) included (among many others) the legend of the great dragon of Wormenhert in his *Gesta Abbatum Monasterii Sancti Albani*, which describes the lives of the first 23 Abbots.

Wormenhert was a cave that was made and inhabited by a great dragon. Connected to a deep ravine, Wormenhert was surrounded by a mountain which stood above the River Ver and the ruined Roman town of Verulamium, known in Saxon times as Werlamceaster.

If the dragon was still at Wormenhert in the time of Ealdred, the eighth Abbot, who succeeded Abbot Leofric about 1007, the *Gesta Abbatum* does not relate. It does, however, tell how Abbot Ealdred, who demolished much of the remaining ruins of Verulamium while collecting stone, brick and other material to rebuild the Abbey, 'flattened as far as he was able' the great ravine and cavern of Wormenhert, 'so dispelling for ever traces of the serpent's lair'.

The imagery of the dragon as a creature of great strength and great evil flourished in Hertfordshire in medieval mysticism and metaphysics. In the writings of Matthew Paris and other monks of the Abbey, as well as in secular works, notably the *Travels* of Matthew Paris's Hertfordshire contemporary Sir John Mandeville – said to have been born at St Albans and to have set out from thence in 1322 on his fabulous 34-year journey to the Holy Land – fact and myth existed side by side, and in a useful partnership.

Just as, for example, the struggle of the English against the Danes is a factor of great importance in early Hertfordshire history – the boundary between the English kingdom of Mercia and the Danelaw ran through the county along the river Lea – so it was a fruitful source of Hertfordshire legend. Nor was it less than fitting for Matthew Paris in the history *Chronica Majora* to record the popular visions of fearsome dragons seen in the skies before the Danish invasions.

The medieval bridge between scholarship and popular tradition was one that all men might cross, if only for the illiterate majority by way of the spoken word, the picture, and the image. Great use was made of real and fanciful beasts such as the dragon, the wyvern, and the unicorn – many of which had derived from earlier pagan tradition – to illustrate Christian belief and morality. Allegorical tales of animals, known collectively as Bestiaries, were used by the clergy not only in religious foundations such as St Albans and Ashridge, but in the parish churches, where deeds of the local patron saint such as the dragon slayers St George and St Andrew were not only read out to assembled parishioners, but painted up in bright colours on whitewashed walls and pillars for all to see.

In some places, as at Berkhamsted, the story of the saint and the snakes long survived as a legend the obliteration of the wall painting of St George and the dragon on a pillar in the parish church. In others, notably St Albans Abbey, fragments of wall paintings remain to tell their own stories of piety and martyrdom. More elusive, if perhaps even more revealing, are the graffiti scratched into the stone of the churches and other ancient buildings which portray as contemporary folk art parish traditions and happenings: thus at St Albans Abbey there are graffiti of dragon-like creatures and grotesques. The Hatfield church of St Etheldreda has a wyvern on one pillar, balanced upright on its two legs and tail and Graveley church a mythical unicorn on the south pier of the tower.

Dragons and other monsters from the Bestiaries were carved in the soft Hertfordshire limestone known as 'clunch' and set up in church fabrics as capitals, corbels, label stops, and gargoyles, and used as heraldic motifs on chantries and tombs. At Tring one of a series of corbels disparaging mendicant friars shows the dragon killing St

George. There were dragons, too, fashioned in wood as bench-ends, misericords – an especially fine dragon is still to be seen at Bishop's Stortford – and other furniture decoration.

It is not surprising that local legends were woven around these prominently displayed yet half mysterious objects, and that they have been preserved at least in part in modern times by tradition. Among those that have survived in Hertfordshire is the legendary 'Old Dog' of Codicote church. The 'Old Dog' is a medieval wood-carving – which perhaps began as a bench-end – a fantastic creature with the head of a monkey, the ears of a bat, the mane of a horse, the body of a dragon, the tail of a lion, and the legs and cloven hooves of a cow. To keep him in his proper place, moreover, and from working any mischief, the 'Old Dog' is held fast by the carved wooden collar around his neck attached to a stout chain. For those with the courage to pat him, the 'Old Dog' is said to bring good luck.

If in Hertfordshire folklore there is no tradition of dragons as guardians of treasure hoards, dragons whether regarded as protective or merely as the imagery of popular legend were common enough on secular buildings of the middle ages and later. The inn sign of the dragon or the dragon and St George is still one of the commonest in the County. Dragons were often carved on oaken corner posts and brackets, and on the barge boards that keep the gable ends of roof timbers from the weather.

The use of dragons on barge boards appears to link them with the ancient belief in the use of images on roofs – apart from charms such as the house-leek (see below, Chapter 8) to ward off lightning – witchcraft, and other evils. In the old market town of Hitchin evidence of this type of belief is still to be seen. A small house, now a shop, standing by the medieval bridge over the river Hiz in Bridge Street has a set of early sixteenth-century barge boards carved in low relief with a line of dragons, newly repainted in green. Preserved at Hitchin museum is one of the last of the two terra-cotta ridge tiles surmounted by figures of armed men on horseback that were set up on the gables of the fifteenth-century Brotherhood House, once a guildhall, in Bancroft, and which were faithfully renewed in recent years. (For the drawing, see below, Chapter 7.) It is said that on the stroke of midnight by St Mary's church clock these horsemen begin to ride their nightly patrol along the gables of the Brotherhood House, until dawn breaks and they resume their places at the top.

In Hertfordshire as in other places during the middle ages miracle plays about St George overcoming the forces of evil portrayed by a dragon were very popular. The largest known production of a miracle play associated with the county was 'The Holy Martyr St George' given on St Margaret's Day, 1511, at Basssingbourn on the Cambridgeshire border, which included part of the present Hertfordshire parish of Royston. It was a joint effort of some 28 parishes in north Hertfordshire and Cambridgeshire, and the leading contributors to expenses were the town of Royston, the parish of Therfield, and the neighbouring Cambridgeshire parishes of Melbourn and Litlington. The Bassingbourn Churchwardens' accounts recorded all the expenses of this production, including such 'garments and propertys' as the dragon, St George, and the king and queen, commissioned to be made at Saffron Walden, in Essex, as well as the feasting and entertainment of the spectators and actors which followed.

Apart from special productions, most large Hertfordshire towns had their own dragons, usually in the care of the parish church wardens. These were prominent figures in religious processions such as those on Corpus Christi Day, and on perambulations of the parish boundaries as well as in the plays performed by the town guilds on festival days.

The Bishop's Stortford dragon first appears in the Churchwardens' accounts in 1482, when perhaps because of the zeal of St George, he was in need of repair:

> Item Payd to Wyllm Northach
> for mending of dragon and for
> his labour . . . . iiij d.

The Stortford dragon was made of canvas stretched over hoops with room inside for men to move him about. Besides performing in the Stortford processions and plays, which raised money for church repairs and other charitable purposes (the 'Pley' brought in 26s. 7d., in 1490, 33s. in 1523) the dragon was also 'let out' from time to time by the thrifty churchwardens to neighbouring parishes, including Sawbridgeworth and Braughing. In 1504 the Stortford dragon earned 4d. for taking part 'in the Braughing playe'. The Stortford dragon finally fell a victim to the Edwardian church reformers: he is last heard of as church property in an inventory dated 1549 among other items of furniture sold – but 'w^t owte the assent of the parisshoners ther'.

After the Reformation the popular characters of St George and the dragon appeared in the folk plays of mummers and 'guisers, which continued in rural parts of Hertfordshire well into the nineteenth century. A well executed graffito of a knight in armour at Wallington church may relate to a now-forgotten George-and-Dragon play which included a hobby-horse: there is a companion graffito of a full-size hobby-horse on the wall of the church porch where he may have been kept between performances.

In Hertfordshire there were doubtless those who subscribed to the traditional rhyme collected by John Aubrey in the seventeenth century:

To save a mayd St. George the Dragon slew –
A pretty tale, if all is told be true.
Most say there are no dragons, and 'tis sayd
There was no George; pray God there was a mayd.

Believed or not, except perhaps for Jack O'Legs, the Weston giant, no Hertfordshire folk character has so captured the popular imagination as Piers Shonks, who slew the great dragon of Brent Pelham. A small rural parish in the east of the county on the Essex border, Brent Pelham is said to owe its name – as distinct from the neighbouring parishes of Stocking Pelham and Furneaux Pelham – to a fire that all but destroyed the village in the reign of Henry I.

From the sixteenth century – if not earlier – the legend has centred upon the elaborate tomb of Piers Shonks in a recess in the north wall of the nave of St Mary's parish church. The slab of black marble covering the tomb is carved in high relief with the winged symbols of the four Evangelists in the corners: the Angel (St Matthew); the Lion (St Mark); the Eagle (St John); and the Bull (St Luke). At the top is an angel bearing Shonk's soul up to heaven, and in the centre a large foliate cross thrusts its staff into the jaws of a dragon coiled at the foot. On the wall behind the tomb is this inscription, believed by the historian Nathanial Salmon (*History of Hertfordshire*, 1728) to have been written by the Rev. Raphael Keen, who died in 1614 after nearly 76 years as Vicar of Brent Pelham:

Tantum fama manet Cadmi sanctique Georgi
Posthuma; tempus edax ossa sepulcha vorat.
Hoc tamen in muro tutus, qui perdidit anguem
Invito positus Daemone, Shonkus erat.

O PIERS SHONKS
WHO DIED ANNO 1086

Nothing of Cadmus nor St George, those names
Of great renown, survives them but their fames:
Time was so sharp set as to make no Bones
Of theirs, nor of their monumental Stones.
But Shonks, one serpent kills, t'other defies,
And in this wall, as in a fortress, lies.

The story of Piers Shonks was first recorded in print by John Weever (*Ancient Funerall Monuments*) in 1621, where it appears as the story of Shonks the giant, who dwelt in the parish of Brent Pelham, and fought with another giant from the neighbouring parish of Barkway, 'and worsted him, upon which Barkway hath paid a Quit-Rent to Pelham ever since'.

The version which has survived as a popular legend, however, follows the inscription at the back of Shonks' tomb that describes him as a dragon-slayer, and this one was very generally known in Hertfordshire at the end of the nineteenth century. Herbert W. Tomkins in *Highways and Byways in Hertfordshire* (1902), tells of meeting a man at Hadham – Much and Little Hadham are three and four parishes to the south of Brent Pelham – who knew the tale of Piers Shonks. 'Sir,' said the countryman, inclined to be sceptical, 'it's one of the rummiest stories I ever heard, like, that 'ere story of old Piercy Shonkey, and if I hadn't seen the place in the wall with my own eyes I wouldn't believe nothing about it.'

The lair of the Brent Pelham dragon was a cave under the roots of a great and ancient yew tree that once stood on the boundary of Great Pepsells and Little Pepsells fields. A terror to the neighbourhood, this dragon was said to have been a favourite of the Devil himself.

One day, so the story goes, Piers Shonks, the lord of Pelham, who lived in the moated manor house the ruins of which are still known as 'Shonkes', said by some to be a giant, and by most a mighty hunter, set out to destroy the evil monster. In full armour, with sword and spear, Shonks was accompanied by an attendant and three favourite hounds, so swift of foot they were thought to be winged. Shonks at length found the dragon, and after a terrible struggle thrust his spear down the monster's throat, giving him a mortal wound. The forces of evil, however, had not been overcome, for the Devil himself now appeared and cried vengeance upon Shonks for the killing of his minion. The Devil vowed to have Shonks' body and soul, when he died, were he buried within Pelham church, or outside it. Nothing daunted, Shonks defied the Devil, saying that his soul was in the Lord's keeping, and that his body would rest where he himself chose. Years later, when Shonks lay dying, and having it in mind to outwit the Devil at the last, he called for his bow, and shot an arrow that struck the north wall of the nave of Pelham church. There Shonks' tomb was made, and, as he had foretold, his body rests in peace beyond the devil's reach: neither within Pelham church nor outside it.

The conqueror of the Pelham dragon and the defier of another whose identity has been lost, Piers Shonks as a folk hero grew larger than life. The old belief that Shonks was a giant, too, gained new acceptance in the nineteenth century when his tomb was opened in 1861 and large bones were found. Some were taken away by the curious, but were said 'to give no peace', a common belief attaching to stolen articles, until they were returned.

Even in death Shonks is said to work for the triumph of good over evil in the district, and still lays a firm hand upon malefactors. One moonlit night, so the story goes, when Jack O'Pelham had stolen his neighbour's faggot, and had almost reached home with it on his back, the load of wood suddenly grew so heavy that Jack was thrown to the ground. As he struggled to his feet, there before him stood Piers Shonks the dragon slayer, and Jack counted himself lucky all his days that he had then fainted away with fright. There are few in Pelham even now who for any gain would run the risk of seeing Piers Shonks a second time.

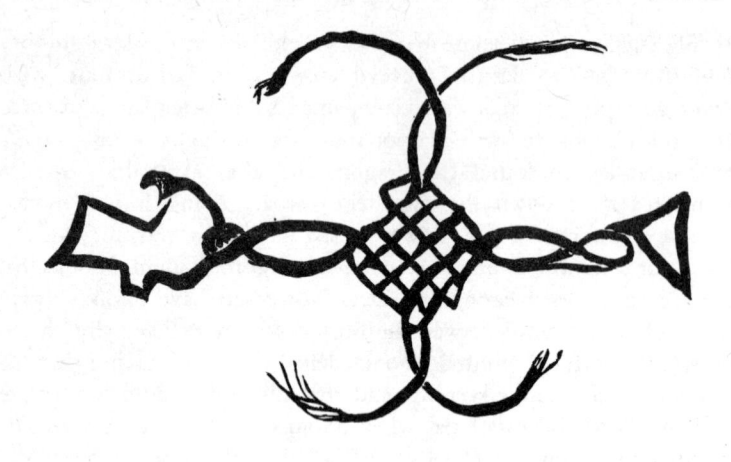

True Lover's Knot, graffito, D'Amores House, Hertingfordbury

5 From the Cradle to the Grave

> One is for sorrow,
> Two for mirth,
> Three for a wedding,
> Four for a birth.

IN HERTFORDSHIRE, as elsewhere, apart from religious and secular ceremonies, traditional beliefs and customs, often very old, surrounded the great turning points in the cycle of life: birth, marriage, and death.

It was said that to rock an empty cradle would bring a baby before long – one belief in particular still current today both here and in New England colonial towns such as Deerfield and Stockbridge where Hertfordshire people settled. As in the rhyme above the gathering of magpies was watched to forecast a birth. If four were seen together, a birth was certain to happen soon.

The sex of the coming child was always important. Boys especially were hoped for, to carry on the name, to inherit titles and property, to join in the work of a profession or trade, and to help on the farm. Four crows meant a boy:

> One Crow sorrow,
> Two Crows joy.
> Three Crows a letter,
> Four Crows a boy.
> Five Crows silver,
> Six Crows gold.
> Seven Crows a secret,
> That never should be told.

There was more or less celebration after a birth, depending upon the outcome. In the nineteenth century a squire of Bayfordbury planted an acorn for each son born, and an inscribed stone was set near by to record the event.

It was customary to bring gifts to a new baby to give it a good start. Gold sovereigns were popular for this purpose, or a piece of silver, for 'money in the pocket' all through life. A silver threepenny bit is still remembered as the well-off cottagers' gift.

Among the old notions not yet wholly lost is the idea that a baby must first be 'carried up' before it is 'carried down'. In case of negligence in this matter, I was told not long ago, the bad fortune sure to follow could be headed off by performing this ritual at the first opportunity, and the child would live to grow up.

The ancient custom of Churching women after childbirth – usually at their first journey from the house after confinement – long held an obligation by the church, was a relic of the barbarous supposition that women at that time were 'unclean' and the harbourers of evil spirits. Although today many women, even those not habitual church-goers, do still often attend soon after a birth and before the christening, the idea is usually to give thanks for a safe delivery. In the popular mind, however, the expedition to church, when undertaken, is still associated with the recovery of strength by the mother.

Religious belief apart, there are few today who do not have their babies christened – and as early as possible – to be seen thus as launching them properly in the world. Few remember the old danger that unbaptized children were believed to be especially liable to be stolen away by witches. Baptism is still thought by some to be beneficial to the health of a child, while many continue to regard it as most unlucky to give out the name of the child before the ceremony.

It is still taken as a favourable sign if the child cries during the baptism – known as 'letting the Devil out', who was supposed to leave the church through the north, or Devil's, door. In some parishes the north door was left open for this purpose.

In past times – and to perhaps a lesser degree today – christenings were important social occasions, and it was usual for the family to give a dinner or other refreshment afterward for the godparents and other guests as elaborate as their social and financial position allowed. John Izzard Pryor of Clay Hall, Walkern, described a christening dinner in a neighbouring parish, 10 September 1834: 'We dined at Mr and Mrs Nath. Chauncey's at Green Elms, Little Munden. Their youngest child was christened in the morning by Mr Jollonds the clergyman there who made one of the party. We had an excellent dinner, turtle soup, fish, etc. and spent a pleasant evening and had a rubber at short whist at which I lost 5s.'

For a girl no stage of life was more hedged about with mystery and folk belief than courtship and marriage. Whether one were fated to marry, and whom, the future of a romance, these were all-important when the woman's place in society generally was so largely one of dependence.

Certain times of the year were believed especially favourable for discovering the name of one's true love. The year began with the hopeful girl stealing out alone to look at the first new moon in January over a gate, followed by prayers on St Agnes' Eve (20 January) which if answered would cause her lover to appear that night in a dream, and later prayers 'to the good St Mark' on 24 April. The girl was certain to help her cause by gathering May Dew at daybreak on May Day, as the old rhyme said:

> Maid who on the first of May
> Goeth afield at break of day;
> Wash thy face in dew off the hawthorn tree
> And ever after a fair maid shall be.

A number of spells and divinations – including the magical 'Midsummer Men' – might be tried on 23 June, Midsummer's Eve, and on All Hallows, or 'Nutcrack Night', 31 October.

In Hertfordshire the time for courting was whenever the gorse was in bloom:

> When the gorse is out of bloom
> Then kissing is out of tune.

In fact the gorse is seldom out of flower in this relatively southern county. Courting couples were said to be 'walking out' or 'keeping company'. To 'talk' was to make love. Those who became engaged were 'tokened', and a 'keeper' was an engagement ring.

In Hertfordshire, as in other counties, the upper classes by custom married largely within the County, while the majority of other folk chose within walking distance and the parish. A plentiful supply of bachelors was one of the assets of Ashwell town, as pointed out in the traditional boasting rhyme:

> The houses they stand thick and thin,
> Young men there are in plenty.
> Young ladies they can have their choice,
> For there ain't such a place in twenty

There was a lively and deep-seated prejudice against young men coming courting from other parishes – but one facet of the ancient rivalry between them, which in a mild form still exists today, especially in rural parts of the county. People from Weston were noted for being inbred, and nicknamed the 'Weston Partners'. Their neighbours, the 'Graveley Grinders', were so-called because if they caught a man from Weston or any other 'furrin' parish 'walking-out' they were reputed to grind his backside on the stone at the smithy.

Girls, on the other hand, with a mind to the best husband, appear to have been far less parochial in their outlook, and in this respect at least had far more spirit of adventure – as related in the traditional Hertfordshire 'Sneezing Rhyme':

> ... Sneeze on a Tuesday, kiss a stranger.
> Sneeze on a Wednesday, sneeze for a letter,
> Sneeze on a Thursday, for something better.
> ... Sneeze on a Saturday, see your sweetheart tomorrow ...

The Marrying Times appointed by the Church before the Reformation set a pattern generally followed by custom for centuries afterward:

> Advent marriage doth deny,
> But Hilary gives the liberty;
> Septuagesima says thee nay,
> Eight days from Easter says you may;
> Rogation bids thee to contain,
> But Trinity sets thee free again.

In rural parishes today there is still a lingering notion that it is 'unlucky to marry between hay and harvest'. A century ago the County historian John Cussans found in the Parish Registers of Abbot's Langley that 'during the reign of Elizabeth, marriages were not only solemnized in Lent, but even on Good Friday'. Under the date 12th April, 1566, which was Good Friday, occurs the following:

> Thomas Robertte hanged himselfe uppon an Appletree
> in ye Churchfeild belonging to ye heires of James
> Hayward for the Love of Johane Hayward their Widdow
> unto whome the said Thomas was betrothed, And should
> have married as uppon Goodffriedaie in the Morninge.

Today in Hertfordshire it is almost the universal custom to have the parish church bells ring a joyful wedding peal before and after the ceremony. Not so in times past, however, for it was thought most unwise to have the bells rung for a wedding since, if a rope chanced to break, misfortune would follow the married couple thenceforth.

In some places, such as Baldock, it was the happy custom to give refreshment and good wishes to wedding parties after the ceremony at the churchyard gate. At Baldock this was called 'keeping Dick Taylor'. This referred to a famous silver half-gallon tankard inscribed with the name of its first owner – Richard Taylor, a brewer of Baldock – and called after him, as the custom was. Dick Taylor was presented to all wedding parties to drink from at the churchyard gates, or at the George Inn gateway on their return from church – and a fine of a shilling – used to refill the tankard for the pleasure of the presenters – was levied upon all who used both hands to lift Dick Taylor to drink. Dick Taylor, kept at the George and Dragon Inn, was used as well on other festive occasions in the town. On the Eve of Old Baldock Fair (20 September), known as Cheese and Onion Fair, the stall-holders would bring out Dick Taylor and invite their friends to drink – with the same forfeit for using two hands to raise it, and another for forgetting to shut down the lid afterwards.

Weddings among the upper classes were generally grand affairs in which it was the custom for all the parish, and particularly tenants and workpeople, to share in the celebrations. John Izzard Pryor of Clay Hall, Walkern, described such a wedding in the early years of Victoria's reign:

June 16, 1842. Dined at 7:30 o'clock, dressing afterwards to attend the Soiree given by Mr. Chauncey at Dane End to which 150 persons had invitations. The dejeuner took place at Green Elms after the wedding, Mr. Nathaniel Chauncey's daughter being married to a Mr. Maples about 11 in the forenoon at which a large family party attended. The church path and the church were strewed by young girls of the village dressed in white and a substantial dinner given to the poor.

We arrived at 9 o'clock and found the carriages coming in very thick. Dancing began directly afterwards and was kept up with great spirit. Quadrilles and waltzes were the prevalent dances. A most elegant supper was served up in an apartment nearly adjoining at 12 o'clock. Plenty of ices, champagne etc. and dancing resumed until 3 in the morning. We left about half past 2.

An instrument called the Choramcisicon, uniting the organ, pianoforte and harp, being equal to a complete band, was played by the person who owned it.

Cottage weddings were usually 'walking weddings'. Edwin Grey, writing of his youth in Harpenden in the 1860s said:

'I have known wedding-parties walk over two miles to and from the Parish Church, their homes being quite on the outskirts of the parish; maybe there were occasions when the wedding-party would arrive at church from these outlying parts by farm cart or pony trap, but I do not remember them. The bridal party would start off two by two, the bride to be and best man being first, the prospective bridegroom and the attendant bridesmaid following. As the little procession passed along the road one might have heard women's voices here and there, calling out from the doorways of the roadside cottages, expressing best wishes for good luck and happiness, for the young people would in nearly every case be well known by them all. . . . Not many people would attend the service at the church; a few intimate friends of the bride or maybe friends living near the church. On their return, the newly wedded pair would walk first, the best man and bridesmaid following, the expressions of goodwill and congratulations called out from cottage doorways as they passed along homeward being now if possible more hearty than before.

The wedding festivities were, as at the present day, generally held at the home of the bride's parents. . . . Here the guests, who were mostly members of the newly-married couple's families, and maybe two or three more intimate friends would assemble for the after ceremony meal . . . a good substantial meal with, as a rule, plenty of beer for those who drank it (and there were few who didn't) and maybe a bottle or two of home-made wine wherewith to drink the healths of the newly wed. . . .

The wedding-dinner was naturally prolonged, but when over, the wedded couple would, with their attendant groom and maid, if the weather was fine, go for a long walk or stroll across the Common or down the then country lanes, and they would still proceed two by two, as in the little wedding procession from the Church. . . . In the meantime the women guests would set-to, wash up, and get the place cleared up, ready for the evening or tea-time meal, for it must be borne in mind that there was only the one front room in which the assembly could be held, the second room or back house for the time being, having to serve for scullery, wash-house, larder etc.

This meal was generally delayed, so that any members of either family who had been at work on the farm would have by this time arrived home, and having washed and spruced up a bit, would now be able to be present at this pleasant tea-time meal. . . . A special cake was made for the occasion; among the cottage classes this was generally home-made, and baked in the community oven, being neither iced nor otherwise decorated . . . but this special wedding cake was easily recognized by its size and place of honour in the centre of the tea table.

In the evening, perhaps, a few more young men friends from the farms would also come along, and everything movable was pushed on one side, thus making as much seating room as possible, the evening passing pleasantly; for one might have heard songs (as a rule unaccompanied) rendered by both men and women friends, and there would be pleasant chatter and conversation; and maybe some young man in the company a bit more accomplished than the others, would give a mouth organ or jew's harp solo; he might even attempt to play an accompaniment to one or the other of the singers, or perhaps play for a step dance, the dance being performed by one of his mates. . . .

In any marriage there is a dominant member, and as often as not it was the wife. In Hertfordshire one traditional outward sign of this was a thriving rosemary bush in the garden. 'That be rosemary, sir,' said a cottager in reply to a query, 'and they do say it only grows where the missis is master, and it do grow here like wildfire.' This belief is still current in most rural parishes where a rosemary bush that 'does well' is certain to be remarked upon and the saying recalled.

Unhappiness, domestic strife, and immorality were as common in Hertfordshire as anywhere: ill-assorted marriages, husbands and sometimes wives who were drunkards – it is still remembered in Whitwell how those who could not stand were carried home from the seven pubs in wheel barrows – men who beat their wives and children, lewd women who upset the peace of the neighbourhood, and so on. When abuses were flagrant, however, the community showed its disapproval. Mild warnings were first given, but these always made pointed reference to the offence: a common warning to a wife-beater was a quantity of straw thrown upon the doorstep, 'all thrashed'. If these were ignored the community used the traditional expedient called 'Rough Music' or the 'Rough Music Parade', which was the final notice to desist or be run-out of the parish.

Edwin Grey in his *Cottage Life in a Hertfordshire Village* described 'Rough Music' in the neighbourhood of Harpenden in the 1860s:

. . . when it became known that so-and-so were to be given 'the rough music' on a certain night at a certain time, the news spread like magic; by whose authority the night and the time for the demonstration was fixed no one knew, but somehow everybody did know it, so that at the appointed time one might have seen a very mixed-up gang, composed of men, youths, and women, gathered outside the offenders' house, each member of the gang carrying some sort of article whereby he or she could make discordant noises; old kettles with stones inside, old tea-trays and sticks, bells, whistles, clackers, etc. At a given signal all would get in procession and march to and fro past the house, rattling the kettles, banging the tea trays, clanging the bells, twirling the clackers, etc., as they paraded up and down, thus making a most terrific and earsplitting din, for about an hour or so, and this for three successive nights sometimes, but generally one or two nights were sufficient for letting off the steam. I have witnessed three of these performances in my time, though I have heard of others. I was told that here they carried an effigy or effigies of the offending person or persons, which effigies, after the rough music parades were over, were taken on to the Common and burnt; here on the Common, the music makers were able to give vent to their feelings and shower abuse on the effigy to their heart's content. I understood the unwritten law concerning these affairs to be that the music makers could, if they so wished, perform on three successive nights, that they must keep on the move, that one could make as much noise as one wished, but that the names of the offenders or the nature of the offence must not be shouted out. With these conditions observed, it was affirmed that no police officer could interfere; if this was so, I cannot say, but certainly no police or any other officer interfered or made an appearance, so far as I can remember at any of the rough music parades that I witnessed.

The authorities, however, did not abstain everywhere, as the diary of John Izzard Pryor shows:

January 31, 1848. A great row took place in the village this evening in consequence of a gang of working men going about with rough music, intending to give a bad woman a ducking. She was a notoriously bad woman, and in the family way, and was saying she would swear the child to someone though she confessed she had been connected with many.

February 1, 1848. Three of the policemen that were engaged last night in taking into custody a riotous mob that were parading the village with rough music were very much cut about. Warrants are granted for several to appear before the Bench of magistrates at Hitchin tomorrow. It has been an old custom to go to the house of a notorious character with rough music, as they call it. They say that they should not have made any riot, had not the police set on them. It is a sad business and I think several will be comitted.

Most people in Hertfordshire, as elsewhere, made do with their fate and the responsibilities of marriage and family, encouraged, no doubt, by the fact that no divorce was recognized by the church, and that the cost of legal separation was beyond the reach of all but the well-to-do. Before the Reformation patient and dutiful wives afflicted with troublesome husbands prayed to St Uncumber (Wilgefortis) to be rid of them. 'For a peck of oats', as Sir Thomas More observed of her shrine and image in St Paul's, much frequented, as he said, by the matrons of London. One of the five lights in the church of St Lawrence, Bovingdon, was to St Uncumber, which was served by a Warden and Brotherhood that was not disbanded until 1545.

A master of accommodation to circumstance in Hertfordshire must surely be Reginald Hine's tale of the ownerless breeches that were cried for lost in Hitchin Market, taken from a newspaper of 31 May, 1775:

On Saturday, May 20th, a Tanner, who lives within twenty miles of Hitchin Back-Street, returning late from his Work, found his Wife was gone to Bed, but had forgot to lock the Door. The Husband, blundering in the Dark, just gave Time to another, who had supplied his Place, to get under the Bed. The Husband had put off his Clothes and was getting also into Bed when his Wife complained she was exceedingly ill, and should be glad of some Aniseed Water, but feared the Publick Houses were all shut up except the Sun Inn which was at the greatest Distance. The honest Man put on his Clothes, and went into the Sun, where, putting his Hand into his Pocket for a shilling to pay for the Water, the Waiter returned it to him, telling him he could not change his Guinea. The Man, amazed to hear Mention of a Guinea (knowing he had but a few shillings) hastily put his Hand again into his Pocket and pulled out nine more, with a Ten-Pound Bank-Note, and on further Examination found he had got a new Pair of Breeches and fine Watch. Comprehending the whole then in an instant, he observed with the coolness of a Philosopher, that the affair was over before this, and that what was done could not be undone. As his Wife, therefore, had been so industrious in putting him into so much Ready Money, he would have a Bottle of Wine first, and then carry her the Aniseed Water. The Tanner had the Breeches cried on Tuesday in the open Market, but has not yet found an Owner.

It was said that the bells of Hatfield church told the old story of wife-swapping. It is a curiosity that when change-ringers ring – in the same order for a time the bells soon begin to make a jumble of words, and this verse is one traditionally 'spoken' by the Hatfield bells:

Lend me your wife today,
I'll lend you mine tomorrow.
No, I'll be like the chimes of Ware,
I'll neither lend nor borrow.

If some – usually men – for whom marriage or other circumstances had become intolerable absconded, thus leaving responsibility and family upon the charity of the parish, others resorted to the old practice of selling their wives. As often as not when relations had reached such a stage no doubt both parties wished to try their luck for a better bargain. In any case, the procedure was for the man to exhibit his wife for sale at a market with a halter around her neck and to deliver her to the highest bidder. The halter symbolized the man's supposed proprietary right in his wife – a belief widely held among labouring people until fairly recently – not so far-fetched, if no less barbarous, an idea when one considers that again until recent years, upon marriage control of the woman's property passed to her husband. In Hertfordshire this was called 'apern-string-'old'.

The church, required as it was in the past to enforce much of the civil law concerning the family, did its best to stamp out the practice of wife-selling, as the records, among others, of the Archdeaconry of St Albans show. On 3 November, 1584, the Vicar of Rickmansworth, John Sterne, and the churchwardens, signed a certificate that Thomas Griffen, presented to the Archdeacon's Court for 'buying' the wife of Richard Baldwin had satisfied the congregation by acknowledging his fault. On 14 November, less than a fortnight later, a similar certificate was given stating that Richard Baldwin, of Rickmansworth, 'hath acknowledged and confessed his faulte which was committed by him in selling of his wife'.

The last of the great stages in life is the leaving of it. When, for most people, life was brief and little was to be done to touch the inexorability of it, omens of death, not strangely, were to be found everywhere. Meeting a funeral is still thought unlucky, particularly meeting it head-on. To avoid or to postpone fate one had to turn and walk or ride along with the procession, slowly, until one had been 'outwalked' or left behind by it. A Hertfordshire lady of Regency times is still remembered for her habit, when driving out, of always taking with her a supply of pins so that, whenever her carriage was met by a funeral, she had some to throw out of the window.

Animals in distress or acting strangely were well-known death omens: a cow lowing continually passing along a village street, and especially by the cottage of someone who was ill; a dog howling in the night; a hare looking in at a cottage or barn door. Seeing but one magpie, too, was the worst of omens, even if one showed proper respect by taking off one's hat or bowing when it appeared on one's left side. Some of the loveliest flowers signalled death if brought into the house, among these the May blossom, or hawthorn, and lilac, especially white lilac. Snowdrops and primroses, too, were only thought safe if picked in bunches.

In the last century an old woman at Essendon remarked, on hearing of the passing of a neighbour, that 'she was not at all surprised to hear of the death, as the church clock struck while they were singing in church on Sunday'. An empty grave on the Sabbath was said to invite another death in the parish before the week was out. Candles that 'spun winding sheets' and 'corpse lights' dancing by a cottage were other signs.

More fearsome still in Hertfordshire were the death omens that were ghosts. Among these were the large black funeral hearses which carried the coffins of squires and the rich to their last resting places: legend says that one of these with a headless coachman and black horses is to be seen 'when someone is about to die' driving toward St Paul's Walden Bury along the road from St Albans to Hitchin that once cut across the meadow known as Dove House Close. Another death omen in recent years more often heard than seen is the 'plague cart' that creaks its slow and deliberate way around Datchworth Green.

Some omens were attached to families or to family homes. Most notorious of these in Hertfordshire is the death warning of the Lyttons of Knebworth House, the spectre of a 'shining boy'. Among others the spectre is said to have appeared to Lord Castlereagh who was a guest at Knebworth shortly before his suicide in Kent in 1818, and because its coming was so frightful to have been the reason for the creation of Hertfordshire's best-known fictional ghost: Jenny Spinner.

There were those, however, who might safely ignore any omen. People in Wallington, still a small and isolated village hidden away in the chalk downs near Baldock, are said to live as long as they please.

The 'Passing Bell', thought to protect the soul of the deceased on its journey to the hereafter, was tolled usually for about half an hour to announce a death in the parish. The number varied from parish to parish, and told the sex of the person: at Harpenden it was three tolls for a man, two for a woman, and one for a child. In Hertfordshire the more downright referred to the deceased as 'gorn dead', but others said the person had 'passed over' or more graphically 'slipped through the hedge'. After death and before burial one was said to 'lie by the walls'.

Like their weddings, cottagers' funerals were generally 'walking' affairs. The coffin was carried on men's shoulders, in large parishes often for a distance of several miles. There were usually eight bearers, four carrying and four 'reliefs' walking by the side of the coffin, and the heads and shoulders of the bearers were covered over with a pall.

When the deceased was a tradesman it was customary for the bearers – usually friends belonging to the same trade – to wear the full dress of their calling. Thus at Hertford in the 1830s it was observed that at the funeral of a butcher the bearers wore blue smocks each with a band of black crepe tied around their arms, while the bearers for a blacksmith were dressed in white leather aprons.

The mourners walked behind the coffin in order of relationship, and last came friends and neighbours. In the mid-nineteenth century 'it was customary for a widow to wear a lot of crape, a widow's veil, trimming on dress, bonnet, etc., for the more they could smother themselves in this particular material the more grief and respect for the departed was supposed to be shown; in many cases the excess of mourning garb could be but ill afforded'.

Continuing his description of cottage funerals as he had known them in his youth at Harpenden, Edwin Grey wrote:

... no matter how poor the family of the deceased might be, some bread, cheese, and beer was always provided for the bearers, and partaken of before the start of the funeral procession; in cases of cottagers in somewhat better circumstances, ham or some other sort of meat would be provided. . . . After the procession had gone from the cottage, a friend or neighbour would then, as now, put the living room in order and set tea ready for the mourners on their return; sometimes if it could be afforded there would be what is now called 'high tea' provided. An old lady from a village near Harpenden attended a funeral of a relative or friend at another village a short distance away. Next day her neighbours asked her how she got on at the funeral. 'Not much,' she said, 'I didn't enjoy meself a bit; it was a very poor set out, there was only biscuits and sich. Why,' continued she, 'I've buried three 'usbands and I buried 'em all with 'am.'

More elaborate and elegant were the funerals of the County magnates. John Carrington of Bacon's Farm, Bramfield, described the funeral of the third Earl Cowper:

... He was brot back to Cole Green House to be buried on tusday 16 of Feby & Lay in State that night at Cole Green & was buried the next day, Wednesday, the 17th 1790, wich was this year Ash Wednesday, at the Familey Vault Hardingfordbury Church about 12 clock noon Herce wth 6 horses, 4 Coaches with 6 horses, all Scutchings & his Corrinett carred on Horseback on a Velvet Cushen before the Herce, the men bear head, & about 20 of his Tenants road before with (black) silk Bands & sashes. . . .

Among other traditional funeral customs was the 'funeral garland', a wreath of flowers made of wood, wax, silk, feathers, and other materials carried by young girls at funerals – these were called virgin garlands when the deceased was an unmarried woman – and later hung in the church. A garland long kept in the Watch Loft, in St Albans Abbey, is said to have been carried at the funeral of Sir Ralph de Rayne, who was murdered while on his way to his wedding in the Abbey. His bride was Lilian Grey, a ward of Sopwell Nunnery.

It was part of traditional belief that when a death occurred in the family the creatures that worked for it should be told. These included the plough horses, and, more commonly, the bees. One of the early collectors of Hertfordshire folklore, Edith Rinder, described the custom of 'telling the bees' in an article in the *Hertfordshire Illustrated Review* in 1894:

> Here, as elsewhere, it is considered essential to apprise them of the death of any prominent inmate of the household to which they belong; the ceremony generally takes place upon the day of the death after sunset, when an old servant or other esteemed member of the establishment taps three times at the different hives, and, in a voice audible to the whole community, tells of the sad event that has occurred. On occasions the bees are even regaled with wine and cake, but this is by no means usual. Anyone failing to inform the bees after this manner will, it is said, lose them all, whether by death or flight, and more than one instance in the County is brought forward in corroboration of this curious belief.

The Sunday after a burial it is still the custom, especially in rural parishes, for the family of the deceased and other mourners who can, to attend morning service in the parish church. In the last century and earlier, in the case of 'Walking Funerals', the mourners walked again in procession to the church, as nearly as possible in the same order as at the funeral. It is thought that this is a relic of the pre-Reformation practice of having special masses said for the soul of the dead at this time.

Clibbon's Post, Tewin Parish, 1976

6 Graves and Ghosts

> At Burnham Green just where the recent dead
> Ride a White Horse without a Head
> A Post is fixed along a Ditch....
>
> <div align="right">William Nobbs, 'The Parish Bounds
of Welwyn', <i>c.</i> 1820</div>

IT WAS THE HOPE that the souls of the dead would depart in peace and that once buried the body would remain in its grave, nor as spirit nor spectre rise again to trouble the living.

Hertfordshire being as near as it was to London, the advances in the study of anatomy brought fears of body-snatchers, best known as the 'resurrection men' who were particularly active here in Regency times. Burials in isolated village churchyards were most watched for, and if a grave were left unguarded for several nights after a funeral – or until decay had surely set in – there was great risk that the body would be got up, stuffed into a sack and driven quickly up to

London in the hay-carts that made regular journeys in the season, carrier's waggons, or even as freight in the boots of coaches. There was a good living to be made in this gruesome calling, so it was said, and a Whitwell man once boasted openly that he had stolen the body of his grandmother, saying that she would rather he got the money for the job than some stranger. The 'resurrection men' were not always successful, however. Relatives or friends of the deceased would take it in turn to watch the grave at night, and many a time they were disturbed by passers-by before their quarry was secured. In November, 1824, the body of John Gootheridge, a farmer of Nup End and Churchwarden of Codicote was found several days after his funeral lying in the churchyard. He was buried a second time, one week after the first, and his grave rail still proclaims. It was, moreover, a trick of the body-snatchers – as of smugglers, robbers, and others who were up to no good after dark – to revive or put about tales of churchyard ghosts so that they might ply their trades unmolested, thus adding to the vigour of local legend. Nor did the presence of grave-watchers in the churchyards, shadowy figures with their lanterns, lessen the traditional dread of such places.

For many the greatest fear was burial alive, and stories of unaccountable rappings from tombs – particularly the 'altar' tombs so prominent in churches and churchyards – and gravediggers' tales of skeletons being found in odd positions were passed down in a parish for generations if not centuries. The conviction was that not many were so fortunate as Matthew Wall, the sixteenth-century farmer of Braughing, who was being carried along Fleece Lane in his coffin when one of the bearers slipped and the coffin fell to the ground. Wall was revived by the jolt, and lived for some years thereafter, a noted figure in the neighbourhood. His will dated 1595 endowed the doles of 'Old Man's Day' and proclamations remembering the wonderful deliverance in Braughing and neighbouring parishes each year on the anniversary, 2 October.

The well-to-do often took elaborate precautions against premature burial. The Rev. Richard Orme, Rector of Essendon and Bayford and Vicar of All Saints, Hertford, by leaving nothing to chance became a legend. He was buried, according to instructions, in a tomb above the ground in Essendon churchyard against the Rectory garden, the fence being removed along that part of the boundary. The tomb had a door which was fitted with a lock: one key was buried in the coffin with the Rector, along with a loaf of bread and a bottle of wine. He was buried in October 1845, and while the gap in the hedge was some years later replanted, the fence was not replaced nor the door of the tomb finally sealed until 1881.

Small wonder that in Hertfordshire altar tombs in particular have 'resurrection' legends attached to them. Among the best known of these today is the belief, mostly current among the children, that running a certain number of times around a tomb will cause the deceased – or the Devil – to appear. At Aston the story is still told that running at midnight around a tomb on the north side of the churchyard seven times will make an old lady come out; at St Nicholas' churchyard, Stevenage, a circuit of twelve times around the tombstone to the left of the belfry door will bring out the Devil. There was a saying about the grave of Robert Snooks at Boxmoor, supposed to have been the last highwayman hanged in England, 11 March 1802. If one ran around it three times, and shouted 'Snooks' three times, he would pop his head up.

> Sitting in the meadow
> Among the buttercups
> Atishoo, atishoo
> We all jump up!

In four Hertfordshire churchyards, according to legend, there are tombs which testify to the truth of the Resurrection: Aldenham, Cheshunt, Tewin and Watford. At Tewin Lady Anne Grimston, who died in 1710, is supposed to have called upon those present to witness that, if scripture did indeed prove true, then seven trees would grow from her grave: and so they did, ash and sycamores.

At Watford it is called the Fig Tree Tomb, but it belongs to Ben Wangford. The *Parish Magazine* of September 1898, tells the story:

Ben Wangford as he was generally called, lived about the middle of the last century. I can't say if he was a native of Watford, or if married. But he was buried in St Mary's churchyard and had a handsome tomb for that period. He was a man of enormous size; it is said that his boots could contain a bushel of corn. He did not believe in a hereafter state and wished, when buried, to have something placed with his remains that would germinate and then his relations would know that his soul was alive. If nothing appeared they might know that his opinion was correct. I have not heard what was placed in the coffin, but a fig tree appeared and for years was passed unnoticed by strangers. Now it is very much talked of, and people travel miles to visit the tomb.

They still do.

Fear of burial alive was so great in one case that no grave or tomb was made at all. On 15 October 1724, was proved the strange will of Henry Trigg of Stevenage, a grocer by trade and a churchwarden and overseer. In 1722 Trigg had offered the parish, at a small yearly rent, the use of his barn at the rear of his shop in the High Street for a workhouse, the parish at its own expense to make it fit for habitation. The project was never carried out, but after Trigg's death not long afterward his barn gained much notoriety from the curious provision concerning it in Trigg's will: 'As to my body, I commit it to the west end of my hovel to be decently laid there upon a floor erected by my executor upon the purloyne [purlin].' For more than two and a half centuries Trigg's remains have rested in the barn as he directed, an object of great curiosity to the people of Stevenage – he is probably the best-known person ever to live there – and to the many travellers passing up and down the Great North Road. In 1774 Henry Trigg's house and shop became the Old Castle Inn, with the famous John Ray as landlord. The Castle did a flourishing trade as a staging place for the Oundle and other coaches on the Great North Road, and as a stop for cross-country traffic and the mail coach running from Hertford to Biggleswade in Bedfordshire. Yet, in spite of all this activity, mystery hung about the place, and with it the legend of Trigg and his bones still to be seen, and many looked, in the coffin out in the barn. Why was it, people asked, that in the great Stevenage fire in 1807 'Henry Trigg's House' escaped when all around it the buildings were destroyed? The Devil looking after his own? Trigg's coffin remains in its place to this day, and his ghost is still seen from time to time walking on tours of inspection.

Of those buried in consecrated ground, and many were not, not all thus blessed by the church were quiet souls departed. It was the ever-lasting duty of the first buried in any churchyard to guard it against evil: thus in legend every old Hertfordshire churchyard has one ghost at least, if only the large black dog – with fiery eyes – put in first by the Sexton in more modern times, as at St Nicholas's Church, Stevenage, and St Lawrence's at Bovingdon where he walks along the top of the churchyard wall. At Tring they say that Mother Shipton is buried under the church.

In Hertfordshire the upper classes, and those who would pay were buried within the church; in carved altar tombs, many of them with life-size effigies on the top; in arched 'founders' sepulchres let in to the walls; or, more prosaically, in family vaults in the crypt. Such tombs, especially those of founders or medieval benefactors, as with other prominent or curious features in churches, attracted legend. In the church of St Botolph at Eastwick the large recumbent effigy of a knight in chain mail used to be pointed out as the giant who protected the village. At Albury the tomb of Sir Walter de la Lee (d.1396) and his wife Margaret is known as the Adam and Eve tomb. In the church of St Mary the Great at Sawbridgeworth, according to legend, the hole in the armour of the effigy of Sir John Leventhorpe shows the place where a sword thrust is supposed to have killed him.

The tomb of Piers Shonks in the wall of Brent Pelham Church, inscribed with his feats in killing one dragon and defying another, no doubt did much to perpetuate his legend as an east Hertfordshire folk hero. Burial in a church wall, in any case, was said to give immunity from claims both from God and the Devil.

Burial of the bones of a ghost in a churchyard or other consecrated ground, on the other hand, is still believed to put an end to its haunting. Such a tale is remembered of the headless pedlar who, at the end of the eighteenth century, was a terror to travellers along the road through the warren at Bygrave. The pedlar had sold his stock of cloth at Baldock fair at a good profit and was riding home alone on the Ashwell road, when a great storm broke and he sought shelter nearby at Bygrave Farm. Here Thomas Fossey, the ne'er-do-well farmer, seeing his chance, murdered the pedlar for the money he was carrying. To prevent identification Fossey cut the pedlar's head off and threw the body down a dumb well. From that time the ghost of the pedlar was seen walking along the road carrying his lost head under his arm. Nor did this haunting stop until, many years later, his remains were given Christian burial; the pedlar's skeleton was found by chance in the dumb-well, and his skull at Wallington Farm in the next parish where Fossey, aided by the pedlar's money, had moved soon after the murder. At Whitwell the medieval Bull Inn in the High Street was long troubled by a ghost, said to be a recruiting officer done to death there in the time of the Napoleonic Wars. When, during alterations to the first floor in the 1930s, a walled-up cupboard was discovered, his bones were found and quietly buried in the churchyard – and this ghost has never been seen since.

Particular care was taken as well in the reburial of bodies exhumed by the authorities to confront suspects accused of their murder. It was believed that by certain signs of coming back to life they would incriminate the guilty. The following deposition was taken down by Sir John Maynard in the course of a murder trial at Hertford Assizes in 1629:

> That the Body being taken out of the Grave thirty Days after the party's death, and lying on the Grass, and the four defendants being required, each of them touched the dead Body, whereupon the Brow of the dead, which before was of a livid and carrion colour, began to have a dew or gentle sweat arise on it, which encreased by degrees, till the sweat ran down in drops on the face; the brow turn'd to a lively and fresh colour; and the deceased opened one of her Eyes, and shut it again three several times: she likewise thrust out the Ring or Marriage Finger three times, and pulled it in again, and the Finger dropt blood upon the Grass.

Although in popular belief, if not in Christian dogma, burial outside consecrated ground meant a denial of salvation and the likelihood of becoming an unquiet spirit or a ghost, there were those who chose it. Among them was Sir John Jocelyn, Bart., from an ancient and honourable family of Hyde Hall, Sawbridgeworth, who died on 1 November 1741. This Sir John was an eccentric, who had more than one falling-out with the Vicar, and in the end refused burial in the churchyard. He left careful instructions for burial at sunset with his horse in the circle of yew trees in the grand avenue leading to Hyde Hall, and for his best ox to be slaughtered and given to the poor of Sawbridgeworth as a feast. Nor was anyone in the neighbourhood surprised when Sir John's ghost was later seen, mounted on his white (grey) hunter, galloping down the avenue towards Hyde Hall – as it has done from time to time to this day.

Another whom legend says wished to be buried outside the churchyard was Sissavernes, the wicked farmer of Codicote. He is supposed to have sworn never to leave his own land, and when he died his body was buried there on a hill-top. Another version of the tale is that this spot was chosen because here his bier became so heavy that the horses could not draw it on to the churchyard. If this was for the great weight of his sins in life, it accords best with Sissavernes' later character as a ghost, portrayed in the rhymed directions for beating the bounds of the adjacent parish of Welwyn, written by the Welwyn Parish Clerk, William Nobbs, about 1820:

> To Sissafernes, where many a tale was told
> Of fam'd old Sis, renowned in days of old,
> Who play'd such pranks they say in days of yore
> No other ghost had power to play before.
> And as he rose from out the Stygian shades
> He fed the horses and he kiss'd the maids.
> There was a maid, perhaps her name was Beck,
> She would not let him, so he broke her neck.
> Grandames of him did tell most wondrous tales
> To frighten children from the lonely vales. . . .

Those denied Christian burial in consecrated ground included suicides, the insane, and felons. The best these could hope for, before the 1823 Act of Parliament ordered parishes to set aside a piece of unconsecrated land for them, was burial by a crossroads. Here in many cases wayside crosses had stood before the Reformation, and the places were hallowed by tradition long after memory of the crosses and their benevolent shadows had been lost. Near Bishop's Stortford at the top of Holloway Hill on the site of Wayte's Cross (one of the four medieval crosses of Bishop's Stortford) was a place greatly dreaded by those who had to pass that way after dark. The gruesome stories told about it received due confirmation when, during road alterations, some skeletons were dug up there. Legend, too, is the story of Tommy Deacon of Wiggen Hall, Watford, who rode so furiously down the hill which now bears his name that he broke his neck – and was buried at the foot by the crossroads. Another version has it that Tommy Deacon lies near the top of the hill, and that in the wettest weather his grave, like Gideon's fleece, is always dry.

In Hertfordshire bodies buried in unhallowed ground often had a stake driven through 'to hold them down' and stop the corpse walking as a ghost. Best known of these for the better part of 200 years is the grave of Walter Clibborn, the piemaker-turned-footpad of Wareside, who murdered more than one while robbing his chosen victims, farmers and merchants carrying large sums from Hertford market. Clibborn's grave is in Oakenvalley Bottom by the Bull's Green Road in the parish of Tewin, and his stake, known as 'Clibborn's Post', has been renewed carefully in the belief that otherwise so 'wicked' a man must surely walk. Clibborn, in the way of rogues, has become a well-known folk figure in Hertfordshire, though not so notorious as the highwaymen Dick Turpin or James Whitney, and his story has gathered to itself the exploits of many another robber in the neighbourhood. Clibborn was shot dead while trying to rob Benjamin Whittenbury of Queen Hoo Hall on 28 December 1782, and was buried by the roadside where he fell.

In spite of careful precautions, Hertfordshire had ghosts of all kinds — as it still does — in every parish and from every age. The benevolent antiquarian Henry Nash (d.1899) whose little shop in Castle Street supplied leather to bootmakers, explained in his *Reminiscences of Berkhamsted* printed in 1890:

> We are apt to smile sometimes at the primitive habits of our forefathers who retired to rest as the shades of evening closed around them; still there was some wisdom in it in those days: they avoided many evils that are bred in darkness, and escaped many unpleasant encounters to which they would have been otherwise exposed. After the closing of the shops, which had then only a dismal apology for lighting, the town was left in total darkness, save one solitary oil lamp in front of the King's Arms — the effect of this was to intensify the surrounding gloom. Occasionally one might meet some aged persons bearing before them the old horn lantern, endeavouring to illumine their pathway by aid of a rushlight; seen in the distance this would flicker hither and thither like a will-o-the-wisp on the marshy moor, leaving one long in doubt as to the object they were about to approach. Feeble as were these lights, they served a useful purpose in preventing collisions, which in their absence were of frequent occurrence. There were many places in the town of evil repute, and of which timid folk

had a natural dread; almost every lane and dark corner were said to be haunts of supernatural beings, and the churchyard with its ghostly visitants, impelled many to hasten their speed as they passed it in the darkness. The uneducated class, which was much the larger, were nearly all trained by tradition to believe in supernatural appearances, and one was thought to have had little experience in the world if they had not in some form or other met with these strange beings.

Belief in ghosts and spirits, however, was common enough among the upper levels of society. In the latter part of the eighteenth century the Royston Dissenting Book Club, with a membership of clergymen, lawyers, doctors and successful tradesmen from the district – and their wives – debated among other propositions of current interest: 'Is there any foundation in fact for the popular belief of ghosts and apparitions?' The voting showed 15 in favour and 26 against, which a century later prompted the Royston historian Alfred Kingston – who made little use of oral tradition – to observe: 'If fifteen men of education voted for the ghosts can we wonder at the stronghold they had among the common people?'

Ghosts known to history, being in part at least associated with folk-memory, often very old, of events or living people, on the whole have evoked less fear. Nell Gwynne appears as a beautiful grey lady at the moated manor house, Salisbury Hall, at London Colney; Lord Capel, 1631-83, one of those implicated in the Rye House (Broxbourne Parish) Plot to shoot Charles II and the Duke of York as they journeyed to London from Newmarket Races in the spring of 1683, walks on the anniversary of his death at his seat, Cassiobury Park, Watford; one of Hertfordshire's greatest eccentrics, High Sheriff in 1661, the noted Levantine traveller Sir Henry Blount, 1602-82, is still to be seen in his mansion of Tyttenhanger, in the parish of Ridge, his satin dressing gown rustling as he walks along the passage to his study on the second floor. John Evelyn, described Sir Henry in his *Diary* (30 September 1659) as 'the famous Traveller and water-drinker' – he had acquired the then curious habit of taking coffee while in Turkey. Lord Anson, known to history as the circumnavigator (1740-44) and naval commander in the rout of the French fleet off Cape Finisterre in 1747, retired to Moor Park, at

Rickmansworth, where he built the stone Temple of the Winds, of which his friend Dr Samuel Johnson wrote:

> A grateful wind I praise;
> All to the winds he owed,
> And so upon the winds
> A temple he bestowed.

The Temple was blown down in a gale in the early part of this century, but the old Admiral's ghost still takes its daily walk among the ruins.

Among the most agreeable of ghostly phenomena in Hertfordshire must be the game of bowls played on the green that used to run down to the little River Hiz behind the Sun Inn at Hitchin. Here, on fine summer evenings in the eighteenth century was a game between two gentlemen scholars: Mark Hildesley, 1698-1772, one of the best-loved Vicars of Hitchin and later Bishop of Sodor and Man; and Edward Young, 1683-1765, Rector of Welwyn and author of the elegiac poem 'Night Thoughts', in which appears the line 'Procrastination is the thief of time ...'. The two still play at bowls in the right season of the year, it is said, when heard again are the 'chink' and 'kiss' of the woods, and Young's deep voice as he disputes the score.

Strife and conflict and the agonies connected with disaster and death, evoking as they do great emotion, however, appear by numbers at least to have contributed most to ghost lore in Hertfordshire. In a strategic position, one day's march north of London, Hertfordshire has seen its share and more of ancient battles, most of which, if parish legend is questioned even today, have left spectres of the event behind them.

Shadowy figures of Roman soldiers walk by the Icknield Way at Miswell, and elsewhere, in Tring parish at sunset, wounded from a ghostly battle between the Romans and the Iceni along Duncombe Terrace are brought down to the waters of the Bulbourne. It was at Welwyn, in the Danelaw a few miles north of the River Lea, that there began an uprising of the English against the Danes instigated by Ethelred the Unready, on St Brice's Day, 13 November 1002. William Vallens, a native of Ware, recorded the event in his description of the River Lea and its tributaries, *A Tale of Two Swannes* (1589):

... And then to Welwine, passing well beknowne,
And noted for a worthie stratagem:
I meane the Danes, who on St Bryce's night
Were stoughtly murdered by their women foes. ...

To this day White Horse Lane, on the Welwyn parish boundary with Datchworth, is haunted by a headless white horse which is heard galloping down from Burnham Green – ridden, says legend, by the formless ghosts of the dead. At best of times the Lane is an 'unkid' (melancholy) place, as countrymen say, and to be avoided, nor with kindly persuasion can horses or dogs be induced to go along it.

Three major battles in the Wars of the Roses were fought in Hertfordshire: the struggle began with the First Battle of St Albans (22 May 1455); a second battle was fought at St Albans on 17 February 1461; and another at Barnet on Easter Day, 14 April 1471. In St Albans sounds of the fighting can still be heard on Holywell Hill by the place between the Checquers Inn and the old Cross Keys, where the Yorkists forced a bloody entry to the town 'blowing up his trumpets and shouting with a great voice "A-Warwick! A-Warwick!"'. There are those who say that a thick mist comes to Barnet on the anniversary of the battle, as it did when raised to help the forces of Edward IV by the wizard Friar Bungay, who worked this magic from the tower of Hadley church.

The Civil War in Hertfordshire was, in contrast, an ordeal of minor incidents, marching and skirmishing, hit-and-run cavalry raids along the western border, hapless queues of bedraggled prisoners, herded for safe-keeping at night into the churches, come from Colchester to cross the county westward after the fall of the Royalist stronghold in 1648. All are to be found in parish tales of hauntings: phantom Royalist soldiers – some of whom left graffiti in the churches as well – at Watton-at-Stone and Graveley; a whole detachment of marching Roundheads in the Berkhamsted lane still known as Soldiers Bottom whose helmets and pikes can be seen glittering as the sun sets. Local people in this neighbourhood persist in the legend that it was from high ground at Wigginton – an adjoining parish – that Cromwell's men, the villains after the Restoration, trained their cannon on the town of Berkhamsted and destroyed the Castle.

One of the best-known west Hertfordshire ghosts is the fugitive cavalier known as Goring, a relic of the threatened Royalist invasion of the county in the summer of 1644. Goring, who had been wounded in a skirmish was given shelter by Henry Docwra at High Down House, near Pirton. When Parliament troopers came up, they searched the house and found nothing, but as they came away they discovered Goring hiding in the hollow of a Wych-elm by the gate – and killed him in cold blood. On the night of 15 June every year, the anniversary of his murder, so it is said, Goring rides headless on a white horse to Hitchin Priory, where he disappears.

Later wars, too, have left their ghosts: from the Napoleonic Wars comes the ghost at the White Hart, Hemel Hempstead, a tall young man who would not become a recruit, or reneged upon the King's Shilling, and was killed at the foot of the staircase; from the Second World War the tank which drives slowly from Knebworth House lodge gate toward Codicote, with its hatch open and a soldier in a steel helmet motioning all on the road to take cover, presumably from a German air raid.

There are numbers of monkish ghosts which in Hertfordshire as in other places are associated with most pre-Reformation religious foundations. Long settled now as members of the community – the ghostly monks of St Albans Abbey are good examples – they are even said to be omens of good luck. Such are the five errant monks of Braughing that walk at Horse Cross one night every five years; by local reckoning they should appear next in May 1981. The ghostly walk is said to be penance for eating trout caught without leave in the River Rib – which poisoned them for their transgression.

For grave infringement of discipline monks and nuns were walled up alive, and the horror of their fate makes these among the most dreadful of all ghost legends. Hinxworth Place, built as a monastery for the White Monks (Cistercians) in the eleventh century, has one of these. The haunting takes place along one of the small staircases leading to the attic where this message is inscribed on the wall:

> This is where a monk
> was buried alive in this wall.
> His cries can be heard sometimes
> at midnight. 1770.

Most of the ghostly monks of Hertfordshire, however, are merely going about their accustomed duties, as at St Albans Abbey where they are often heard singing Matins at the ancient time of 2 a.m. At Little Wymondley the ghost of the last Prior, Richard Atow, still walks the paths of the box orchard, some say grieving for the destruction of the monasteries. It is a paradox that, according to legend, the wickedest of all Hertfordshire men, Sir Geoffrey de Mandeville, Earl of Essex, who lived at South Mimms Castle in the time of King Stephen, laid a terrible curse upon those who had seized the lands he had given as founder to Walden Abbey (Essex) for the monks to say masses for his soul. Until these are returned, moreover, Sir Geoffrey's ghost walks his former domains from South Mimms to East Barnet every six years near Christmas dressed in full armour and a red cloak and followed by a spectral dog.

Every age has its particular ghosts, and those becoming popular in the telling are not long in making a place in local legend; modern stock-character additions to County lore include the phantom hitchhiker and the ghostly car broken down on a motorway – there is a notorious instance of one of these along the Watford Bypass. Best of all, perhaps, is the ghost of the Great Northern engine driver.

'Three years ago, sir,' said the retired railwayman toward the end of the last century,

'I was driving the 8:30 train to the North, and left King's Cross four minutes behind time. I can't tell you what it was, but I never felt nervousness but once on an engine, and that was on the night I'm talking about.

Now, sir, I don't know nothing about ghosts or spirits, or apparitions – call 'em what you like – but I'm ready to swear before any judge today that I saw something of the kind that night, and no amount of argument will change my belief. It was just when we were passing through Hatfield when, I would take my oath for all I am worth that a man stepped from the platform to the footplate, just as easily as though we weren't travelling about fifty-five miles an hour. Ay, I can see his face and dress to this day. It was the saddest face I ever come across. The eyes seemed to look you through and through; and when on top of that I saw that he was all in black, I never was so afraid in my life.

The curious thing is that Dick, my fireman, saw nothing of it. He coaled up for the hill by Welwyn just as natural as though all was fair sailing, and when I tried to shout to him, I felt a great lump in my throat, and not a word could I speak. I soon noticed that the strange-comer never went to any other part of the footplate except to the spot whereon I stood, and he even hedged up so close to me that I went cold all over, and my feet were like lumps of ice. I think I must have acted mechanically, for I watched the man put his hand upon the regulator, and I put mine on with him. The touch of it was like the touch of snow, but I couldn't loose it, and before I knew what I'd done, the steam was cut off and the train was slowing.

Dick, I know, thought I was mad. He'd been away on the tender, breaking up the coal, but he came down and craned his neck when steam was off, and he saw, as I saw, that the distant signal was off, and after that the home signal stood for line clear. You won't believe, perhaps, but its Gospel truth, that though I knew the way was right, I was compelled to stop that express, and stop her I did outside Hitchin Station.

For nothing you say; well, Heaven alone knows how, but it proved to be for a great deal. There were two trucks across the main line, and although the signals were off, the way was blocked, so that me and the passengers behind me, wouldn't be living to tell the story if I hadn't been compelled to pull up as I did. . . .'

The White Horse of Burnham Green, Inn sign, 1976

Lightning Charm roof tile, now at Hitchin Museum

7 Cures, Charms and Healers

> It is the garden of England for delight, and men commonly say that such who buy a house in Hertfordshire pay two years' purchase for the air thereof.
>
> Thomas Fuller, *Worthies of England*, 1662

HERTFORDSHIRE WAS KNOWN as a resort for health: for royalty in Tudor and Stuart times with their residences at Hatfield and Theobalds and the 'hunting box' of James I at Royston; for Londoners whose riches came from City trade at their many country seats. Post-boys who brought 'round the horses for riders and coaches sang:

> Who rides a mare through Hertfordshire
> Pays two-thirds value to the air.

Other verses paid tribute to 'who builds a house', the saying traditional by Fuller's time, and 'who weds a maid'.

If Hertfordshire people were reputedly healthier than most, in illness they had no better cures and healers than the knowledge of the times provided. It is only within very recent years that people expected cures to be as kindly and painless as possible, and medicines palatable, that they found confidence in the practices and practitioners of science rather than traditional cures and charms and folk-healers.

Folk medicine depended for its effectiveness upon the expulsion from the afflicted person of the evil or devil whose invasion of the body was believed to be the cause of all illness and debility, whatever their visible symptoms. The more the pain and discomfort, or bad tasting and revolting the remedy, the more certain the cure.

Of all the traditional cures, most widely and most recently resorted to in Hertfordshire with its many chalk-fed streams and springs, was the waters of certain sacred wells. Certainly no other agency is as well known in oral tradition or written records. One of the oldest Hertfordshire legends tells of the spring that burst forth at the top of the hill overlooking the River Ver by command of St Alban that he might drink before he was done to death by the Romans. Ever after the place has been called Holywell Hill, and it was here that the great Benedictine Abbey dedicated to St Alban was later built. St Alban's shrine rivalled in popularity that of Our Lady of Walsingham as a place of pilgrimage for the sick and troubled before the Reformation.

At the bottom of Holywell Hill, at a little distance from the walls of the Roman city of Verulamium, was an ancient well said to have healed the wounds of the Christian leader Uther Pendragon, father of King Arthur. The chronicler Brompton, who lived in the time of Richard II, wrote:

> Now during these conflicts [between the English and the Saxons] no mention is made of Verulam, nor of any transaction there, although it had been a capital city of the Romans; except this, that Uter Pendragon, a British prince, had fought the Saxons in a great battle at this place, and received a dangerous wound: and lay a long time confined to his bed: and that he was cured at length by resorting to a well or spring not far distant from the City, at that time reputed salubrious; and for that reason, and for the cures thereby performed, esteemed holy; and blessed in a peculiar manner with the flavour of Heaven....

In 1815, when Shaw the bookseller published his *History of Verulam and St Albans*, the 'Holy-well' was 'still held in some estimation, for its purity and salubrious qualities'.

Pre-Christian curative wells were dedicated to Christian saints in Hertfordshire as in other places. Cadwell at Ickleford and Chad's Well springs, in the meadows between Hertford and Ware, both noted for the treatment of eye diseases, were named for St Chad, missionary to the East Saxons and patron of the blind and of medicinal springs. Chad's Well, a source of the New River brought to London by Sir Hugh Myddleton in 1613, was the more valued for the benefits of its water. The Holy Well at Bishop's Stortford was dedicated to St Osyth, founder of a nunnery in Essex who was killed by marauding Danes in AD 635 and greatly venerated afterward in East Anglia. A chalybeate spring, it, too, was said to have special curative affects upon eye diseases – and made the best pea soup for miles around.

The legend is still told of how a monk at Berkhamsted had a dream that the waters of the pagan spring were to be blessed and dedicated to Christian healing under the patronage of St John the Evangelist, and of how a shrine was built and a hospice for pilgrims and a community of monks. The waters of St John's Well were thought to cure a variety of diseases; among these leprosy and scrofula (the King's Evil) as well as sore eyes. There was also a persistent belief that clothing washed in its water would impart good health to the wearers. Washerwomen were prosecuted for polluting the well in 1400, and wardens were afterward appointed to see that St John's Well was used only for drinking.

One of the best known of Hertfordshire's magical wells was that of St Faith at Hexton. This well, with its shrine and the customs attached to it before the Reformation, were described by the seventeenth-century lord of the manor, Francis Taverner. A zealous Protestant opponent of 'superstition', Taverner ordered the destruction of shrine and well, and this was carried out so thoroughly that the site has not since been found:

> There is a small perscell of ground adjoyning to the Churchyard, called St ffaith's wick ... the greatest parte standing upon a bedde of springs, and undrained was very boggye, towards the Churchyard. But the West side of the wick, being higher ground

... neer adjoyning unto which ... the Craftye Priests had made a Well, about a yard deep and very cleere in the bottome, and curbed about, which they called St Faith's Well.

Now over this Well, they built an Howse, and in this Howse they placed the image or statue of St Faith and a Cawsey they had made ... for the people to passe, who resorted thither from farr and neere to visit our Lady and to perform there devotions, reverently kissing a fine Colloured stone placed in her toe (it seems the good ladye was troubled with Cornes in her feet ...)

The people that came to offer did cast some thing into the Well, which if it swamme above they were accepted and theire Petition granted, but if it suncke, then rejected, which the experienced Prieste had arts enowe to cause to swymme or sincke according as him selfe was pleased with the Partye, or rather with the offring made by the Partie. ...

Following reports by local clergy, Hugh of Grenoble, Bishop of Lincoln (1186-1200), journeyed among other places to Berkhamsted to stop people from worshipping the nymphs and sprites in St John's Well, dancing around it by moonlight and dressing the well with flowers and garlands.

Unlike Hexton, most of the curative wells in the County outlasted the destruction of the Reformation, and were patronized by seekers after health even in modern times. Writing in 1700 Sir Henry Chauncy, the historian, described the benefits to be had from the 'waters' at Barnet, "Northall" and Cuffley:

There are in this County some Waters or Springs that are physical, one in the Common near Barnet, another in the common at Northall, and a third at Cuffley in the same Parish: These purge most by Siege; the Mineral they are impregnated with is supposed to be Alom, but most certainly a mixt fixt Salt, of which 'tis hard to determine. They purge very kindly, and are of great Use in most Weakly Bodies; especially those that are hypocondriacl or hysterical. They dissolve acid tough Flegm in the Stomach and Guts, with sharp Choler, much better than other Purgers; and are of great Efficacy in Cholicks, proceeding from both those Humours; in short, for most Diseases that proceed from sharp and hot humours (if they pass freely) they prove excellent safe Purgers.

Some waters in Hertfordshire were avoided for their bad reputation. The flowing of 'woe-waters' foretold pestilence, famine, war, and other disasters. 'At Redbourne', wrote Chauncy,

> the Ver was joined by a small brook called Wenmer or Womer, which sometimes breaks forth, and 'tis observed forerunneth a Dearth, or some Extremity of dangerous Import, thence streaming by the Ruins of Old Verulam, did heretofore feed a great Fishpool, between that Place and St Albans, afterwards watering the Nunnery at Sopwell.

Among other 'woe-waters' are the Kine, which once ran through Kimpton Bottom, and the Bourne Gutter, which 'flows in times of war or rumours of war' past Berkhamsted, for a mile or two along the boundary with Buckinghamshire, to join the Bulbourne at Bourne End.

Stones are still valued in Hertfordshire for their rarity – much of the land is clay, gravel, or loam overlaying chalk-with-flints or the soft limestone known as 'clunch' – and mysterious powers. Two ancient town 'guardian' stones remain, 'Dixie's Stone', which stood across the road from Dixie's farm gate at Ashwell; and the Roysstone, from which the town is said to have taken its name, still to be seen in the town centre at Royston Cross.

The very rare Hertfordshire 'Plumb-Pudding Stones', lumps of conglomerate, glacial gravel and pebbles cemented together with calcium carbonate, were much prized as charms against evil, and stood in prominent places, against gates, and the like. Flints, found everywhere and in great numbers, were also thought to possess supernatural powers. Flints with holes in them – quite rare – were used as charms against illness and kept carefully: I was told that a large holed flint edging the lawn in front of my house 'would not stop there long' and that I 'should take better care of it, hang it in the garage'. Holed flints were hung in barns or with brasses on harness as charms against diseases in horses. Holed flints, too, were said to prevent horses from sweating by keeping away the dread 'night-hags' that got into stables at night, took the horses and galloped them over the fields, or hunted them about all night in the stables before returning them, lathered with sweat, to their stalls.

Few Hertfordshire countrymen were without one or two 'God-stones', small pebbles of a whitish colour, transparent or opaque, carried in their pockets for luck and to keep away sickness, particularly rheumatism. When these could not be found – they usually came from gravel pits – small potatoes about the size of a walnut were used instead. Reginald Hine, the lawyer and historian of Hitchin, wrote in 1929 that he knew 'four quite ordinary people who carry flints from Minsden Chapel (i.e. consecrated stones) about with them wherever they go', and that 'one of them ascribed her recovery from a serious illness entirely to the healing power of the talisman beside her bed'.

Traditions associated with trees and plants persist. It is still rare to find mistletoe and holly in church decorations at Christmas, though most contrive to have them in their homes, and, however poor, no one now – or in the past – would burn elder wood which grows so readily in the County as to be called by some the Hertfordshire weed. Most people have forgotten that this is because to burn elder is a sure way of raising the Devil.

Young ash trees were used for the cure of hernia, and rickets and other bone deformities in children. The child would be passed one or more times through a split in the tree, which was afterward bound together, and, as it knit together, the child's affliction would likewise disappear.

Acorns were kept in the pocket as health-giving charms, those from Gospel Oaks or other trees along the parish boundaries being thought most effective. The story is still told with regret about the great oak in the grounds of Hatfield House where, according to legend, Queen Elizabeth received news of her accession, and of how Queen Victoria in the middle of the last century took away what proved to be the last of its acorns for planting at Windsor – since her visit the tree has produced no more.

Here and there were curative trees. Near Berkhamsted there was an old oak known as the Cross Oak which stood in a group of trees near a crossroads. People who suffered from ague would go to this charmed tree, peg a lock of their hair to it, and with a sudden jerk leave the hair – and the ague – firmly attached to the tree.

Before the time of scientific medicine cures were thus compounded largely of magic and luck. They were based upon such beliefs as like remedy curing like symptoms and an affliction's capability of being transferred from a person to an animal or inanimate object. There was little to distinguish in their nostrums between physicians and white, or good, wizards, cunning men, and wise women.

One of the best known of medieval English 'Men of Physick' was a Hertfordshire man, John of Gaddesden. Royal physician and friend of Chaucer, he appears in the Prologue to the *Canterbury Tales*. Gaddesden's book, *Rosa Anglicia*, with its five parts – fevers, injuries, general hygiene, diet, materia medica, and treatment by drugs – enjoyed a great vogue in its time. It may be that *Rosa Anglicia* was, as the critic Guy de Chauliac later wrote at Paris (1363): 'a foolish English rose which contains no sweetness but only a few old fables'. Certainly it is among the earliest collections of cures and charms that sprang from the County.

For those who could read there were as well the 'commonplace books', inherited or made oneself – which invariably included a sprinkling of useful cures and charms. The commonplace book of Richard Hill, Gentleman, of Hillend, Langley (Hitchin), dating from the first part of the sixteenth century gives directions for such as 'medicen for a doge that is poysent'.

By the mid-eighteenth century William Ellis of Little Gaddesden, a writer noted for his anecdotal style, was including in his books on husbandry and farm management a selection of the traditional Hertfordshire magical charms and cures – seemingly as much for the entertainment as for the enlightenment of his readers, at that time still people of some education. In his *Country Housewife's Family Companion* Ellis described how:

> A Girl at Gaddesden having the Evil in her feet from her infancy, was cured by the advice of a Beggar Woman, who coming to the door said that if they would cut off the hind Leg and the Foreleg on the contrary side of a Toad, and Tie them in a silken Bag about her Neck it would certainly Cure her. She said the Toad was to be turned loose, and as it pin'd, wasted, and dy'd, the Distemper would likewise waste and die; which happened accordingly, for the Girl was intirely cured of it.

Within living memory there have been many who have relied more or less upon the practitioners, charms, and cures of folk medicine. Nor was this trust entirely misplaced. Some traditional cures had undoubted benefits: dried foxglove leaves contain digitalis, the heart stimulant, and poppies, so great a pest in corn fields, opium which dulled pain – to name only two. William Ellis told about the popular use of a concoction made from the ubiquitous Hertfordshire hedgehog as a remedy for deafness. 'A young Man', he wrote, 'was cured ... with Dripping of Hedgehogs, 3 Drops into his Ear at Night, the same in the Morning, and so for two Days, when it cured him', as indeed oil is prescribed by doctors today for simple blockages in the ear.

Some folk cures traded upon the macabre and were resorted to only by the bravest. A bit of the rope which had been used to hang a man, when worn in the hat, was a cure for headache, while it was thought that the touch of the hand of a hanged man would reduce goitre and other growths as the body of the felon decayed upon the gibbet.

Warts were always the province of the charmer. U. B. Chisenhale Marsh, who collected folklore in the Stort Valley and along the Hertfordshire-Essex border at the end of the nineteenth century, wrote:

> An old lady in Thorley told me of an old man who used to be called the 'tu'penny ha'penny man' – his real name was Bonney. He lived in Bishop's Stortford when she was a child, and could charm away warts and sores. She herself had been cured of the former by her schoolmaster, who advised her to count them, take a black snail and stick it on a thorn bush; as the snail perished they would disappear, provided secrecy were observed, 'and they all went, sure enough', she concluded.

Around Harpenden, in West Hertfordshire, a bit of raw meat was rubbed on the warts and then buried in the ground: it was supposed that as the meat rotted so the warts would disappear.

Toothache, was thought to be caused by a tiny wriggling worm in the tooth which, once it had entered, had to be driven out to obtain relief. Charms without number were tried to keep toothache away: one favourite was a live garden snail carried in a pill box in the pocket. Once afflicted, a good smoke of the magical and evil-smelling henbane seed was said to be a cure. Many called upon the saving powers of the Almighty with scriptural charms such as this one which was repeated seven times:

And the Lord said unto Peter,
'Peter what ailest thou? 'And
Peter said, 'Lord, I am sore
troubled with the toothache.'
And the Lord said unto Peter,
'Trouble not, Peter, for the
toothache has departed from
thee.' In the name of the Father,
and of the Son, and of the Holy
Ghost. Amen. Amen. Amen.

Another charm with Biblical associations, this one making use of the tale of the patriarch Jacob's vision of the ladder to Heaven, is still remembered around Pirton as a cure for hiccups:

Take a cup of water, and say:

Hiccups, Hiccups,
Rise up Jacob.
Seven gullups in the cup
Cure Hiccups.

Boys at the Hertford Blue Coat School suffering from cramp in unheated dormitories would jump out of bed and say:

The Devil is tying a knot in my leg,
Mark, Luke, and John, unloose it, I beg,
Crosses three we make to ease us,
Two for the thieves and one for Christ Jesus.

The specifics for folk cures and remedies were many. For consumption there was the Hertfordshire 'Great Roman Snail', eaten raw and thought by some to equal oysters in flavour. Another prescribed a visit to the fields in the early morning, while the dew was still on the grass. The sufferer was to dig a hole in the ground large enough for his face, and then lie down with his face in the hole, breathing deeply the smell of newly turned earth.

While sore eyes could be prevented by wearing 'sleepers', a form of ear-ring, sore eyes and sties would go away if rubbed with a gold wedding ring. Rings were the Hertfordshire cure for fits. Fit-rings were made from 7, sometimes 8, silver three- or four-penny pieces obtained as gifts or from the communion plate, and worn on the third finger of the right hand.

Asthma was cured in West Hertfordshire by swallowing young frogs, and an exotic relief from piles could be obtained by sitting over the smoke of burning Frankincense and Pomegranite shells. For jaundice the cures all had the yellowish colour of the symptoms: tar-water to be drunk, a dish of stewed earthworms, or nine lice or again the magical seven, to be taken every morning for a week, in a little ale. For shingles some resorted to a mixture of the blood of a black cat's tail – a black cat was lucky in Hertfordshire – with the juice of houseleek and cream, warmed and applied to the blisters three times a day. No prudent cottager was without houseleek, a charm against lightning when growing on the roof, and an ingredient of many folk remedies: a bit broken off and rubbed on a whitlow was said to cure it.

For sore throats there was the woollen sock, preferably red, sweaty and warm, wound around the neck before going to bed. Red, the colour of warmth, was thought to have a magical curative power all its own, and particularly red flannel. In his *Country Housewife's Family Companion* (1750) William Ellis gives a simple 'to cure a sprained Wrist in Harvest. It is common', he wrote, 'for Men to sprain their Wrists the first or second Day, by reaping, in Harvest, before they are much used to it; some dip a *red* Cloth in Verjuice, and wrap it going to bed about the Wrist. Or in Want thereof, dip it in Urine mixt with Salt.'

Of the childhood diseases one of the worst and longest lasting was 'chin' or whooping cough, and the general belief was that no matter what time of year the child became infected the cough would persist until the following May. There were many remedies for whooping cough. Most common, perhaps, was the mouse, skinned and fried. People in Much and Little Hadham passed an afflicted child through a 'living arch', usually a bramble frond that had re-rooted. In North Hertfordshire it was believed that, if a black beetle of the field variety were shut in a box and buried the whooping cough would disappear as the beetle wasted away. The hair sandwich was a standby in some places. A tiny bit of the child's hair was put between two small pieces of buttered bread, and given to a cat to eat. 'But the strangest thing about the whole affair', according to Edwin Grey of Harpenden, 'was that in some cases the said cats who had eaten the treacherous dainties given them gradually began to wheeze and cough, eventually becoming thin and emaciated, so much so that in two or three cases . . . the animals had to be destroyed, whilst in other cases the cats seemed not in the least affected.'

Herbal ingredients for the popular folk cures and for salves, potions and purges in common use were readily to be found in woods, hedgerows and fields. These were known as yarbs in Hertfordshire: stewed groundsel for poultices; marshmallow leaves and flowers made an ointment for boils; lily leaves healed cuts; dock leaves relieved galled feet; green broom was used for kidney and liver troubles; coltsfoot leaves for asthma and bronchitis; rue in making tonics – and many more.

Good for health generally and as a preventative was Yarb Tea. It was usually made from leaves of camomile, yarrow, and agrimony, simmmered with sugar to taste, and drunk at home, by workmen in the fields from their tea-cans, or bottled for later need. Tea made from young nettle shoots was widely used as a spring tonic.

Some put their faith in cure-alls, nasty tasting pills, potions, and tonics which could be bought in the towns on market days. Martha Weeden, the Pirton Medicine Woman, is still remembered. Dressed in her straw bonnet and cloak she went round the village taking orders for such popular concoctions as Daffy's Elixir before pushing her van – an old pram – the four or five miles into Hitchin. There she collected her remedies before walking back again, delivering her bottles at cottage doors along the way for a half-penny or farthing each.

Mountebanks and quack doctors sold their stock-in-trade of cure-alls at markets and fairs to crowds of country people. Lady Mary Carbery described the appeal of the quack at Harpenden Race Meetings in the last century:

> . . . The Windmill Man is selling whirligigs by the score, and someone very like the Pots and Pans Man, has a barrel of beer on a dray and dozens of mugs, knowing he can count on a good thirst all 'round this lovely day. Not everyone can afford to go to the refreshment tent, and even respectable women need 'jist a sip to 'elp swaller down th' 'ealth an' beauty pills they'd got off o' th'

doctor,' who is a cheap-jack in a top hat and black coat, shouting from a cart about his mirryaculous cure-all 'ealth pills. . . .

Hertfordshire folk could no more be fooled than any other, however, for all their nickname of 'thick heads'. For sellers of cures, magical or not, incompetence brought a disastrous end. Thomas Harding, the 'cunning man' of Ickleford, was one of these. So many of his potions and charms proved useless – including a scroll of parchment hung around the neck as a charm against the plague – that in 1590 Harding was taken to the county jail at Hertford and prosecuted for fraud.

Holed-flint stable charm, Dixie's Farm, Ashwell, now at Ashwell Museum

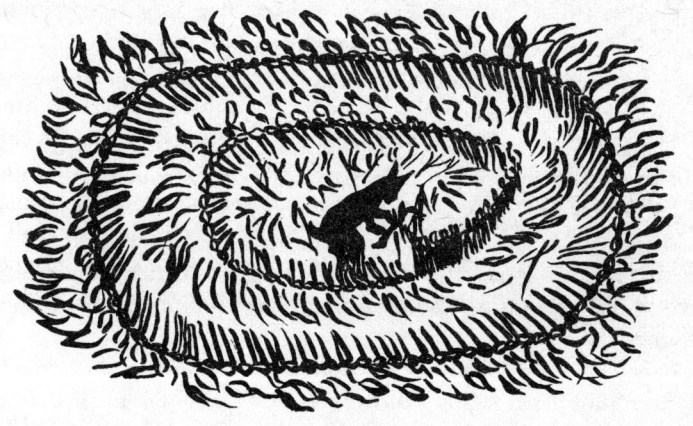

The Mowing Devil, woodcut, The Mowing Devil, or Strange News out of Hartford-Shire, *1678*

8 The Devil

THE DEVIL, it is said, must have a special liking for Hertfordshire – so many of his evil works and mischievous deeds were done here.

In Hertfordshire the Devil is a source of mischief, nuisances, and awkward things of all kinds. He deceived travellers. Roads were ways, and with them, as in everything, the Devil had his share. Of the dozen or so kinds of way at least three belonged to the Devil: wicked ways which were rutty, muddy lanes, and 'ten Devil's' and 'twenty Devil's' ways – practically impassable roads.

To farmers and gardeners weeds are still the Devil's plants: 'Twas th' deev'l as sowed 'em in 'arf'dsheer: thizzles an' nittles, darnock an' docks, cockledrakes, hawdoddles, kedlocks an'goolds, langley-beef, dog-fennel, deev'l's guts, beggars'-lice, an' a two-three 'undered moer.'

The Devil interfered, too, with the growing of crops: parsley seeds, notoriously slow to sprout, were thought to go down to the Devil seven or nine times before they could sprout. The prudent, however, sowed their parsley on Good Friday when the moon was full and the seed out of the Devil's power. It was out of spite, they said, that the Devil cursed the brambles each year and made them unfit to eat on Old Michaelmas Day (11 October), the anniversary of his fall from Heaven.

The Devil has his door to Hertfordshire churches: the north door, seldom used, leading to his own north side of the churchyard. Colder and with less sun, it was shunned by people living in the parish and used mainly for the burial of paupers, felons, and travellers. It may be that stories about the Devil's side of the parish churches are derived from the siting of many to the south of pre-Christian burial grounds.

In any case, the Devil left his thunderbolts and toenails behind in Hertfordshire, the fossils called Belemnites and Gryphaeas. If the Devil claims the upper part of Cuffley Brook in Northaw, which is called Grime's Brook, his name is most often attached to unnatural creations. According to Hertfordshire legend it was the Devil himself who built the prehistoric earthworks about the county, a number of which still survive.

At the western edge of Royston Heath is the 'Devil's Hopscotch', a series of ridges – lynchets – running up Church Hill.

Some way to the south the Devil dug with a great shovel in Whomerley Wood, at Stevenage, throwing up the earth into six large mounds known as the Six Hills near the Great North Road. The seventh shovel-full, however, miscarried, and flying through the air a mile or more knocked the steeple off Graveley Church, forming the steep hill close by the churchyard.

The Devil's greatest efforts at building, however, were in the west: the Devil's Ditch in the parish of St Michael's, St Albans, to the north-west of Verulam by the park of Gorhambury; the Devil's Dyke near Wheathampstead; and, largest of all, Grim's Dyke, on the far western county border, which enters Hertfordshire about two miles south of Tring, curves in a south-easterly direction through the parishes of Wigginton and Northchurch, crosses Berkhamsted Common where it is lost, only to reappear as a bank on the old Middlesex boundary at Bushey.

Traditional stories of the Devil follow the course of these works from parish to parish, but as they proceed out of the still remote parishes in the Chiltern Hills south-eastward toward Middlesex the Devil as a folk-figure becomes less menacing.

The Devil's Dyke near Wheathampstead was the downfall of Marford John. One Saturday night John lingered over his drink, and it was late when he left the inn. His way home lay across the Dyke, and before he had climbed quite over John knew that Satan himself was following. He knew it would be folly to look around, but without thinking swore a great oath which put him in the Devil's power, who pushed John flat upon the ground. Too frightened to move, John presently fell asleep, and knew no more until the spell was broken by the bells of St Helen's church in Wheathampstead ringing for morning service. John continued his walk home to Marford, and though afterward he was always careful to leave the inn in good time, he would tell his tale of meeting with the Devil on the Dyke.

Grim's Dyke, as it enters Hertfordshire from the direction of the Wendover Gap, is said to be the creation of a diabolical wizard, and has a number of Devil tales associated with it. According to some this wizard was Sir Guy de Gravade, an alchemist, who had bartered his soul to the Devil in return for miraculous knowledge. Sir Guy lived in an ancient castle near the place now called Tring Station, just within the boundary of Aldbury parish.

The Devil himself is said to rattle his chains in the hollow-way known as Hastoe Lane in Tring parish, and further along the route of Grim's Dyke, on Berkhamsted Common, near the Potten End water tower.

At Bushey, on the Middlesex border, the Devil is a man of culture. On moonlight nights he sits upon a style in Little Bushey Lane playing his fiddle. After a time, and still playing, the Devil may be seen walking slowly along the footpath through the wood, only to disappear in the ditch that runs toward Coldharbour.

For those brave or foolhardy enough to put their fate to the test there was the ancient sport of Devil-raising. In Hertfordshire this usually took the form of a trial in which those who would meet the Devil must run a certain number of times around a prominent landmark. Often the direction was set against the sun. In modern times and within living memory these tests for the Devil had lost much of their terror, and they are now largely childrens' games.

At Aston it was believed that running seven times around an old alter tomb on the north or Devil's side of the churchyard would cause him to appear.

A similar tale is told at Tewin of the tomb of the wicked Lady Anne Grimston – she died in 1717 – who disbelieved in the Resurrection and said that if it proved to be true the sign would be that trees would grow from her grave – which they have done. On New Year's Eve, however, the Devil by tradition appears by his own power in Tewin churchyard. It was then the custom of the ringers to have one among them chime the church bell for midnight while the rest set out to cheat the Devil by running seven times around the church before the twelfth stroke ceased to be heard. The Devil, who lay in wait, made away with the stragglers.

In some cases the task of running around the object was made all but impossible. According to legend, if one could run a giddy fifty times around the tall obelisk in Tring Park Wood blood would spurt out from the top.

Sabbath-breaking was another sure way of making the Devil appear, besides, as in past times, when it was a legal offence attracting the unfavourable attention of the local magistrate. For the Devil, however, useful work was more than plying one's trade or profession: it was labour of any kind on the Christian sabbath, particularly gleaning or scavenging, and he was ready at hand to tempt and aid anyone in committing such wickedness. Those who tried to pick fruit and nuts from the hedgerows, for example, would find that the Devil had come and was holding the branches down for them. It was not the Devil, but the Man-in-the-Moon who punished people who went a-woodin' on a Sunday. Countrymen have little dependence nowadays on food gathered from hedgerows, and the threat of the Devil as a means of stopping the more enterprising from stealing a march on their neighbours has little force. It is a sign of the times that in rural Hertfordshire parishes, such as my own of St Paul's Walden, local residents take care to gather the best of the hedgerow fruit and nuts before they are lost to greedy Londoners and other town folks, as they are called, who drive out for gleaning Sundays in the late summer and autumn.

Those who would see the Devil every day of the week had only to cut their nails on a Sunday – a belief not yet dead.

It was generally agreed in Hertfordshire that, however it might appear, the Devil's work never truly prospered, and that in any case it was inviting danger and disaster to invoke his aid.

At Walkern the story is told of how, during one very wet season, a farmer viewing his crops is said to have expressed a wish that the Almighty would go to sleep for six weeks until it was time for harvest. Suddenly he fell into a trance and could not be awakened for that entire period: even horses could not move the farmer's body from the spot where he lay, and a shed had to be built over him.

Another farmer, at Gaddesden, was looking over one of his fields when a man walked by and said: 'You have a nice field of corn there.' 'Yes,' replied the farmer, 'if the Almighty would only leave it alone.' He did, and in the charge of the Devil the corn neither grew nor ripened, but remained green as a testament to the farmer's impiety.

It was more disastrous still to ask directly for Satan's aid, as in the tale of the 'Mowing Devil', which was printed as a fly-sheet dated 22 August 1678:

THE MOWING DEVIL:
OR, STRANGE NEWS OUT OF
HARTFORD-SHIRE

Being a True Relation of a Farmer, who Bargaining with a Poor Mower, about the Cutting down Three Half Acres of Oats; upon the Mower's asking too much, the Farmer swore *That the Devil should Mow it rather than He.* And so it fell out, that very Night, the Crop of Oat shew'd as if it had been all of a Flame; but next Morning appear'd so neatly mow'd by the Devil or some Infernal Spirit, that no Mortal Man was able to do the like.

Also, How the said Oats ly now in the Field, and the Owner has not Power to fetch them away.

The hazards being what they were the Devil was never a popular sign for innkeepers, but at least one in Hertfordshire was bold enough to do business under the patronage of the Prince of Darkness. At Royston in the middle of the last century there was a public house called the Devil's Head. It had no signboard but a carved head projecting from the side of the building, with the name painted underneath.

In Hertfordshire, as in other places, there were few clever or unscrupulous enough to confront the Devil and outwit him. The popular medieval folk-hero Piers Shonks of Brent Pelham, who killed the Devil's dragon, only just escaped the Devil's revenge and saved his soul by being buried in the Pelham church wall.

St Dunstan, tempted by the Devil, seized him by the nose with red-hot tongs. There are no stories that he ever came to Hertfordshire, although the story is well known and the church at Hunsdon is dedicated to him. To this day, however, there is a pub in the Tring hamlet of Long Marston in the Chiltern Hills, near the border with Buckinghamshire, with the sign of the Boot, which recalls a similar feat of daring. The tale of how Sir John Shorne, rector of North Marston (1290-1314) conjured the Devil into his boot was the great medieval legend of the district, and made North Marston a popular place of pilgrimage for miles around, especially for those seeking relief from the ague at the chalybeate well known as St John's well. The souvenir sold to votaries, commemorating Sir John's capture of the Devil, was the first Jack-in-the-box, still a favourite with children.

On the other side of the County, the people of south Hertfordshire around Barnet and Totteridge and the great ancient forest of Enfield Chase were as much amused by the fabulous pranks of the 'Merry Devil' of Edmonton as they were later by that other Edmonton stalwart, John Gilpin, and his famous ride on his wedding day to Ware. It was the 'Merry Devil', Peter Fabell – already legendary when the poem 'Fabyl's Ghoste' was printed by John Rastell in 1533 – who cheated the Devil, and unlike most, got away with it.

At St Albans they claimed that when the Devil appeared in the town he was caught and killed by a butcher. A pamphlet printed in 1648 was entitled: *The Devil seen at St Albans, being a true Relation, how the Devil was seen there in a Cellar, in the likeness of a Ram, and how a Butcher came and cut his Throat and sold some of it and dressed the rest for himself, inviting many to Supper who ate of it. Attested by divers Letters of Men of very good Credit in the Town. Printed for the Confutation of those that believe there are no such things as Spirits or Devils.*

Children and others in search of adventure might play at 'Devil-raising', but on the whole the Devil as the embodiment of evil things was taken seriously in Hertfordshire. While the expression 'the Deev'l 'tis' was often heard, many avoided tempting fate – and still do – by speaking his name indirectly. People saw to it that they had charms to keep away the Devil and his minions, witches, wizards, and the like – horseshoes with the ends pointing upward to keep the luck in, horse brasses, holed flints, house-leeks on the roof, knives (iron) buried by thresholds, and many more. Nor was it an accident that in Hertfordshire those who left nothing to chance by attending both church and chapel were called Deev'l-Dodgers.

Horned Devil, graffito, Stevenage Church

Witch with the body of a swan, graffito, Wheathampstead Church

9 Witches and Wizards

WITHIN LIVING MEMORY many Hertfordshire parishes had their witch, wizard, cunning man or wise woman who dispensed of spells, potions and advice on problems of all kinds. Witches, usually women, were of two kinds: evil – or black – witches that dealt in sorcery and enchantment, bewitching man and animals, causing them sickness, ill-luck, death, or other misfortune; and good – or white – witches, who set up to be respectable and to be of use to their neighbours, and – for a fee – were supposed to be able to remove spells cast by black witches, to do such other useful things as finding lost or stolen property, and by the use of magical charms and remedies to cure the sick.

On Easter Eve, 13 April 1471 the famous necromancer Friar Bungay travelled out from London to Barnet Common with the Yorkist army of his patron Edward IV, having in charge the deposed Henry VI. On the night before the battle with the Earl of Warwick and the Lancastrians, the sorcerer promised Edward that he would raise thick mists and vapours which would give him the victory. The

Friar's prophecy was fulfilled: as dawn broke a heavy mist hung over Barnet Common and the fate of the battle turned upon the confusion in the gloom by Warwick's men of the star-with-rays worn by followers of the Earl of Oxford, his chief lieutenant, with the sun badge of Edward IV.

The better to bewitch, or intimidate, or escape pursuit, Hertfordshire witches had powers to transform themselves into a variety of animals. The powerful witch Mother Haggy of St Albans could turn herself into a lion, a hen, or a cat, besides the more commonplace hare. She could not, however, it was said, turn herself into a male creature nor walk over two crossed straws. At Rabley Heath they still tell of the local witch who turned herself into a hare – only to be shot by a courageous gamekeeper; she was never seen again.

One seventeenth-century witch, had up before the justices, testified that she 'was sure not to die yet, for all the mischief I have done is in transforming myself into the shape of a Bumble Bee, and Biting the Maid's thread often in pieces as she spun....'

The belief that witches have the ability to transform themselves still persists in Hertfordshire. A man still living in 1948 had accused his next-door neighbours, a man and his wife, of being witches and of entering his house at night in the shape of rats, with the intention of bewitching him.

Rosina Massey, wife of the nineteenth-century poet Gerald Massey, who lived in an old cottage at Witchcraft Bottom, Little Gaddesden, got her three-legged stool to run errands for her. She was also seen through her cottage window with hands outstretched, conducting the cups and saucers around her table in a sprightly dance.

Hertfordshire witches were noted for their powers to 'fly or subsist in the ambient air'. Mother Haggy of St Albans was said to ride at full gallop on a broomstick at midday: she 'swam' across the River Ver on a kettle-drum. The favourite mode of transport for Hertfordshire witches, however, was not the broomstick but the hurdle, a rectangular frame made of small branches inter-twined and strengthened with cross pieces, used as temporary fencing to pen sheep and other livestock. On windy nights Rosina Massey would ride a hurdle from the bottom of her garden at Little Gaddesden across the valley to the village of Studham and back.

In the 1820s William Nobbs, the Parish Clerk of Welwyn, recorded, with much other local tradition, the proficiency of the witches in the neighbouring parish of Datchworth at riding hurdles in his versified directions for beating the bounds of Welwyn parish:

> ... Datchworth, whose witches, ancient Dames declare,
> With Wheatcock Hats rode through the ambient air
> On Hurdles plac'd. ...

Hertfordshire witches could also transport other persons for good or evil purposes. Some drew upon this ability as a service to favoured clients, the practice of the 'Cunning Man' of Wiggington. Vicars Bell, schoolmaster of Little Gaddesden, told the story in *Little Gaddesden*, 1949, of Joe Swaby, an under-gamekeeper who lived near the Monument. Finding one day that his savings had disappeared, he decided to visit the Cunning Man of Wiggington:

> It was late when he arrived at the white wizard's cottage, and it took a little time for the 'Cunning man' to diagnose the case. But at length he was able to tell Joe Swaby that his money had been stolen. He gave him the name of the thief and told him how to recover the money.
> So it was long past bedtime when Joe stepped out into the night to begin his long walk home through the darkness.
> 'Now', says the 'Cunning Man', 'how should you like to go home? High or low?'
> 'High, if you please', says Joe.
> And at that there was a mighty puff and a roaring in Joe's ears. He raised his dizzy head to the sky and saw that in a moment of time he had been whirled across the wide valley and landed at his doorstep.

Foretelling the future was an important part of the witches' magical powers. Among the slain at the First Battle of St Albans, 22 May 1455, the opening engagement of the Wars of the Roses, was the Lancastrian Duke of Somerset, whose body was found on the steps of the Castle Inn, which stood on the corner of Victoria Street. He had been warned by a soothsayer to shun castles, and the fulfillment of this prophecy immortalised the sign of the Castle at St Albans, as Shakespeare wrote:

For underneath an ale-house' paltry sign
The Castle in Saint-Albans, Somerset
Hath made the Wizard famous in his death. . . .

Witches were applied to for news of good fortune, and perhaps by none more anxiously than girls seeking to discover their true-loves. Joseph Strutt, the eighteenth-century antiquary, in his romance set at the Tudor mansion of Queen Hoo Hall, Tewin, describes the visit of two girls from that village to Dame Sad, the notorious witch of the neighbouring parish of Datchworth. Strutt had lived for about four years at Bramfield, and knew this part of Hertfordshire and its legends well. There is no better description of an old Hertfordshire witch than the following that appears in Chapter 4 of *Queen Hoo Hall* titled 'The History of an Old Witch, and an important Adventure at her solitary Cell'. The girls, wrote Strutt, had 'determined to visit a weird woman, who resided upon Datchworth Green, at the distance of four miles, or somewhat more, in order to learn of a certainty which of her two lovers was destined to be her husband, and what good fortune awaited her in the future'.

Setting out to walk from Tewin, the two girls found it was near noon by the time they reached the old hag's hut, which stood by the side of a coppice, in a narrow dirty lane that bore no mark of having been a thoroughfare for centuries back. The cot itself seemed to be of great antiquity. Half its covering was carried away by the devastations of the weather, and the deficiency of the mud danking upon the walls admitted the wind from every quarter. In short, the outside of this deplorable habitation was so squalid and ruinous, that our two adventurers hesitated a while, and neither the one nor the other dared to knock at the door, fearing that some evil goblin, instead of a woman, should open it for their reception.

When at length the girls found the courage to knock and enter, the oraculous cell was fully exposed to their view, and the Pythoness herself, who was seated upon a wooden tripod by the side of a few expiring embers, which she was turning over with her stick. Her head was wrapped about with a volpure, so disguised with filth that its original colour could not possibly be discriminated, and through the torn places, which were numerous enough, her white locks stood up on end, for she had neither a veil nor a wimple to cover them. Her dress was an old threadbare courtpie, patched with different kinds of cloth, and besmattered with dirt, so that it was perfectly rigid.

Her flesh was the colour of smoke-dried bacon, and her ferret eyes, which looked askance, were bloated with hovering over the wood embers. Upon the tip of her nose, which was very thin and prominent, she wore a large pair of barnacles, and they made no small addition to the uncomeliness of her long lank visage. The moment the door opened she elevated her head, which was shaken by the palsey, and, surveying the damsels, cried out, 'Come in, and shut the door.'

Fear and dread of the powers of witches to do evil, to lay harmful spells upon people and animals bringing sickness and even death has not yet departed from Hertfordshire, particularly in the rural areas. Many now living, even in market towns, can remember being told by parents not to cross or trouble certain dangerous men or women and thus invite their displeasure and revenge. Nor can the name of the last witch in many villages be discovered, the truthful reply from those who will talk about this forbidden subject being that 'the time has not yet come'.

Places where witches were even reputed to have lived are still avoided from fear of lingering evil. One of the most notorious of these was a disused chalk pit in a wood along the old road from Bramfield to Datchworth known as Sally Rainbow's Dell. Here in one of the chalk caves lived the old woman known to legend as Sally Rainbow, greatly dreaded by people in the neighbourhood and especially the farmers, who would let her have anything she wanted in the belief that otherwise she would overlook their cattle and bring the fatal murrain. The highwayman Dick Turpin made good use of the story of Sally Rainbow. One of his best-known haunts along the North Road was the ancient hollow-way below Sherrard's Wood, near the Red Lion Inn on Digswell Hill, where his seat by the fireside is still shown. After robbing any fashionable coach or chaise Turpin would ride across country by Harmer Green and Burnham Green to the Dell, where he could hide undisturbed, protected by the witch's legend.

After the 1563 Act of Parliament made the casting of spells a crime punishable by hanging there were many prosecutions for witchcraft in England, including a considerable number in Hertfordshire. The campaign against witches, which reached a climax in the 1640s with the appointment by Parliament of the Witch-Finder General, Matthew Hopkins, who had settled in Manningtree, Essex, however, never reached the pitch of fervour in Hertfordshire as in the neighbouring counties of Essex, Cambridgeshire and Bedfordshire, where he carried out his investigations. If any such invitation came from the Corporation of a Hertfordshire town, none was acted upon.

An early prosecution for witchcraft, recorded among the others in the Hertfordshire Sessions Rolls, was that of Joan Danne of Hitchin:

> 1579-80. The Jurors for the Queen present that Joan Danne of Hytchen, spinster, being a common sorceress and enchantress, as well of men as of beasts and other things, not having the fear of God before her eyes, but instigated and seduced by the Devil and of her malice aforethought on 1 November [anno] 21 Elizabeth by force and arms bewitched and enchanted a certain John Sympson of Hytchen, yeoman, by reason of which the said John Sympson from the said 1 November until the last day of January then next following greatly languished, against the peace and form of the Statute....

In 1591 at Hertford Summer Sessions, Alice Crutch of Tring, said to have bewitched a horse to death, was later condemned to be hanged for bewitching Hugh Walden, who languished and died.

In 1649 John Palmer of Norton, and Elizabeth Knott, said to be notorious witches, were condemned at the Sessions of Oyer and Terminer at St Albans. Palmer was accused of practising his black art in the neighbourhood of Norton for over sixty years, aided by two familiars, one in the form of a dog that he called George, and the other in the likeness of a woman whom he called Jezabell.

Palmer's greatest reputation, however, rested upon his skill in destroying enemies by that simple and ancient expedient of framing pictures of them in the clay and then burning these. It was said, for example, of Goodwife Pearls of Norton that 'whilst her image was consuming, she lay in miserable torment, and when it was quite consumed, she died'. Palmer's anger had been occasioned by Goodwife Pearls' visits pressing him as her tenant to pay his arrears of rent.

Allied against witchcraft also were clergymen and doctors, and the removal of evil spells and spirits was regarded as an essential part of their duties. Dr Christopher Woodhouse, Bailiff of the Borough of Berkhamsted, was renowned for the success of his 'stinking suffumigations' that were said to be powerful enough to drive out the Devil himself.

Dr William Drage of Hitchin, 'Apothecary' and 'Practitioner in Physick' (1637-68) included a treatise on 'Diseases from Witchcraft' in his successful medical book which ran through three editions in the author's short lifetime: *Physical Experiments, Being a plain description of the Causes, Signes and Cures of most Diseases incident to the Body of Man. Faithfully collected from Ancient and Modern Writers and partly experimented by William Drage, Practitioner in Physick at Hitchin in Hertfordshire* (2nd. edn.) 1668.

Describing the signs and symptoms of cases of demoniacal possession or bewitchment he had encountered, Drage referred to the prevalence of witchcraft in Hertfordshire, and declared it would be 'too tedious to write fully all the Examinations and Informations I have took concerning our Countrey Witches'.

Among cases of possession, Dr Drage tells of Elizabeth Day of Hitchin 'whom I well knew', and of her 'running up the walls with her feet laying no hand, and on the Seiling with her head downwards'. She was cured by a 'suffumigation' and some 'ceremonies', whereupon the evil spirit 'leapt forth like a mouse' from her mouth.

At Baldock Dr Drage heard about two witches who were ducked in that town 'divers years since'. One 'sunk presently down right; the other, though tyed Toes and Thumbs together, could not be made to sink'. Neither could the witch he described at St Albans, 'though she strove by putting her head under the water and was thrust down with Poles.... As she confessed, one of her imps leaped upon her breast in the water and she could not sink.' Persons suspected of witchcraft were made to undergo the ordeal of ducking to determine their guilt or innocence: the guilty floated, while the innocent sank honestly to the bottom of the local pond or stream – and oblivion.

A Hertfordshire woman, Jane Wenham, of Walkern, was the last person to be tried – and found guilty of witchcraft – in England. She was accused among other acts of 'having a conversation with the devil in the shape of a cat', and the case was tried before the historian of Hertfordshire and Recorder of Hertford, Sir Henry Chauncy. Judgement was given against Jane Wenham at Hertford in 1711 by Mr Justice Powell, but the sentence of death was never carried out. She later received a free pardon, and lived in a small cottage at Gilston, dying at Hertingfordbury in 1730. Jane Wenham's case gave rise to a spate of pamphlets largely condemning the penalty of death for witchcraft, and did much to prepare the way for passage of the Witchcraft Act of 1736 which finally stopped legal prosecution.

Public opinion as a whole, however, was another matter: people continued their belief in witches, and when the law no longer viewed witchcraft as a crime, they took the law into their own hands. In 1751, some fifteen years after the Witchcraft Act, the town criers of Hemel Hempstead, Leighton Buzzard, and Winslow announced that on 22 April, '... Monday next, a man and a woman are to be publicly ducked at Tring, in this County, for their wicked crimes. ...' These were alleged to be bewitchment to death of a local farmer some five years before. Ruth and John Osborne, two elderly people, died as a result of their ducking in the village pond at Gubblecote, near Tring, while an approving crowd looked on.

The local justices, however, knew their duty, and the ringleader, Thomas Colley, a chimney sweep, was tried and found guilty of murder. He was duly hanged, and, in accord with the traditional practice in the case of murderers, gibbetted near the scene of his crime, at Gubblecote.

While the gibbet stood, and long after it had fallen into decay and disappeared, the clanking of Colley's chains could be heard as his skeleton – no longer there – swung in the wind. The spot has been haunted ever since, moreover, by the spectre of a giant black dog. The village schoolmaster was one of many who saw the ghost:

> I was returning home late at night in a gig with a person who was driving. When we came near the spot, where a portion of the gibbet had lately stood, he saw on the roadside bank a flame of fire as large as a man's hat. 'What's that!' I exclaimed. 'Hush', said my companion, and suddenly pulling in his horse, made a dead stop. I then saw an immense black dog just in front of our horse, the strangest-looking creature I ever beheld. He was as big as a Newfoundland, but very gaunt, and shaggy, with long ears and

tail, eyes like balls of fire and large, long teeth, for he opened his mouth and seemed to grin at us. In a few minutes the dog disappeared, seeming to vanish like a shadow or to sink into the earth, and we drove over the spot where he had lain.

The most notorious of Hertfordshire's witches-turned-spectres was Mother Haggy of St Albans, who lived in the reign of James I. She was married to a yeoman of St Albans, and enjoyed a good reputation for many years, but later became a black witch and played many 'mighty pranks'. These she continued after her death, much to the terror of the neighbourhood: flying through the air on her broomstick, swimming the River Ver on a kettle-drum as it was said, and many more.

At Kensworth, on the Bedfordshire border, a witch (and a headless milkmaid) are said to haunt the path that runs over Bury Hill to Kensworth Church. Around Hatching Green, near Harpenden, there was the 'Agdell Ghost', Edwin Grey recalled talking '... to an old lady, a cottager, who had lived all her life in the Hatching Green vicinity ... "I often think," said she, "of the time when I was a young girl, and of how we girls were afraid to go down Agdell path to the village on a dark night, for fear we might meet the ghost of old Ann Weatherhead" ... this wandering spirit was said to be that of an old witch or hag who lived years ago somewhere in Agdell.'

One at least of Hertfordshire's sorcerers and alchemists became a ghost. In a castle where the hamlet of Tring Station now stands, just inside the parish of Aldbury, there lived in the time of Edward III a knight called Sir Guy de Gravade. Like Faust and many others Sir Guy had made a pact with the Devil, bartering his soul for knowledge of necromancy and alchemy, and by practising these arts had grown wonderfully rich. Disaster overtook the knight, however, when his servant, John Bond, tried to rob him by using one of Sir Guy's own spells. Sir Guy, discovering this treachery, called upon his master, the Devil, for aid. In an instant and with a great rumble of thunder, alchemist, servant, castle and all vanished, taken forever, it was said, to the Kingdom of Darkness – though allowed to return as spectres one day a year on the anniversary of their destruction.

Near the village of Lilley, in the early years of the nineteenth century, lived John Kellerman, called the last of the alchemists, who with diabolical aid practised the 'black Egyptian arts' and claimed to have turned base metals into gold. Many a tale was told in the district of how, on dark stormy nights, people watching from the roadside saw clouds of smoke and fumes coming from Kellerman's laboratory lit up by the glowing fire beneath, and of how at times these clouds took the form of a gigantic being which quickly vanished down the shaft whence it came.

Kellerman was visited by Sir Richard Phillips, who wrote an account of it in *A Personal Tour through the United Kingdom* (1828):

> On enquiring for curiosities at Luton, I heard of a living one, who excited in me an intense interest. He is an alchemist, who lives at the village of Lilley, midway between Luton and Hitchin. It was four miles out of my road, but I thought a modern alchemist worthy of a visit, particularly as several inhabitants of Luton gravely assured me, that he had succeeded in discovering the Philosopher's Stone, and also the Universal Solvent.... I learnt that he had been a man of fashion, and at one time largely concerned in adventures on the turf, but that for many years he had devoted himself to his present pursuits; while for some time past, he had been inaccessible and invisible to the world, the house being shut and barricaded, and the walls of his grounds protected with hurdles, with spring-guns so planted as to resist intrusion in every direction....
>
> The appearance of the premises did not belie vulgar report.... Contrary, however, to my expectation, I found a young man who appeared to belong to the outbuildings, and he took charge of my card for his master.... In a minute the front door was opened, and Mr Kellerman presented himself.... He was about six feet high, and of athletic make: on his head was a white night-cap, and his dress consisted of a long great-coat once green, and he had a sort of jockey waistcoat with three tiers of pockets. His manner was extremely polite and graceful, but my attention was chiefly absorbed by his singular physiognomy. His complexion was deep sallow, and his eyes large, black, and rolling. He conducted me into a very large parlour with a window looking backward, and having locked the door, and put the key in his pocket, he desired me to be seated in one of two large arm chairs covered with sheep skins.... The floor was covered with retorts, crucibles, alembics,

jars, bottles in various shapes, intermingled with old books piled upon each other, with a sufficient quantity of dust and cobwebs. Different shelves were filled in the same manner, and on one side stood his bed....

In proceeding through some solitary new enclosures after I left Lilley, I felt the strongest emotions from the extraordinary scene I had just witnessed.... Let no man laugh at Kellerman, who himself believes that bodies, as in the pretended power of attraction act on each other.... On arriving at Silsoe I learnt that there anciently existed a vein of gold in the neighbourhood, and it appeared that he had sent for some of the earth to operate upon....

On 29 March 1614 Robert Cropwell, Vicar of Great Gaddesden, reported to the Archdeacon, and among the particulars he gave was: '... We have no recusants in our parish, but three that are counted bewitched, who are excommunicated....' Within sight of the old manor house at Ayot St Lawrence is a haunted clump of trees just beyond Brimstone Wood said to mark the spot where a witch was burned. Traditional beliefs in witches and wizards still linger in Hertfordshire, if kept so largely hidden by all but a few. Of those who do not admit to belief in witchcraft, moreover, many still follow in this as in other things the old Hertfordshire admonitions 'to keep out of harm's way' and to 'let well enough alone'.

Running hare, graffito, St Albans Abbey

The Stortford Dragon, misericord, Church of St Michael, Bishop's Stortford

10 The Turning Year

JANUARY

MANY HERTFORDSHIRE churches still ring in the New Year with midnight peals, although not many now remember the old beliefs that this was to drive away evil and to bring luck to the parish for the coming year. The medieval tradition of gift-giving at the New Year, in the family and among friends, between master and man, tenant and landlord, moved long ago to Christmas, but the custom of celebrating to welcome the New Year, or doing what one wishes to do again when the next New Year comes around – a belief similar to that still associated with first hearing the cuckoo, the herald of spring – still persists.

A New Year carol in the early sixteenth-century *Commonplace Book* of Richard Hill, of Hillend, Langley in the parish of Hitchin, a London grocer, begins:

What Cher? Gud Cher, gud cher, gud cher!
Be mery and glad this gud New Yere!
Lyft up your hartis and be glad
In Chrystis byrth, the Angell bad;
Say eche to order, yf any be sade:
         What cher?

I tell you all with hart so fre:
Ryght welcum ye be to me;
Be glad and mery, for charite!
         What cher?

  . . .   . . .
What Cher? Gud Cher, gud cher, gud cher!
Be mery and glad this gud New Yere!

On New Year's Day it was the custom for spiced Pope Lady Buns to be cried in the streets of St Albans and other market towns. As one traveller wrote in Regency times:

On returning from the country I happened to sleep at St Albans on the night of the 31st December last, and was awakened early the next morning by a confused noise of boys and girls in the street, crying for sale 'Popladys!! Popladys!!' Inquiring at breakfast time the meaning of these words, I was informed that it was an ancient practice in the town to cry and sell in the streets and in the baker's shops, on New Year's Day, a species of cake or bun called 'Poplady,' one of which was brought in to me.

It was a plain cake, like the cross-buns sold on Good Friday, but, instead of being circular, it was long and narrow, rudely resembling the human figure with two dried raisins or currants to represent eyes and another for the mouth, the lower part being formed rather like the outer case of an Egyptian mummy. . . .

For generations after the introduction of the Gregorian Calendar in 1752 the traditional-minded in Hertfordshire kept Christmas, and the other ancient holidays as well, on their customary (or Old Style) dates: there were thus particular festivities on 5 January, Old Christmas Eve, or Twelfth Night, and the day following, Old

Christmas, the feast of the Epiphany. There are still those who believe that rosemary blooms and that cattle turn toward the east at midnight on Old Christmas Eve in memory of the birth of Christ.

Old Christmas, or Epiphany, was the season for the Wassailers to make their rounds of the parish, to be rewarded for singing carols, and at farms to serenade the apple and other fruit trees, and the beehives, to assure fertility and a good crop in the coming year. These visits of the Wassailers are generally recorded in the account books of Hertfordshire squires who by custom gave gifts of money as well as refreshments of the season. In the late seventeenth century James Forrester of Broadfield Hall, Cottered, noted:

> Gave the fidlers and Wasellers, 1s 6d

The custom of wassailing the beehives was kept up in some parts of the County until the last years of the nineteenth century, if not later still. The Rev. Canon John Catterick, the present Rector of Ashwell, collected the words of this traditional song from one of the last of Ashwell's Morris Men:

> Bees, oh bees of Paradise,
> Does the work of Jesus Christ,
> Does the work which no man can.
> God made bees,
> And bees made honey,
> God made man,
> And man made money.
> God made trees,
> And trees made branches,
> God made young men,
> To love little wenches.

On Plough Sunday (the first after Twelfth Night) ploughs were brought to the churches to be blessed before spring work on the farm was begun. Although kept in few rural parishes since the First World War, this custom has been revived in a number of places in recent years, notably at Cottered and Flamstead, where in the Order of Service (1956) the following was sung:

God speed the plough,
The plough and the ploughman,
The farm and the farmer,
Machine and beast and man.

God speed the plough,
The beam and the mouldboard,
The share and the colters.

God speed the plough,
In fair weather and foul,
In success and disappointment,
In rain and wind,
Or in frost and sunshine.
God speed the plough. . . .

In some parishes, including Clothall where farming is still virtually the only occupation, a traditional old Hertfordshire Wheel plough – long outmoded – is kept in the churchyard for the annual ceremony of blessing the plough.

Plough Monday, the day following, was a holiday for the ploughmen, who made the rounds of neighbouring villages and towns drawing a plough decorated with ribbands, bells, and other ornaments, begging money for their traditional evening's celebration at the local inn. In Hertfordshire these companies of ploughmen were known as the 'plough witches',. In some places they were accompanied by all the traditional parish performers, including Morris Dancers and Mummers, known as Guisers, portraying such old favourites as St George and the Dragon, and 'Wodehouse', the legendary wild man, often called Jack-in-the-Green.

The Plough Monday celebrations continued in some rural parishes until the First World War. They are notable for some of the last recorded appearances of the Wodehouse in Hertfordshire. The colourful Jack-in-the-Green which now appears at the Aldbury May Festival is a mid-twentieth-century revival.

No one expected January to be anything but a bleak month, cold and stormy, with dark days. Unseasonable weather was viewed with suspicion as harmful to crops and a forecast of difficult times and hardship through the year. People said:

If the grass grows in Janiveer,
It grows the worse for it all the year

and

A kindly good Janiveer
Freezeth the pot by the fire.

FEBRUARY

February was a time of storms and winter. Still well known, although so many hedgerow ditches are being filled in, is the saying 'February fill-dyke'. By Candlemas, 2 February, the days were well along, as countrymen say, in 'picking out', although the lengthening hours of daylight were supposed to bring the most severe frosts, as on the feast of St Dorothea, 6 February, the 'day of snows'. At Candlemas people looked, as they still do, for signs of spring: the first snowdrops, called 'February Fair Maids', and for the 'drop' that, hanging on the hedges, promises a good crop of peas and beans.

Although always so largely dependent upon agriculture, Hertfordshire owed much of the prosperity of its towns in Medieval and Tudor times to the wool trade, and the festival of St Blase, patron of wool combers and wax chandlers was kept as a holiday in Hitchin, Bishop's Stortford, and other important wool towns. Here the wool staplers, wool combers, shepherds, sheep-shearers, comb-makers and others connected with the wool trade went in colourful procession through the streets carrying banners and staves and wearing the liveries of their guilds. St Blase was usually portrayed as a man on horseback, dressed as a bishop, with a book in one hand and a comb in the other. His attendants were real or mythological characters connected in some way with the wool trade: shepherds, Jason and the Golden Fleece, the Argonauts, and so on.

13 February, the Eve of St Valentine, is called Moat Lady's Night at Much Hadham. Every year, so it is said, the ghostly Moat Lady came out from the ancient moat at Moat Farm to claim a human victim, pulled in and drowned beneath the waters. Each year someone venturing that way would be sure to die, on that night, or at least within the week – until the moat is dragged and the bones

of the Moat Lady found, where they were hidden by her murderer, and given Christian burial.

In the middle of the last century, writes Edwin Grey,

> the custom amongst the young people [around Harpenden] of sending valentines to the object of their affection on February 14th was very popular, these love tokens being dainty little affairs made up of paper lace, artificial rosebuds, violets, lillies of the valley, or other artificial flowers, together with Cupid's hearts and darts, with a tender or sloppy message printed under the design. . . .

St Valentine's was among the foremost perambulation and begging days for Hertfordshire children, with its traditional chanted or 'singing' rhyme. 'A Lady', thought to have been Matilda Lucas, a Quakeress, of Hitchin, contributed the following description to the antiquary William Hone's *Year Book* of 1832.

On the fourteenth of February it is customary, in many parts of Hertfordshire, for the poor and middling classes of children to assemble together in some part of the town or village where they live, whence they proceed in a body to the house of the chief personage of the place, who throws them wreaths and true lovers' knots from the window, with which they entirely adorn themselves. Two or three of the girls then select one of the youngest amongst them (generally a boy), whom they deck out more gaily than the rest, and, placing him at their head, march forward in the greatest state imaginable, at the same time playfully singing,

> Good morrow to you, Valentine;
> Curl your locks as I do mine,
> Two before and three behind,
> Good morrow to you, Valentine.

This they repeat under the windows of all the houses they pass, and the inhabitant is seldom known to refuse a mite towards the merry solicitings of these juvenile serenaders. I have experienced much pleasure from witnessing their mirth. They begin as early as six o'clock in the morning.

At the beginning of this century the children at Breachwood

Green, in King's Walden Parish, still made their rounds on St Valentine's Day singing a two-verse version of the traditional Hertfordshire ditty:

> Good Morning, ma'am, 'tis Valentine;
> Curl your locks as I do mine,
> Two before and two behind,
> Good morning, ma'am, 'tis Valentine.
>
> Good Morning, ma'am, 'tis Valentine;
> There are no grapes upon the vine,
> There will be some in summertime,
> So pray, ma'am, give me a Valentine.

Pennies, half-pennies, or more often apples were the usual Valentines given to the children of Breachwood Green, and one woman is still remembered for having kept some of her best Blenheims for 'the singing boys and girls'.

The two-verse Valentine rhyme from Breachwood Green is very similar to the one which was sung over the Cambridgeshire border to this tune:

February marked the beginning of Lent, the great penitential season of the Christian year. Shrove Sunday was the popular name for Quinquagesima, the next sunday before Shrove-tide, which included Collop Monday, Shrove Tuesday, and Fritters or Ash, Wednesday. On Collop Monday eggs and slices of bacon, pork, or other meat were traditional fare; such fresh meat as remained in the larder thereafter was cut into collops (steaks) for salting and hanging up to cure in the kitchen chimney until the fasting of Lent was past.

Shrove Tuesday was Pancake Day and Dough-nut Day in Hertfordshire.

William Hove notes in his *Every Day Book*:

> At Hoddesdon in Hertfordshire the old Curfew-bell, which was anciently rung in that town for the extinction and re-lighting of 'all fire and candle light' still exists [1826], and has from time

immemorial been regularly rung on the morning of Shrove Tuesday at four o'clock, after which hour the inhabitants are at liberty to make and eat pancakes, until the bell rings again at eight o'clock at night. This custom is observed so closely, that after that hour not a pancake remains in the town.'

Until the First World War the pancake bell was still rung at Hatfield, where 'at mid-day an old man of the name of Buff was wont to ascent the tower of the church in order to ring the pancake bell, a signal to housewives to get ready the batter for the pancakes. For this service he used to receive from the churchwardens the sum of one shilling'.

The best-known maker of Shrove Tuesday pancakes in Hertfordshire, however, was no mortal but the 'Pancake Witch' of Toddington, a small rural parish along the Bedfordshire border. She still fries her yearly batch deep inside Conger Hill. The Toddington village school bell rings at five minutes before noon to give the children time to scurry along to the top of the hill nearby. Here, putting their ears to the ground, they listen for the sizzle of the pancakes as they fry in the old witch's pan.

Shrove Tuesday was another of the perambulating and begging days, activities that were so much a part of the old Hertfordshire calendar festivals. In Victorian times the children chanted this rhyme around the market town of Baldock, which was noted for its cheeses:

> I've come a-shrovin'
> Vor a little pancaik
> A bit of bread of your baikin'
> Or a little truckle cheese o' your maikin';
> If you gi me a little, I'll ax no more,
> If you don't gi me nothin', I'll rottle your door.

A few miles to the south, in the rural hamlet of Breachwood Green, the children relied upon persuasion in a verse which is still remembered:

> Pancake in a pan,
> Pray, ma'am, give me some,
> You've got some and I've got none,
> So pray, ma'am, give me some.

As at Valentine's Day the hope was for pennies, but the usual – and welcome – gift was apples.

Stoning or clubbing cocks to death was the high point of medieval Shrove-tide celebration, and many parishes had a place set aside for it, as at Ashwell where Cock Throwing Close adjoined the orchard and pasture – surrounded by a moat – where one of the four ancient fairs was held on Old St Peter's Day (10 July). In the mid-eighteenth century Shrove Tuesday was the greatest day for cock-fighting. Such was the popularity of the sport that it was carried on in secret long after it had been outlawed, to within living memory in such out-of-the-way places as Royston Heath, Nomansland, between Sandridge and Wheathampstead, and the spinney called The Cockpit along the path from Wigginton to Tring Station. It is still said that a Wigginton Man is never lost so long as he can see a cockpit.

Ash Wednesday, the first of the 40 days of Lent, was called Fritters Wednesday from the old custom of eating fritters on this day. At Baldock and other places in North Hertfordshire it was Dough-Nut Day. Baldock Dough-Nuts were probably as famous as the local cheeses described by Samuel Pepys and other travellers. The traditional Baldock Dough-Nut was made of a spiced dough fried in hogs lard in a brass frying-pan until golden brown. Properly made these Dough-Nuts were very light and quite small, no bigger than large walnuts. They were at their best eaten when still hot from the pan.

MARCH

The arrival of March meant that spring was at hand. Early March was known in Hertfordshire as 'prim-e-rose' time, primroses usually being in bloom then in the woods and under hedgerows sheltered by last year's fallen leaves. For the enterprising housewife primrose flowers and tender new leaves were much sought after for use as salads and pot-herbs, as well as for 'bringing the spring' into the house. For the cottage housewife, struggling to make ends meet, primroses were the first of the wild flower vending season. People still alive remember going 'prim-e-rosing' early in the morning to gather the flowers with the dew to keep them fresh, making the flowers and new leaves into bunches, and crying them for sale at nearby villages and market towns for a penny or ha-penny each.

The cries of the Hertfordshire primrose vendors have been lost; perhaps they were less elaborate and tuneful than those used by sellers of daffodils, called in Hertfordshire Lent lillies and Daffy-down-dillys, which, in their season, followed next:

> Daff-a-down dilly
> Has now come to town,
> In a yellow petticoat
> And a green gown.
> Daff-a-down dilly
> That grows in the dell,
> My father's a tinker,
> My mother can tell.
> My sister's a lady,
> And wears a gold ring,
> My brother's a drummer,
> And drums for the King.

March and better weather brought new season's produce from the farm, and it marked the first of the year's large fairs – an exception being Redbourn January Fair, held in the first week – notably Baldock Fair on 7 March, for cheeses, cattle, and household goods.

In March the curfew bells, protectors against fires breaking out in the villages and towns on long winter nights, ceased to be rung. From 11 March the Baldock bell was silent until the next Norton Fair Night, 30 October. As most often happens, a custom which is endowed outlasts even those that continue to give pleasure, and the ringing of the curfew at Baldock, thus supported, continued into modern times. According to tradition a gentleman became lost on the road near Baldock, but, upon hearing the eight-o'clock Curfew Bell, was able to find his way to the town. In gratitude for his deliverance he left a piece of land in Willian Parish to Baldock Church, the yearly rent to go to the ringing of the bell forever. The land in question – between Weston Way and Willian Road – was known as 'Bell Acre' until it was sold a few years ago, and the income from the reinvested capital is still known in Baldock as 'The Bell-Acre Rent'.

Mid-Lent Sunday, the fourth in Lent, was popularly known in Hertfordshire, as elsewhere, as Mothering Sunday. Before the

Reformation it was the custom to visit one's parish, or 'Mother', church to receive its blessing and make special offerings at the high altar. Later these visits were made to parents, and to mothers especially, by children of the less well-to-do, often working, or in the case of girls 'in service', at some distance from home. Traditional gifts brought by children at this time were the rich plum cakes with saffron-yellow crust called Simnels.

Fish in an inland county such as Hertfordshire was always scarce and dear, and, as a staple of the Lenten diet, a particular hardship for the poor. Mid-Lent Sunday was thus often chosen for bequests or doles of fish to the parish: at Meesden in the eighteenth century 'three shillings and four pence' were paid out of the rent of an acre called 'Salmon's Acre' in West-field for herrings for the poor on mid-Lent Sunday; while at Braughing Mr. Jennings, a member of the Fishmongers Company in London, provided in his will:

> Herrings for the Poor in Lent, £2.
> For Carriage of the Herrings, 4d.
> To the Poor in Bread, £2 12s.

Payment was enjoined upon the Fishmongers' Company from the rent of the Chequer and Horseshoe Inn at the corner of Thames Street. 'The herrings are brought yearly into the vestry at Braughing', wrote the historian Nathaniel Salmon, 'some Red, some White, and punctually distributed tho' they have indeed outlasted Lent'.

Palm Sunday, the next before Easter, was known as Fig Sunday in Hertfordshire, a reference, so it is said, to the parable of the barren fig tree that withered away when cursed by Jesus after His triumphal entry into Jerusalem (Mark 11:12-14). It was the custom to 'keep warsel' – to celebrate with family and friends on this day, and stewed figs and rice and fig puddings were traditional dishes to be eaten by all for good fortune. Kimpton, Bushey, Watford, and Abbot's Langley were noted for their 'keeping warsel' on Fig Sunday, and people in Whitwell can still remember buying figs from the old village shop in blue sugar-bags. More figs were sold in Hertfordshire the week before Palm Sunday than in all the rest of the year. Today, however, there are not many, even in the most rural parishes, who keep the old custom of eating figs, although if the weather in fine on Palm Sunday this is still a popular day to take your best girl-friend out in the afternoon.

APRIL

On Good Friday, the anniversary of the Crucifixion, only the milking and other necessary tasks were done on the farms, shops and offices were closed, and almost everyone went to church. Good Friday was one of the great 'ringing days', and many churches had special customs, as at Ayot St Lawrence, where, beginning at three o'clock in the afternoon, the 'cemetery bell' was tolled 33 times, marking the years of Our Lord's life.

At dawn in the market towns vendors began their rounds carrying trays piled high with steaming Hot Cross Buns, crying:

> One a-penny, two a-penny,
>   Hot Cross Buns;
> If you have no daughters,
>   Give them to your sons;
> But if you have none of these merry little elves,
> Then you may keep them all for yourselves.
> One a-penny, two a-penny,
>   Hot Cross Buns. . . .

At the least it was – and still is – thought bad luck not to eat Hot Cross Buns on Good Friday. Hertfordshire buns had all the traditional powers of 'holy bread'; they were said never to mould, and housewives who could afford one extra kept it to bring luck to the home in the coming year. Although Baldock was noted for its bakers, the Hot Cross Buns of St Albans were most prized. Long after the Reformation the bakers there claimed to be making 'magical' buns from the very recipe used by the baker of St Albans Abbey, Father Rocliff. On Good Friday, 1361, he is thought to have begun the custom of giving to each person who came to the Abbey Gate in need that day one small sweet spiced cake in addition to the usual dole of a basin of soup.

Good Friday after church and dinner for most people became what it largely is today, the first public holiday of the year. Those who could took their pleasure at Stevenage Good Friday Fair, a lively and colourful gathering with its cattle market, hawkers and pedlars and sellers of new season's cheese. This was one of the three annual Stevenage fairs granted by James I in 1625 to the Bishop of London,

Lord of the Manor, and the inhabitants; the others were held on the Feast of the Ascension of Our Lord, and the Feast of St Swithin. The Stevenage fairs and markets prospered until the coming of the railway in the mid-nineteenth century which, as in other Hertfordshire market towns, killed the cattle market and eventually all but the pleasure trade at the fairs.

Hexton had its Good Friday 'bush' fair with stalls and booths on the nearby Pegsdon Hills, part of the Chilterns, beyond the Fairy Hole where Roaring Meg and the Burwell (pronounced 'Burrl') Brook used to flow, feeding the now lost miraculous well of St Faith, patron of the Parish. It is still remembered that people walked to Hexton from Lilley, Pirton, Hitchin and other places miles away.

Among the attractions for children at Hexton Fair was the rolling of oranges down the grassy slopes. Possibly as well – as often happened when oranges were not available – hard-boiled and coloured Easter Eggs. Little has been recorded about Easter Eggs in Hertfordshire, and few of the oldest people remember having them as children before the First World War.

Good Friday afternoon was the traditional time to begin planting potatoes in the cottage garden: beans and peas, and especially parsley, had to be sown or they 'would never prosper'. Even then, it was believed, parsley seed had to go seven times to the Devil and back again before coming up, a matter of fact to all who sow this seed even today.

Easter Eve, popularly called Holy Saturday, was one of the great flower-gathering days of the year, for Easter decoration in homes and churches. Particularly looked for was the dainty *Anemonie Pulsatilla*, the legendary Pasque, or Easter, flower of the chalk downs, which flourished on Royston Heath, Arbury Banks, the hills above Pirton and Hexton, and Aldbury Nowers, near Tring. This *Anemonie* was also called 'Dane's Blood', from the popular belief that it only grew where battles had been fought between the English and the Danes – among the oldest, perhaps, of Hertfordshire legends. There were those too, it is said, who used the *Anemonie Pulsatilla* for its green dye in colouring Easter Eggs.

Easter Day, the Resurrection, was one of the greatest festivals of the year, and welcomed – as in some parishes it still is – by early morning peals. Everyone went to church – many still do who seldom attend at other times during the year – and those who could went in new clothes, particularly for women and girls, new hats, for luck. Traditional dishes for Easter Sunday dinner are lamb and mint sauce and the first rhubarb. Rhubarb and mint, so easy to grow, are still to be found in many gardens, even in the towns. The traditional green tansy puddings are now known to few.

Easter Day was one of the times watched for signs of weather in the coming season. People used to say:

A good deal of rain on Easter-Day,
Gives a crop of good grass, but little good hay.

Easter week was a busy time for traditional parish activities: doles and endowed sermons at Hitchin and King's Langley and that model of parish government, when officers were chosen, the annual vestry. The cost of the Vestry Dinner which followed was met by private bequests in fortunate parishes, as at Braughing, where a London fishmonger named Jennings left 20s. for a Vestry 'dinner on every wednesday in Easter Week'. At Codicote Easter Monday was sports day and a holiday. The last event traditionally was a contest to climb a greasy pole for the prize of a large leg of pork. There were fairs, too. Before the Reformation the Hitchin Guild of St Mary held the first of its two annual fairs on Wednesday in Easter Week, and the two days following.

April 14th was 'Cuckoo Day' in Hertfordshire, when one was supposed to hear the first Cuckoo of the spring. When the first note was heard people turned their money for luck – and many still do. Nearly everyone carried a holed coin of some sort so as never to be caught out with an empty pocket. They still say that whatever one is doing when first the Cuckoo sings, one will do again the next year.

There were a number of versions of the Hertfordshire Cuckoo Song:

> In April
> Come he will;
> In May
> He sings all day;
> In June
> He changes his tune;

In July
Begins to fly;
In August
Go he must.

Hock Day, or *Quindena Paschae* as it was called by Matthew Paris, the thirteenth-century chronicler of St Albans Abbey, was kept on the second Monday and Tuesday after Easter. In some parts of Hertfordshire Hock Day survived the Reformation, and continued, as at Hexton, 'for some few yeares within the reigne of Queene Elizabeth ...'. It was customary for collections known as Hockmoney to be made by the churchwardens. Tuesday was the principal day of the celebrations: Hock Monday was for the men, and Hock Tuesday for the women. On both days, the men and women alternately strung ropes across the roads, and pulled travellers to them, from whom they collected the money, which was used for suitable expenses such as church repairs.

The fullest account of Hock Day in Hertfordshire now known was written by Francis Taverner, lord of the manor of Hexton in the early seventeenth century. Each year the people of Hexton gathered on the top of Wayting Hill, where a team of women tried to upend

> a very strong ashen pole fastened into the ground ... striving with all their force to bring it down the hill, which the men did defend ... and thus they laboured insessantly two or three hours, not giving over till they had brought the pole and set it up at the Cross by the Town House door, where a great number of people were attending their coming. And then, the women having provided good cheer, they brought it to the Town House, and did there all eat and drink together.... And after they had eaten, then the hockers did gather money of every one what they pleased to give, part of it then given to the poor, the remaining money the hockers delivered unto the churchwardens, who layed out the same in reparation of the church and bells....

There were sports in the afternoon, in some of which the women of Hexton again competed against the men.

MAY

May Day was the greatest secular festival of the year. It began before dawn with groups of young people, usually accompanied by local musicians, gathering the traditional May boughs and flowers – nettles, too, for those who had annoyed them in some way – and later distributing them door-to-door in the villages and towns.

Miss Louisa Hinde, of Bancroft in Hitchin, is said to have written this account of May Day for William Hone's *Every Day Book* of 1826: 'May Day at Hitchin in Hertfordshire'.

Soon after three o'clock in the morning, a large party of town people and neighbouring labourers parade the town, singing the 'Mayers Song'. They carry in their hands branches of may, and they affix one either upon or at the side of the doors of nearly every respectable house in the town; where there are knockers, they place these branches within the handles; that which was put into our knocker was so large that the servant could not open the door till the gardener came and took it out. The larger the branch that is placed at the door, the more honour to the house, or rather to the servants of the house. If in the course of the year a servant has given offence to any of the Mayers, then instead of a branch of May, a branch of elder with a bunch of nettles is affixed to her door: this is considered a great disgrace, and the unfortunate subject of it is exposed to the jeers of her rivals.

On May morning, therefore, the girls look with some anxiety for their May-branch, and rise very early to ascertain their good or ill fortune. The houses were all thus decorated by four o'clock in the morning. Throughout the day parties of these Mayers are seen dancing and frolicking in various parts of the town. The group that I saw today, which remained in Bancroft for more than an hour, was composed as follows: First came two men with their faces blackened, one of them with a birch broom in his hand and a large artificial hump on his back; the other dressed as a woman all in rags and tatters, with a large straw bonnet on and carrying a ladle: these are called 'Mad Moll and her husband'; next came two men, one most fantastically dressed with ribbons and a great variety of gaudy coloured silk handkerchiefs tied round his arms from the shoulder to the wrists and down the thighs and legs to the ankles; he carried in his hand a drawn sword; leaning upon his arm was a youth dressed as a fine lady in white muslin, and profusely decked from top to toe with gay ribbons; these, I understood, were called the 'Lord and Lady' of the company; after these followed six or seven couples more, attired much in the same style as the 'Lord and Lady', only the men were without swords.

When this group received a satisfactory contribution at any house, the music struck up from a violin, clarionet, and fife, accompanied by the long drum, and they began the merry dance, and very well they danced, I assure you; the men-women looked and footed it so much like real women, that I stood in great doubt as to which sex they belonged, till I was assured that women were not permitted to mingle in these sports. While the dancers were merrily footing it, the principal amusement to the populace was caused by the grimaces and clownish tricks of Mad Moll and her husband. When the circle of spectators became so contracted as to interrupt the dancers, then Mad Moll's husband went to work with his broom, and swept the road-dust all round the circle, into the faces of the crowd, and when any pretended affronts were offered (and many were offered) to his wife, he pursued the offenders, broom in hand; if he could not overtake them, whether they were male or female, he flung his broom at them. These fights and pursuits caused an abundance of merriment.

From such accounts as survive it appears that the traditional celebrations of May Day in Hertfordshire varied, often considerably, from town to town. At Baldock, only about six miles north of Hitchin, the May Lord and Lady were portrayed as effigies in tableaux set up before the houses of the less well-to-do. William Hone printed this description in the *Year Book* (1832):

> ... these figures were constructed a-la Guy Fawkes, of rags, pasteboard, old masks, old canvas, straw &c., and were 'dressed up' in the holiday habiliments of their 'fabricators', 'My Lady' in the 'best gown'd' apron, kerchief, and mob cap of 'the dame', and 'my

Lord' in the 'Sunday gear' of her 'master' – to wit, perhaps a nutmeg coat, 'posied' waistcoat, leather breeches, speckled stockings, and half-boots.... The tiring finished, 'the pair' – and sure such a pair were never seen elsewhere – were seated on chairs or joint-stools placed outside the 'cottage door', or on the porch or settle, most lovingly side by side – their bosoms ornamented with large bouquets of May flowers and blossoms. These resemblances ... were the 'supporters' of a hat, into which the contributions of the lookers-on were put ....

At the 'backside', an irregular street of cottages in the suburbs of the town, chiefly tenanted by the poorer working class, the greatest display of 'lords and ladies' was usually exhibited. On many a May Day morning within the recollection of the writer there has been 'on view', at this spot, from five to ten 'couples' or 'knots' of those pseudo-mummings of the 'nobles of the land'. These dumb shows, as may be expected, attracted a crowd of gazers. They varied according to the materials and skill of the constructors. One old woman named Betty Trorn, long since deceased, is still remembered as a capital hand at 'making up' a May Day 'my lord, and my lady'.... The usage just detailed was exclusively confined to the 'good wives' of the labouring poor resident in the town, who were amply compensated for their pains-taking by the 'voluntary contributions' which generally amounted to 'something considerable'.

The spring carol sung by the Mayers, called simply 'The Mayers Song', is probably the best known today of all the old Hertfordshire carols. As with other May Day folk customs this song had different versions from parish to parish. Some two dozen variants are known to have been collected since Louisa Hinde of Hitchin sent the words of the Hitchin May Carol to the antiquarian William Hone in a letter dated at Hitchin, 1 May 1823, which he later printed in *The Every-Day Book* of 1826. The earliest known written version of 'The Mayers Song' is in the early sixteenth-century manuscript Commonplace Book of Richard Hill of Hillend, Langley, in the parish of Hitchin. The longest version, with eighteen verses, was found in a notebook discovered at Buckland Rectory in 1903, which gives the words of the song as it was sung in the neighbouring parish of Therfield about 1810:

1.

Remember me, poor Mayers all,
    For here should we begin
To lead our lives in righteousness,
    Else we shall die in sin.

3.

The moon shines bright, and the stars give light,
    A little before 'tis day;
Our heavenly Father He calls to us all,
    And He bids us wake and pray.

12.

So rise, fair maidens, to your casement,
    And view the bush so fair,
And we will come some other, other day,
    To taste of your brown beer.

14.

For 'tis we have been rambling this long night
    And some part of the day,
And now we are returned and back again
    And we brought you a branch of May.

18.

Now my song is begun and almost done,
    No longer can I stay;
God bless you all, both great and small,
    And send you a joyful May.

    The Mayers Song was sung to a variety of folk tunes. At Hitchin and other places at the beginning of the nineteenth century The Mayers Song – as well as The Old Christmas Song (see below) – was sung to the traditional Hertfordshire air 'Tidings of Comfort and

Joy', a variant of the one collected in London by Dr E. F. Rimbault and printed by him in *A Little Book of Christmas Carols* in 1846, and used today largely as the setting for the Christmas carol 'God Rest You Merry Gentlemen'. A dozen or more tunes for The Mayers Song have been written down in Hertfordshire since the folk song revival that began at the end of the nineteenth century. Among the most notable collectors of folk tunes and words in Hertfordshire during this period were Ralph Vaughan Williams – at the Royston Workhouse – and Lucy Broadwood, who died in 1929, in the neighbourhood of St Albans and King's Langley. Lucy Broadwood and J. A. Fuller Maitland printed two settings for The Mayers Song in their collection *English County Songs* (1893): one from King's Langley and this lesser known tune from mid-Hertfordshire sung by Thomas Gray at Weston:

May Day was the craft festival of the chimney sweeps, who went round the towns with blackened faces asking for money and performing morris dances. The refrain of the song of the Tring sweeps, to the tune of 'Shepherd's Hey', a version similar to that collected by Cecil Sharp and sent by him to Percy Grainger, goes:

> The first of May, the first of May,
> Sweeps go a-dancing all May-Day.

With the sweeps went the Jack-in-the-Green. At Ware in the 1840s one was described as 'a locomotive mass of foliage with his black face shining through an aperture in the leaves, while a clown, two "innocent blacknesses" in the shape of climbing boys, and a drummer who also played upon the pan-pipes, completed the wandering company'. The Jack-in-the-Green has been revived in Hertfordshire from time to time as part of the twentieth-century interest in folklore. The most notable examples in recent years have appeared at the Aldbury Women's Institute May Festival.

Jack-in-the-Green, Aldbury May Festival, 1961

In Hertfordshire it was largely the sweeps and the children, mostly the girls – the most important day when the boys went out begging was Guy Fawkes' – who kept traditions of May Day alive in the latter part of the nineteenth and early twentieth centuries. For children the first of May was Garland Day, and the most careful preparations were made. At Hatfield and other places, before April was out, children who planned to go a-garlanding would call upon well-to-do householders asking for any spare bits of white material for use in making costumes and saying: 'Please, Mum, any ribbants for our garlants?'

At Hatfield, on May Morning, dressed in white and holding bunches of hawthorn or, in late seasons, blackthorn blossoms (the wild sloe) the children sang door-to-door a local version of the May song, which began:

> A bunch of May I bring unto you
> And at your door I stand,
> Come pull out your purse,
> You'll be none the worse
> And give the poor Mayers some money....

The children of Watford and King's Langley were noted for their elaborate garlands. The garland, hung from a pole carried by two of the children, was made from two or more hoops decorated with spring wildflowers – favourites being bluebells and primroses when these could be found – tied with ribbon and topped by a branch of May. At King's Langley it was traditional as well for the garland to have a doll, the May Queen, seated in the middle.

Garlanding, however, went on only until just after noon. Percy Standing described the fate of the garlands in south Hertfordshire at the beginning of this century:

> ... At the larger houses they are regaled with cake, milk, etc., and I remember a recent occasion when they were requested to leave their garlands and posies at the 'big house' to be sent to the London Hospital – a better fate than usually befalls them, when the luckless girls are surrounded by the ungallant small boys of the village (as soon as twelve noon has struck) and their garlands destroyed and scattered. The girls, it is only fair to add, return this compliment with interest on November 5th, when it becomes their privilege, at the same hour of noon, to do their best in destroying the boys' 'guys'.

The King's Langley May Garland Song was generally sung by the girls, except for one verse. It began:

> Good morning, mistress and master:
> We wish you a merry day;
> We've come to show you our garland
> Because it's the first of May

The refrain or burden was sometimes sung after each verse as well as at the end:

The garland, the garland,
The very pretty garland,
It's the finest you could see;
It's fit for Queen Victoria
So please [drawn out for three notes] remember me

The verse asking for money was sung only by the boys:

> May-day, May-day, May-day, May;
> Give us a penny
> And then we'll go away.

> If you haven't got a penny
> A halfpenny will do,
> If you haven't got a halfpenny,
> Then God help you.

At Tring on May Morning the children carried through the streets not a garland but the replica of a May Pole, with bluebells, primroses, or violets in a bunch at the top. They sang:

> May-pole, may-pole, may-pole day,
> Please give me a ha'penny
> Then I'll run away.

The old Hertfordshire maypoles, on May Day decorated with ribbons and a bunch of spring flowers at the top, were described as being 'as high as the mast of a vessel of a hundred tons, painted often in a diagonal or spiral pattern from bottom to top in yellow and black, or often in vertical stripes of red, white, and blue'. After Regency times maypoles appear to have become less popular: at Hoddesdon the maypole stood near the Chapel, with the stocks beside it and the Cage, or lock-up, behind. When the maypole was blown down in a storm about 1820, it was not set up again.

For all the jollifications of its beginning May was known as a hard month in Hertfordshire. A proper May was cold, as they said:

> A cold May and a windy
> Makes a fat barn and a findy.

When the medieval Ice Saints whose days fell in the second week of May (11th, St Mammertus; 12th, St Pancras; 13th, St Servatius; and 14th, St Boniface) were forgotten, everyone knew the meaning of Black-thorn Winter, the cold spell which usually accompanies the flowering of this tree. For the elderly or the sick, it was May hill to be 'got up' as best one might. May was believed to bring death to the family if carried indoors, and lilac, particularly white lilac, is still thought best left where it blooms.

Rogation Week, beginning the fifth Sunday after Easter, was the traditional time for beating the parish bounds – known as 'processioning'. Always a considerable expense to the parish, these perambulations have largely been discontinued in Hertfordshire since 1914. Once thought essential for upholding the rights of the parish, beating the bounds as a custom added much to County legend. One of the oldest tales of Graveley parish, for example, concerns the haunted plot of ground still known as Parsons' Field, where in the fourteenth century, as Sir Henry Chauncy recorded in 1700, 'by reason of the uncertainty of their bounds sad contentions arose between the incumbents [of the adjoining parishes of Graveley and Chesfield] that they meeting together upon Perambulation, one Parson [John Smyth of Graveley] killed the other [Robert Shorthale of Chesfield]'.

Whitsunday, the Feast of Pentecost, was rung in with early peals from the parish churches, many of which, following tradition, are still decorated with red flowers, supposed to represent the tongues of fire which came down upon the Disciples. Traditional dishes were roast veal with spring greens and new potatoes, followed by a tart made of the first gooseberries, or, in late seasons, from the last summer's preserved 'Hertfordshire Black' cherries.

Whitmonday was a holiday and a time for fairs and traditional celebrations, such as the medieval 'Church Ales', the profits from which kept the parish churches in repair, and later the perambulations of village benefit clubs which 'walked out' with their staves and banners and dined together afterwards. Whitmonday was fair day at Berkhamsted, Braughing, and Royston, to name only three. There were important sheep fairs on Whit-Tuesday, at Hitchin and Whit-Wednesday at Redbourn.

THE INVITATION TO WATTON HORN FAIR,
ON WHITSUN MONDAY
16 May 1796

Tune: *Come, haste to the Wedding*

Ye Lads and ye Lasses who wish to be merry,
   Come on Whitsun-Monday to Watton Horn Fair;
Your Caps and fine Ribbons be sure for to put on,
   Each strive to be one of the first at the Fair.

Chorus: There's Dancing and Singing
   And Fidling and Ringing
   With good Beef and Pudding,
   And plenty of Beer;
   Good Wines
   And plenty to come at,
Let's all haste away to Watton Horn Fair.

See plated Spurs strove for by Donkeys a-Running,
   And fine Holland Smock so push's for by Women,
Then pair of fine Pumps to be run for by Yeomen
   There's no one but wishes to be at the Fair.

   Then next there's a Hat, in
   Large Sacks to be run for,
   And some fine Ribbons by
   Boys to be won, Sir;
   Cuckolds Ride, Bachelors Drawing
   And Tumblers peck in
   To make up our Fair.

On Whitmonday it used to be the custom for people from Tring to walk to Aston Hill, just over the border in Buckinghamshire, to the Shepherd's grave, high up and with a magnificent view even now. Tradition says that a shepherd named Faithful was so delighted with the prospect that he made this his usual resting place while caring for his flocks; he became so attached to it that he made his fellow shepherds promise to bury him here when his time came. This was done, and an epitaph cut into the turf which the local people scoured for many years. In about the year 1847, however, only the word Faithful was legible, and soon afterwards, the ground was ploughed over.

But the story was preserved in folksong, and within living memory the Tring Morris Men still sang:

   Faithful lived and Faithful died
   Faithful shepherd on this hillside.
   The hill so wide, the hill so round,
   On the day of judgement he'll be found.

Queen Victoria's birthday, 24 May, was celebrated as Empire Day. Many Hertfordshire schools gave the children a holiday, or half-holiday, as appears in the rhyme:

> The twenty-fourth of May
> The Queen's birthday.
> If you don't give us a holiday
> We'll all run away.

For Oak-Apple Day, 29 May, commemorating the triumphal entry of Charles II into London on his Restoration in 1660, there were special decorations, oak boughs and oak-apples, often gilded, which recalled his escape from capture after the Battle of Worcester by hiding in the oak tree at Boscobel. The Hon. John Byng on his walking tour from London to Barnet in May 1789, recorded in his *Journal* that: '... every horse, carriage, and carter was adorned with oaken boughs, and apples, in memory of this once-famous day....'

Hertfordshire children sang:

> Twenty ninth May
> Royal Oak Day.
> Give us a holiday
> Or we'll all run away.

At South Mimms, Wheathampstead, and many other places it was Half-day Stinging Day. The children used bunches of newly-gathered nettles to sting the legs of anyone who had not properly remembered King Charles by wearing an oak-apple. 'Roundheads' were greeted with the chant:

> Poor King Charles lies hidden in a tree,
> Poor King Charles lies hidden in a tree,
> Poor King Charles lies hidden in a tree,
>   Show your Oak-apple,
>   Or I'll sting thee.

May 29th was also Mock Mayor's Pageant and Fair Day in the parish of St Michael's, St Albans. Charles Ashdown wrote of it in *St Albans Historical and Picturesque* (1893):

From Gorhambury Lodge to the open spaces about the bridge were annually placed, on 29 May of each year until comparatively recent times, an almost continuous line of stalls and booths, the proprietors being attracted thither by the celebrations that always occurred in St Michael's upon Oak-Apple Day. During these festive occasions, the village street was decorated with flags and branches of oak, the inn signs received special attention at the hands of the loyal inhabitants.

But the principal charm of the celebrations was the procession of 'the Mayor of St Michael's', a feature of which was a man dressed in a most fantastic and gorgeous manner, who rode upon a donkey embellished with the gayest trappings procurable. This important personage arrogated to himself the title of 'Mayor' and was obsequiously waited upon and addressed by that appellation by his grinning attendants. From this holiday pageant probably arose the erroneous supposition (still credited by some of the inhabitants) that a separate mayor at one time represented St Michael's.

JUNE

June was a kindly month that brought the rural festivals of sheep-shearing and hay-harvest, and the ancient revels of Midsummer Eve. As the June days grow warmer people still watch for the blooming of the pink-and-white Dog Rose in the hedgerows that tells of the coming of summer and the beginning of corn harvest in seven weeks' time.

Every third year in the nineteenth century and later the first Monday in June was the Old Kimpton Merrymaking, which was endowed by the will of a John Bassil in 1816. A prize was given to the winner of a young people's game organised by the Minister and churchwardens; there was a dinner for the bell-ringers and the parish clerk, another dinner for the clergy and parish officers, and a third dinner for the six poorest families of Kimpton not having parish relief and considered the most deserving.

Little remains in Hertfordshire to tell of that great pre-Reformation feast day Corpus Christi, the Thursday after Trinity Sunday. There was a Brotherhood of Corpus Christi at Ware which, like the

Brotherhood of Jesus in that town, 'did kepe feaste' together upon its festival day. A member, perhaps, was Thomas Clarke of Ware who, by his will in 1505, left 'To the fraternity of Corpus Christi a brass pot of 4 gallons and a brass pan, 3 spoons of silver' and 12 pence.

Among others it was the custom at Corpus Christi for guilds to make procession through the towns with their banners and staves, and to perform mystery plays on pageants – carts or wagons with stages built over them – drawn from stand to stand in the streets. No cycle of plays has been found for any Hertfordshire town, however, including St Albans with its great medieval Abbey and several guilds – in Queen Elizabeth's time these were reduced to four: the innholders, mercers, shoemakers, and victuallers.

It may be that one survival of the tradition of theatricals at Corpus Christi was the custom of Hertfordshire Morris Men to give open-air performances in June 'before the beginning of mowing and hay-harvest'. These took place, however, not only in nearby villages and towns, but by the most enterprising Morris Men as far away as London. They generally walked up to London, as did the strolling players, dancing wherever they could attract an audience and collect for their expenses. Such an excursion of one team from a village in Hertfordshire to London provides the earliest description of Hertfordshire Morris Men that I have found, an account of the performers in Rosoman Street, Clerkenwell, seen by J. R. P. of Islington, a correspondent of the antiquary William Hone, in June 1826:

> They consisted of eight young men, six of whom were dancers; the seventh played the pipe and tabor; and the eighth, the head of them, collected the pence in his hat, and put the precious metal into the slit of a tin painted box under lock and key, suspended before him. The tune the little rural noted pipe played to the gentle pulsations of the tabor, is called
>
> Moll in the wad and I fell out
> And What d'ye think it was about?

This may be remembered as one of the once popular street songs of the late Charles Dibdin's composition. The dancers wore party-coloured ribands round their hats, arms, and knees, to which a row of small latten bells were appended ... that tinkled with the motions of the wearers.... The 'set-to', as they termed it, expressed a vis-a-vis address; they then turned, returned, clapped their hands before and behind, and made a jerk with the knee and foot alternately.... Crowds collected round them.... The occasional huzza ... almost drowned the 'Morris'.

Lubin Brown, the piper, was an arch dark-featured person; his ear was alive to Doric melody; and he merrily played and tickled the time to his note. When he stopped to take breath, his provincial dialect scattered his wit among the gapers.... I observed his eye ever alert to the movement and weariness of his six choice youths. He was a chivalrous fellow: he had won the prize for 'grinning through a horse collar' at the revel, thrown his antagonist in the 'wrestling ring', and 'jumped twenty yards in a sack' to the mortification of his rivals who lay vanquished on the green. The box-keeper, though less dignified than Mr Spring, of Drury Lane, informed me that 'he and his companions in sport' had charmed the village lasses round the maypole, and they intended sojourning in town a week or two, after which the box would be opened, and an equitable division take place, previously to the commencement of mowing and hay-harvest. He said it was the third year of their pilgrimage; that they had never disputed on the road, and were welcomed home by their sweethearts and friends, to whom they never omit the carrying a seasonable gift in a very humble 'Forget me not!' or 'Friendship's Offering'.

June 11th, the feast of St Barnabas, Apostle, shown in old Almanacs carrying a rake, marked the traditional beginning of hay-harvest. This was the longest day of the year according to the Old calendar – which kept its mystical authority even into this century. People said:

Barnaby bright, Barnaby bright,
The longest day, and the shortest night.

And before the time of effective weed-killers:

When St Barnabas smiles both night and day,
Poor Ragged Robin blooms in the hay.

In Hertfordshire, a farming county, hay was the most important crop even after the internal combustion engine revolutionised transport, and Hertfordshire hay was noted for its high quality and fragrance. The hay was first of all cut by the scythes of mowers led by a Lord, usually the head horse-keeper or ploughman on the farm. Next came the 'tedding': shaking out, turning over, and spreading out to aid in the drying – and then the 'cocking' – making up into little piles. Finally, if the weather kept fine on the fourth day the hay was 'carted' – carried on the large wains to the barns or stacks. Old Hertfordshire hay was said to be

Sweet an' dry an' green as't should be,
An full o'seed an' Jeune flowers.

Passers-by were, by old custom, made free of the hayfield by having their shoes or boots wiped with a handfull of new-mown hay. In return a reward was expected by the ever-thirsty haymakers.

In Hertfordshire haystacks were most often circular, being easier to build and thatch than those which were rectangular, and less exposed to the weather. When each stack was made it was left for a fortnight to allow the hay to settle before thatching, and finished off on top by the traditional ball or plaited crown.

The last waggon load of hay for the farmyard was announced by a boy riding on top waving a green bough and the shouts 'hip, hip,

Hay waggon, graffito, Anstey Church

hurray!' of the haymakers walking the 'hay-home'. It was customary for the farmer to treat the men and their families to a dinner afterward, the first supper of the harvest season.

Hertfordshire waggons were similar in design to the East Anglian box waggons, but shorter, seldom longer than ten feet, and with narrower wheels. They were usually painted brown with buff for the undercarriage, while the smarter road waggons which travelled up to London usually had blue bodies and red undercarriages. Often these waggons had eyes painted on the frontboard as charms against evil or danger.

It is still thought unlucky to meet a waggon loaded with straw approaching in a lane – but meeting a hay-waggon is a sign of good luck to follow. To be sure of its 'working', however, one must make a wish as the waggon passes by – without looking at the load! When in more recent years hay was baled, it is said that the luck waits until the bales are opened.

Mid-June was the time for the annual sheep-shearing after the arrival of warm weather was assured by the blooming of the Dog-rose:

> Must not shear the sheep of its wool
> Before the Dog-rose is at the full.

Although Hertfordshire had no breed of its own the county had sheep in considerable numbers, the largest flocks for the most part in parishes along the Chiltern Hills where they were raised – or merely fattened as they did for cattle brought from Wales and other places – for the London market. For drovers from the north and west Hertfordshire was the last night stop before London, at beer houses with sheep and cattle pens to accommodate the trade such as the old *Cow Rest*, now corrupted to *Cow Roast*, at Wigginton.

After the shearing came the fun of the sheep-shearing supper. Nor is there any better description of this old custom in Hertfordshire than Mary Lamb's recollections of her Great-aunt Gladman's farm at Mackery End about 1779 in her story *The Farmhouse* told by Louisa Manners in *Mrs. Leicester's School* (1807):

> Great preparations were making all day for the sheep-shearing supper. Sarah said, a sheep-shearing was not to be compared to a

harvest-home, that was so much better, for that then the oven was quite full of plum pudding, and the kitchen was very hot indeed with roasting beef; yet I can assure you there was no want at all of either beef, or plum-pudding at the sheep-shearing. My sister and I were permitted to sit up till it was almost dark, to see the company at supper. They sat at a long oak table, which was finely carved, and as bright as a looking glass.... At last grandmama sent us to bed: yet though we went to bed we heard many charming songs sung.

Some of these old songs are still within living memory. The last verse of one of them goes:

> Now the sheep they're all shorn and the wool carried home,
>   Here's a health to our master and flock.
> And if we should stay till the last goes away
>   I'm afraid t'will be past twelve o'clock.
>   I'm afraid t'will be past twelve o'clock.

One of the best known of Hertfordshire's yearly sheep, cattle and horse fairs was held at St Albans on 17 June, the feast of St Alban, patron of the town and the Abbey. Before the Reformation the feast was kept as well through the Hundred of Cashio in which were grouped the extensive landholdings in Hertfordshire which belonged to the Abbey. Among other customary services the tenants of St Albans Abbey in the Soke of Park, which included lands in the parishes of Aldenham, Barnet, Elstree, Northaw, Ridge, and St Peter and St Stephen's, St Albans, were required to send a man to keep watch before the shrine of St Alban in the Abbey on the night of his Vigil each year.

June 17th was also the feast of St Botolph, the Fenland hermit, patron of the churches of Shenley and Eastwick, near the River Stort – but more widely known in Hertfordshire as the 'ole tu'nup man', for it was on this Saint's day that turnips were supposed to be planted.

June 23rd was the eve of the great church feast of St John the Baptist, but in the popular mind it was Midsummer's Eve, a turning point in the year.

Conjurings – both good and evil – were believed to be especially potent. Spinsters wishing to know the name of their future husband would work spells: leave their shoes by the bedside in the form of a T to dream about him; set up 'Midsummer Men' in their room, leaves of the orpine plant whose bending to the right or left would tell by morning whether a lover were true or false; walk alone slowly around the parish church sowing the magical hemp seed and repeat:

> These seeds I sow – swift let them grow,
> Till he who must my husband be
> Shall follow me and mow.

Witches, ghosts, and other restless spirits were thought to be active on Midsummer's Eve, with heightened powers of working mischief. Anyone who fasted on that night and was brave enough to sit and watch in the church porch would on the stroke of midnight see the wraiths of those in the parish who would die in the coming year knock in succession upon the church door.

Among the oldest of Midsummer's Eve customs was the bonfire, usually made at the highest place in the village or parish, which last caught the setting sun. In the Chiltern Hills Hexton had its Bonfirehill Knoll, Pegsdon its Beacon Hill, and many more. As at Whitsun and other festivals churchwardens passed among the revellers collecting what they could for the parish poor and the church. The records of St Michael's, Bishop's Stortford, show among the entries for 1519: 'recyved at dyverse Bonfyers whereof the summe is vijs.ijd.' Worthington Smith wrote in 1904 that 'old folk, sixty years ago ... could just remember bonfires lit on the Downs on June 24 in honour of Midsummer'.

JULY

July with its tradition of warm and settled weather was a month of fruit and fairs. The first Sunday in July was called Gooseberry Pie or Gooseberry Pudding Sunday. More famous than Goosegobs in Hertfordshire, however, were the Mazzards or Hertfordshire Black cherries, a County delicacy to rival any. The Chiltern parishes particularly were noted for their cherry and apple orchards, and the hamlet of Frithsden ('Freezeden') for its annual cherry fair. Frithsden claims to have originated the Cherry Bounce – still the name of a hillside field – the black-cherry pasty and the cherry turnover.

There was Hertford Fair on Old Midsummer's Eve (5 July) for horses and cattle, the Ashwell Feast on Old Midsummer's Day (6 July), the great Royston Cattle Fair, called 'Becket Fair' after the pre-Reformation dedication of Royston Priory to St Thomas à Becket, which began on 7 July and ran for three days. Old St Peter's Eve (9 July) was Tewin Fair Day on the Lower Green, and Old St Peter's Day (10 July), Bennington Fair, described as it was a century ago by the historian John Cussans:

> Bennington Fair is now held a short distance from ... (the churchyard) probably on the same site which it has occupied for upwards of 500 years. The fair in this village is one of the few which have not been suppressed during the last 10 or 20 years. A more picturesque scene than Bennington Fair as it now exists can scarcely be imagined. The caravans, booths, stalls, swings, and other sources of enjoyment, are stationed on the village green at the top of a steep road, leading to and at a short distance east of the church, in what is locally known as a three-wont-way (place where three roads meet), under the shadow of some of the finest elm trees to be seen anywhere in England. The entertainment provided is not, it must be admitted, of a very intellectual character, but it thoroughly comes up to the expectations and desires of those for whom it is designed, and is certainly far less debasing than many of the exhibitions presented in the London theatres ... patronized by the same 'respectable' people who would suppress all innocent, though perhaps unrefined country amusements, in which they take no pleasure themselves. For myself, I am free to confess that I thoroughly enjoyed the rough pleasantries of Bennington Fair....

In mid-July a break in the fine weather was watched out for as an omen for the coming harvest. Still current is the old legend that rain on St Swithin's Day (15 July) will bring with it rain for forty days, though most wish to forget that in bad years 'St Margaret's Flood' (20 July) does terrible damage to ripening crops.

For all the treachery of mid-July weather, the fairs continued, even on St Swithin's, at Anstey, Little Hadham, Hatfield and Stevenage, where in its last years it was known as the 'Cat and Dog Fair'. Tradition goes, that George Mountain, then Bishop of London (1625), was talking about asking for two fairs to be granted Stevenage, one for the sale of broadcloth and one a pleasure fair.

'Ah!' said his friends, 'its well to think about the cloth, but how will you get on without needles, etc.?, so Mountain, taking the hint, asked for another fair on St Swithin's Day, for the sale of peddlery, with free toll, or standing room. . . . This fair on St Swithin's was kept up to within fifty years ago (about 1850). The last man who brought his goods yearly came with a donkey and panniers and took his stand under the chestnut trees opposite the White Lion, together with a woman from Graveley, who was famous for her cheesecakes.

July 25th, the feast of St James the Great, was another fair day at Berkhamsted and Old Fair Day at Ashwell, but known in the County as 'Grotto' ('Grotter') Day. It was the custom for people (in later years mostly children) to set up grottoes, made of heaped-up stones or shells, before their doors in memory of St James, patron of pilgrims travelling to the Holy Land, whose symbol was the shell of the scallop which abounded along the Palestinian shore and returning pilgrims wore on their hats to tell of their pious mission. After the Reformation the Feast of St James became a secular 'begging day', one of the best known and colourful of the Hertfordshire traditional year. Until the Second World War – if not after – children in Barnet and other parishes along the south border of the County would build grottoes against a wall or fence, of moss, little stones and pea-shells, and say to well-to-do passers by:

> Please, remember the grotto,
> Only once a year.
> Father's gone to sea,
> Mother's gone to fetch him home,
> He will soon be here.
>
> So please remember me.
> A penny won't hurt you,
> A ha'penny won't break you,
> A farthing won't put you in the Work'us.

Late July brought the lavender harvest in the fields around Hitchin, still remembered as one of the most pleasant occupations in all the farming year, and one of the best-known County events, Hertford Ringing Feast. John Carrington, of Bacon's Farm, Bramfield, attended a number of these in Regency times:

> Thursday 27 [July 1809] To Hertford Town Hall to Dinner at the Ringing Fiest Ticket 9s. 6d. Dinner Dressed at Mrs. Ramsey's Falkorn. Nothing But Fowle Hamms & Venison No Beef Mutton Lamb or Vial. Wm. Christie Esqr Master of Hodesdon Brewer, Spencer Cowper, & Calvert of Hunsdon, the members for Hertford Dined one on Each Side Master Great plenty of wine 90ty at Diner. I came home with son John 9 clok.

AUGUST

August was the great month of harvest, first rye and oats, then wheat, peas and beans. The first of August was celebrated as Lammas-day, the feast of thanksgiving for the first fruits of the corn, and pasturing of cattle began on Lammas Lands for those with common rights, lasting until the following Lady Day, 25 March.

Within living memory harvestmen were summoned to the fields by church bells or harvest horns, to mark the time for work and for meals. These were established by long tradition: 1. First Breakfast (pronounced 'Brestfust') at 6 a.m. before the men set out for the fields; 2. Breakfast, or Eight-o'clock, eaten in the fields; 3. Beaver, or Lunch, at 10 or 11 a.m.; 4. Dinner, at 12 or 1 p.m.; 5. Cheesing Time, or Fours, at 4 p.m.; 6. Sixes or Tea, at 6 p.m.; and finally 7. Supper, about 8 p.m., at the farmhouse. As at the earlier Hay Harvest, the men were led by a Harvest Lord, and it was the usual custom for farmers to give gloves to their reapers to protect them from the 'thizzles' growing in with the corn.

Even in this century there were customs connected with the cutting of the last sheaf of corn, and bringing home the last load of grain, assuring fertility of the seed and a good crop in the coming year. 'Crying-the-neck' was the old custom of reaping the last sheaves of corn on each farm. When only a small patch of grain was left standing it was tied or plaited together to form a sheaf. The reapers then threw their sickles at it, competing for the honour of the last cut.

This was often followed by 'Crying-the-mare', described as 'a noisy song of triumph' by the harvestmen at the expense of neighbouring farmers who were late in getting in their harvest. It began with the cry:

'I have her'. (All repeated three times)
'What have ye?'
'A Mare.'
'Who's be she?'
(Then was shouted the name of the farm owner)
'Farmer ————.'
'Whither will ye send her?'
'To John a' Nick's.' (Some neighbour who had not yet reaped all his corn)
Finally, a loud cheer from all the harvestmen.

In Hertfordshire, the last sheaf of corn cut was called the Corn Baby, and it was trimmed with late summer flowers and given place of honour on top of the last load home from the fields. The waggon and horses were also dressed for the occasion. The horsekeeper had the honour of driving while the harvest men and boys ran alongside carrying green boughs – ash by tradition – and singing:

> Master he's got in his corn,
> Well mawn, well shorn,
> Ne'er heeled over, ne'er stuck fast,
> Harvest has come home.

Around Hinxworth, a parish particularly noted for keeping old harvest customs until very recent years, the harvestmen sang as the last load approached the farmyard:

> Hip, hip, hurrah, harvest home,
> Three plum-puddings are better than none,
> So, hip, hip, hurrah, harvest home!

The Hockey Load was the name given to the last load of corn

brought in at harvest, and the custom was to 'water it' as it rolled by to ensure a good crop in the coming year. Alfred Kingston described 'hockey watering' near Royston in *Fragments of Two Centuries* (1893):

> Many persons living remember the intense excitement which centred around the precincts of the farmhouse and its approaches, when it was known that the last load of corn was coming home! Generally a small portion, enough to fill the body of the cart, was left for the last load. Upon this the men rode home, shouting 'merry, merry harvest home', which was a well understood challenge to all and sundry to bring out their water! Through the village the light load rattled along at a great pace, while from behind every wall, tree, or gatepost along the route the men, women, and even children, armed with such utensils as came ready to hand, sent after the flying rustics a shower of water which continually increased in volume as the hockey load reached the farm-yard, where capacious buckets and pails charged from the horse pond brought up a climax of indescribable fun and merriment!

After the Hockey Load was stacked it was customary for the farmer to have a beano, or supper, for the harvestmen, usually bread, cheese, onions, and beer. This was in addition to the traditional harvest-home supper, which came later.

The day after Harvest Home was by custom a holiday on the farm. At Brent Pelham, Furneaux Pelham, and other parishes this was popularly called Drinking-Day. A correspondent of William Hone wrote for the *Year Book* of 1832:

> It is, or lately was, a custom in Hertfordshire for the men employed in getting in the corn, to meet in companies on the morning next after the 'Harvest Home' for the purpose of perambulating the neighbourhood of their work, to 'beg a fowlargess', as they term it. Each party is headed by a 'lord o'th harvest', who is generally spokesman for the rest. They solicit from all persons respectably attired, whom they may happen to meet, but they are more urgent in their requests at the dwellings of persons to whom their masters or themselves have been customers

during the past year. In most instances 'largess' is very liberally bestowed both in money and in kind; and the total sum collected is equitably divided at the close of the day.

Drinking Day was carried on well past the mid-nineteenth century. At Brent Pelham and Furneaux Pelham, however, it was ended by the efforts of the Rev. Woolmore Wigram, who became Vicar of both parishes in 1864, and later a Canon of St Albans. In his *Memoirs* (1908) Mr Wigram explained how he 'set himself earnestly to put down the great abuse in the parish of "drinking day".' Like many another Victorian clergyman he was opposed to the drunkenness and other excesses which at that time were a part of so many traditional celebrations.

The Hockey or Harvest Home Supper was the greatest social event of the farming year. The Master and the Missus, the harvestmen and their families, all who in any way had taken part in the harvest, feasted and drank together, sang the traditional harvest songs, and later, when the tables were cleared away, danced the old country dances in barns bright with corn sheaves, flowers, and other harvest-tide decorations. At the beginning of this century Lord Hampden of The Hoo, St Paul's Walden Parish, gave his men the afternoon off for the occasion. Tables for 60 were laid out in the Coach House, and still-remembered dishes were roast beef and the traditional huge harvest rabbit pies, made from rabbits shot in the cornfield stubble. Later there was singing and dancing to the accompaniment of a concertina, a fiddle or two, and other mostly home-made instruments of the Whitwell village band.

An important feature of the Hockey Supper was the toast to the Master and Mistress, and many, like this one popular in west Hertfordshire, were traditionally sung:

> Here's a' 'ealth unto the Master,
>   The founder of the feast;
> I 'opes his sowld in 'eaven may dwell,
>   When he is called ter rest.

The refrain:
> And may his doin's prosper,
>   Whativer he takes in 'and;

> For we are all his sarvants,
> And allus at 'is command.
>
> Here's a 'ealth unto the mistress
> (She's master here at least)
> We 'opes her sowld in 'eaven may dwell,
> When she is called ter rest.

After harvest came the gleaning, usually done by women but often there was a fair sprinkling of children, let off from school for the purpose, and older men. An Act of 1557 allowed nine days to gleaners after the corn was carried from the common fields before cattle might be turned into them for pasture on the stubble. In some Hertfordshire parishes the customary gleaning period was three weeks.

So that none might have an unfair advantage 'gleaning bells' were rung from the parish churches as signals to begin and end work for the day. In the 1890s some 20 Hertfordshire parishes still rang 'gleaners bells': the sixth bell at Hitchin was rung at 9 a.m. and again at 6 p.m., the bell at Stocking Pelham at 9 a.m. and 5 p.m. Payment for ringing varied from parish to parish. The Westmill Churchwarden's Accounts for 1830 show that Adams, the Parish Clerk, 'for Toling the Bell in Harvest' received ten shillings. At Codicote the Churchwardens from 1828 to 1895 paid out for harvest ringing the sum of one pound.

The gleaners in turn organized themselves into groups, each electing a Queen to see that the customary rules of gleaning were kept – the penalty for breaking these was usually forfeit of the day's takings. Order, however, did not always prevail, and some places where there was a conflict of interest, as along disputed parish boundaries, were notorious for gleaner's fights. Parish Clerk William Nobbs' rhymed directions for beating the parish bounds of Welwyn, written about 1820, described one of these:

> When you with Tewin join at Mardelmas
> Keep on to Chalkdale Field, here Gleaners fight
> With Stones and Scratches to maintain their right;
> They tear their hair, their Caps lie on the Plain,
> And on their Heads they hunt the Golden Grain,

Like mad women rave, the echoing Woods resound,
And thundering Voices tear the solid Ground.
How red their Faces, while their Fiery Eyes
Gleam like the vivid Lightning in the Skies. . . .

SEPTEMBER

September was a month of late harvesting and harvest and Statute ('Statty') or hiring fairs.

One of the most curious of the late harvests was gorse and fern on Berkhamsted Common. No cutting was permitted until the first day of September, but by long established custom people gathered on the Common late on the night before. On the stroke of midnight – they listened for the chimes of St Peter's church over a mile away – the cutters pegged out their claims in the manner of gold prospectors, returning at daybreak to do their cutting. Gorse, in particular, was much valued as fuel, especially for firing the old brick baking ovens; the fern was used as well for thatching the rabbit hutches to be found in most cottage yards in the last century.

Notable September harvest fairs in Hertfordshire were held at Hatfield and Stevenage, the Beggar's Bush Fair removed from Theobalds Park to Enfield Chase by James I in 1615, and Barnet Welsh Fair from 4-6 September, one of the largest in all England for cattle and horses. In 1975 this fair was still held 4-6, September, after Barnet Pleasure Fair from 29 August to 6 September.

In coaching times the sale of Welsh black cattle and horses, brought eastward by Welsh drovers, was a prominent feature of Barnet fair, which ended on 6 September with the colourful Welsh Drover's Race. Riding the ponies on which they had made the trip to Barnet, the drovers competed for a saddle and bridle financed by public subscription. The riders were in shirt sleeves, and wore handkerchiefs tied round their heads; sometimes they had saddles, sometimes none, and there were those who used halters only. There was shouting and talking in Welsh at the start, there being generally about ten or a dozen runners. As they came to the straight run to the winning post a second race began with the cattle dealers galloping up the course as hard as they could go, all shouting.

Mid-September brought the Mop or Statty Fairs for the annual hiring of servants, farm workers, and other manual labour. Those seeking jobs wore symbols of their trades at these fairs: carters fastened a piece of whipcord to their hats; shepherds a lock of wool; grooms a piece of sponge; maids carried a broom, a mop, or a pail, and so on. Those hired received a certain sum as 'earnest money' to seal the bargain, and usually showed that they had been spoken for by wearing a streamer or cockade.

Although the main point of the Statty was the hiring of labour, there was always something of the fun-fair about them, and special treats for children. Describing the Harpenden fairs of the 1860s and 1870s, Edwin Grey wrote:

> ... Neither must I pass over the Baked Pear Vender, for all the cottage boys and many of the girls and young people also, patronized her stall; the delights of the Statty would not have been satisfactorily sampled unless we partook of a saucer of her baked pears. Old cottagers, even today, speak with pleasure of the baked pears, which they when boys and girls used to enjoy at her stall; I so well remember this pleasant-faced, neat little old lady, who in black dress, poke bonnet, spotlessly clean white apron, and a little shawl fastened over her shoulders attended this annual fair for a number of years, dealing out ha'poths and pen'orths of pears from a large upright vessel which stood beside her. ...

On Holy Cross Day, 14 September, it was the custom to go nutting in the woods and hedgerows. Mid-September, too, was barley harvest. Few but the very poorest, however, went barley gleaning: rewards were generally small, and 'no one liked the job'.

The feast of St Matthew on 21 September was the day for Old Baldock Fair, known as Baldock Cheese and Onion fair. The district around Baldock was famed for its cheeses, piles could be seen heaped up for sale opposite the White Lion in the broad High Street. Along the other side of the Street, by the Brewery, were the stalls of the onion vendors.

September was Mayor-Making at Hertford (on St Matthew's Day, 21 September) and at St Albans (at Michaelmas, 29 September), when Mayors and Magistrates were sworn, and the Mayor's Feasts held. At St Albans in 1731:

> After the installation and swearing-in of the new Mayor, he went

the rounds with the Constables, and tipped them five shillings. He then gave a dinner to the Recorder and various gentlemen, and it cost one pound ten shillings. During the Year he gave five Dinners, three of them for Quarter Sessions.

In Hertfordshire it was thought most unlucky not to eat a 'stubble' goose at Michaelmas – it foreshadowed hard times for the family in the coming year. John Carrington of Bacon's Farm, Bramfield, recorded in his Diary for 1807:

Tuesday 29. Dined at Bells with Parker & Capt. Tonyn. fowls & Goose puding &c plenty of wine Brandy & Ginn & water home 9 clock Gave 1sh. No other Reason then being Mixs Day Mr Bell was so minded to ask a frind to partake of a good Goose Mr Bell of West End Farme Bramfield.

Michaelmas was the third Quarter Day, and rents were due. It was traditional for tenants to send a present of a goose to their landlords at Michaelmas. Some tenants, however, bettered this:

It was a long-established custom on the part of the Hitchin tenants of Trinity College (Cambridge) to send their landlords a haunch of buck venison every Michaelmas. 'And on the renewal of their leases', as the great Dr Bentley remarked, 'I believe they have been no loser by it'.

At Michaelmas it was traditional for the Bellmen and Criers of Hertfordshire to begin their winter schedules and to change their 'cries' to the seasonal autumn verses. At Royston the Bellman, by order of the Vestry, remained on duty an extra hour in the darkness of the mornings, until five o'clock.

OCTOBER

October saw the last of the harvest, the County Ploughing Matches – sometimes held in the last few days of September, but before the start of winter ploughing and sowing – late produce and cattle fairs. The poorer women and children, absent from school as the log books show, earned a few much-needed shillings gathering acorns which farmers mixed with salt and kept for winter feed for pigs and sheep. Nutting in the woods and hedgerows, which by tradition began on 14 September, Holy Cross Day, carried on through October until there were no more nuts to be found, but it was the Devil who stopped the Bramble harvest on Old Michaelmas Eve, 10 October, by cursing the bushes and making the fruit bitter.

October 2nd was known as Old Man's Day at Braughing, where every year the church bells were muffled and tolled as if for a funeral, then rung out joyfully in a wedding peal in memory of the deliverance of a sixteenth-century parishioner, Matthew Wall, from the terrible fate of being buried alive. His will, dated 1595, gave rise, perhaps, to the most curious set of endowed customs in Hertfordshire, and all for the annual sum of 20s. charged upon his estate – a messuage and twelve acres of land at Green End, Braughing – paid out as follows:

> One shilling and eight pence each to the Vicar and both Churchwardens; a small sum of money to 20 virtuous poor children and 10 aged and poor parishioners, that all might bless his memory; two shillings and 10d. to the sexton to keep his grave in order and another shilling to ring the bells on October 2nd, the anniversary of his remarkable escape from death; one shilling to a poor man for sweeping the path from Wall's house to the church gate [the footpath now known as Fleece Lane]; eighteen pence to the crier of Bishop's Stortford for announcing on Ascension and Michaelmas Days in the market place that as long as the world shall endure be it known that the Testator left his Estate to one Matthew Wall; one Groat to the Parish Clerk of Hallingbury for a similar proclamation; and finally eight pence to either Mathew or William Wall. . . .

Many considered it unlucky not to dine upon goose as well on Old Michaelmas Day, 11 October.

Every seven years Old Michaelmas was celebrated as Ganging Day at Bishop's Stortford, and nearby villages. This description is from a London newspaper of 18 October 1787:

> On the Morning of this Day, called Ganging Day, a great number of young men assemble in the fields, when a very active fellow is

nominated the leader. This person they are bound to follow, who, for the sake of diversion, generally chooses the route through ponds, ditches, and places of difficult passage. Every person they meet is bumped, male or female; which is performed by two other persons taking them up by their arms, and swinging them against each other. The women in general keep at home at this period, except those of less scrupulous character, who, for the sake of partaking of a gallon of ale and a 'plumb-cake', which every landlord or publican is obliged to furnish the revellers with, generally spend the best part of the night in the fields, if the weather is fair; it being strictly according to ancient usage not to partake of the cheer any where else.

Hatfield autumn or 'tawdry' fair was held from 16-19 October, the vigil and feast of St Etheldreda (Audrey), the patron saint, and the two days following. Before the Reformation Hatfield Manor belonged to the Abbey of Ely, which was founded by Etheldreda (d.679), daughter of Annas, King of the East Angles. The St Audrey Fairs at Hatfield, Ely, and other places associated with this saint were noted for the sale of cheap finery – 'tawdry laces' – hence the word 'tawdry' to describe goods of this kind.

October 30th, Old St Luke's Day, was Norton Fair Night, and from this time until 11 March the old curfew bell at Baldock was rung every evening at 8 p.m.

The last day of October, the 31st, was All Hallow's Eve or Nutcrack night, when girls threw nuts into the fire to discover whether they would marry. If the nut representing the true love burst quickly, it was a good omen, but if it did not burst at all the girl's fate was to be an old maid.

All Hallows was a magical and fearsome time in old Hertfordshire, like Midsummer's Eve, when spirits were believed to walk abroad, and the company of parish ghosts took up their ancient haunts. More feared than these were the witches of the neighbourhood, All Hallows Eve being one of the times in the year when their powers were greatest. Special precautions were taken to prevent the entry of witches and other mischief into the home and shop, even in outbuildings lanterns were kept burning until daybreak, to give the light which kept them away. In this century children around Whitwell and other places begged turnips (tu'nups) or better still the larger 'mangolds' (mangel wurzels) from farmers, which they scooped out and carved with grotesque faces. These with a rushlight or bit of candle inside were hung protectively in the cottage porch or nearby on a gate or fence post.

NOVEMBER

On 1 November, All Saints' Day, a curious and ancient custom was kept at Gosmore, near Hitchin. Reginald Hine wrote:

> In a field near Gosmore called Purgatory Field . . . on the Eve of All Saints [sic] men are said to have assembled at midnight, one of them burning a large fork of straw, whilst the rest knelt in a circle and prayed for the souls of their departed friends. The popular idea was that the dead were released for that one night from the pains of purgatory, but only so long as the straw continued to burn

November 2nd, All Souls' Day, when the faithful departed were remembered in prayer in the churches, was another old Hertfordshire begging day, when the poor and the children went round the villages and towns asking for soul cakes, treats which were usually pennies, apples or nuts, and sang this verse, around Whitwell to the variant of an old tune used also for the 'begging wassail' on Boxing Day - see below:

> A soul, a soul for a soul cake,
> Please, good missus, a soul cake,
> An apple, a pear, a plum, or a cherry,
> Anything else to make us all merry.
> One for Peter, two for Paul,
> Three for Him who made us all.

November 5th was Walkern Fair Day, held every year up to 1889, and in its heyday stalls crowded along Walkern Street from the Red Lion to the White Lion Inns. The great dish on Walkern Fair Night was pumpkin pie made of sweetened vegetable marrow, lemon, apples and currants.

To most, however, 5 November was Guy Fawkes, Bonfire and

Gunpowder Treason Day, and it is still one of the best kept of all the traditional celebrations. Groups of children – no longer just the poor – many with papier-mâché masks instead of the soot-blackened faces customary in many places until the middle of this century, still go from door-to-door in villages and towns with traditional Guys asking 'Penny for the Guy' – with inflation expecting more – for money to buy fireworks, and sometimes for charities. Bonfires on the night of 5 November in people's gardens or in public places are still the centre of festivity, materials for the fire being collected and heaped up well in advance. Bonfire Parties for children are if anything more popular, always including among other delights the traditional baked potatoes, sausages, and fireworks.

Guy Fawkes is altogether a quieter, more ordered festival now than in former years when one great object was the loudest possible noise, rather than as now the visual display of fireworks. Nor was the noise-making done solely by rowdy elements in the villages and towns. John Plomer, Gent., who bought the Blakesware estate in 1682, had bonfires built on Barrow Hill, and provided real gunpowder charges, not, perhaps, to be outdone by his neighbours. His 'Day Booke of Receiptes and Expenses Commencing from Lady Day, 1696' shows: 'Gunpowder att a Bonfire.... 5½d'.

Gone now are the dangerous Guy Fawkes Fireballs. These were made by boys of old rags covered in pitch and rolled into a ball which was slung between two poles, set alight and carried flaming through town and village streets, as the boys begged pennies from householders and well-to-do passers by.

'Membring Parties', as they were called, no longer chant the old Guy Fawkes rhyme, of which there were a number of local versions, this one from Ware:

Please to remember, the fifth of November
The gunpowder treason and plot:
For I see no reason why gunpowder treason
Should ever be forgot.

Guy Fawkes Guy, never come a'nigh,
Hang him on a lamp post and there let him die.
Here comes old Ragged Jack with all his ragged clothes,
Tie him to the lamp post and burn him to his nose.

'Twas God's mercy to be sent
To save our King and Parliament
Three score barrels laid below for Old England's overthrow.
With a lighted candle, with a lighted match.
Boom, boom to let him in.

Stick a pitchfork in his side.
Here comes old Ragged Jack with all his ragged clothes,
Hang him up the lamp-post and burn him to his nose.
A penn'orth of bread to stick in his head,
A penn'orth of cheese to choke him,
A pint of beer to rinse it down,
And a good old faggot to burn him.

Holler boys, holler boys, make the bell ring, ring, ring.
Holler boys, holler boys, God Save the King.
A pocket full of money and a cellar full of beer.

Please remember the old Guy,
Only once a year.

In kindly years Martinmas, 11 November, is still said to bring St Martin's Little Summer, a welcome, if short, spell of fine weather. In times past it was the traditional day for slaughtering cattle, hogs, and other farm animals which, with the old farming methods, there was not fodder to keep alive through the winter.

The feast of St Clement, 23 November, patron of blacksmiths, was another 'begging day' for the poor who went from door to door singing the old rhyme:

Catherine and Clement, be here, be here,
Some of your apples, and some of your beer;
Some for Peter and some for Paul,
And some for Him that made us all.
None of the worst, but some of the best,
And God will send your soul to rest.

In Hertfordshire, however, 25 November, the feast of St Catherine, patron of spinsters and lacemakers, was kept as a craft holiday in some places until the latter part of the nineteenth century. At Ware their traditional procession through the streets included a girl representing St Catherine riding in a waggon with her spinning wheel, and they sang:

> Here comes Queen Catherine, as fine as any Queen,
> With a coach and horses, a-coming to be seen;
> And a-spinning we will go, will go, will go,
> And a-spinning we will go.

According to local belief, handed down among Hertfordshire lace-makers, this art was first brought to the district by Queen Catherine of Aragon during her residence at Ampthill Castle, just over the border in Bedfordshire, in 1532-3, while waiting for her divorce from Henry VIII. Not only is Queen Catherine supposed to have taught local women the art of lace-making: she is also said to have burnt her own stock of laces to give them work when times were hard and bread was dear.

However it began, the making of bone or pillow lace was the most important cottage industry in Hertfordshire in the 17th and centuries. In the nineteenth century, however, owing largely to the invention of efficient lace-making machinery and an instrument for splitting straws quickly and easily, lace-making was superceded by straw-plaiting. Cathar'ning or Keeping Kattern, as it was called, still continued at Wigginton and neighbouring west Hertfordshire parishes. The historian John Cussans wrote in mid-century that '... On St Catherine's Day relations and friends usually meet in social parties with their children, and pass the day much in the same manner as a month later they do Christmas. Of late years, however, this custom appears to have been less strictly observed than was formerly the case'. Traditional fare for these Kattern gatherings were the specially baked Kattern or Kat cakes, eaten hot and buttered, with tea, spiced ale, metheglin, or hot Elderberry wine.

Special festivities for St Catherine's Day, often including a holiday or half-holiday, were held as well at the lace schools, where for a few pence a week children – boys as well as girls – were taught the craft of lace-making. At the better lace schools the children also received some instruction in reading and 'casting sums'. Traditional for Keeping Kattern at the lace schools was the ring dance around the great candlestick which, placed in the centre of the room gave light to work by in the dark of long winter afternoons. These candlesticks were more than two feet high, and many three, with several inches more for the tallow candle at the top. The children formed a ring about the candlestick and sang as they danced around:

> Waly, waly, wallflower, growing up so high,
> We are all maidens, all made to die,
> Excepting Dolly Virden, she's the only one,
> She can hop, she can skip, she can turn the candle stick,
> Oh, oh, oh, what a shame, turn your face to the wall again.

When the verse had been sung the child mentioned turned face outward from the ring, but the rest of the children continued to dance until all had turned – when the difficult feat of jumping the tall candlestick, lighted candle and all, was attempted. This jump was done with great care: if the candle was put out bad luck was sure to follow the jumper for the next twelve months. The game continued until each child had its turn.

A fair number of Hertfordshire churches were dedicated to St Andrew, among them Bramfield, Buckland, Little Berkhamsted, Hertford, Much Hadham, and Totteridge, and St Andrew and St Mary at Watton-at-Stone, and these parishes celebrated his feast day on 30 November. Under a charter granted in 1540 by Henry VIII the town of Hemel Hempstead elected its Bailiff on St Andrew's Day. As part of the festivities which followed it was customary for the new Bailiff to supply mulled port to all and sundry at his own charge. St Andrew's Day marked the distribution of one of Hertfordshire's most generous charities given by Thomas Chapman, Clerk, in the seventeenth century to those in need in his own parish of Stevenage and to three others. Chapman charged a messuage and certain lands in Stevenage with an annual payment of £8 to be given to the poor of the four parishes 'that best visit their church, are sober, and indigent', as follows: 1. To this Parish (Stevenage) 20 yards of yard-wide cloth at 2s. the yard, and 20 dozen of Wheaten Bread; 2. To Ashwell, the same gift as here; 3. To Paul's Walden seven yards of the same cloth and 6 dozen of the same bread; and 4. To Norton the same Gift as to Walden, with a clause of Distress.

DECEMBER

Most Hertfordshire people still think of the last month as did Thomas Tusser who wrote in 1557:

> O dirty December,
> For Christmas, remember.

Like St Andrew, St Nicholas, whose feast came on 6 December, was a popular saint in Hertfordshire; the churches at Elstree, Harpenden, Hinxworth, Great Hormead, Minsden (a chapel-of-ease to Hitchin), Great Munden, Norton, and Stevenage were dedicated to St Nicholas. At Stevenage in particular folk legends which grew up around the patron saint before the Reformation are still told: in the nave of the old parish church the graffito on a pillar of a man wearing a medieval head-dress with liripipium is said to represent St Nicholas. More spectacular is the ghostly knight in shining armour who on St Nicholas' Eve rides the white horse – in this county associated with the dead – out through St Nicholas' churchyard gate and down the still winding 'country' lane as far as the medieval Alms House – where he disappears.

December 11th was Baldock Black Pudding Fair for cheese, cattle, and household goods: but the season of fairs was now largely over. In mid-December, as now, schools broke-up for the Christmas holidays. The venerable grammar schools had annual dinners and orations: the Mayor, one Justice of the Peace, and the Rector of All Saints each received a pair of gloves under an eighteenth-century bequest for attending the Hertford Grammar School dinner. December 16th was the annual founders' birthday dinner for the scholars at Thomas Bourne's School at Berkhamsted, after which, however, the boys had the unfortunate custom of climbing the stairs in the church tower and pelting hapless passers-by in the street below with the oranges and apples they had been given for dessert.

December 21st, the winter solstice, was carefully watched for portents of the weather. It was believed that from whatever direction the wind blew at noon there it would remain for the next lunar quarter. December 21st was the feast of St Thomas the Apostle, another of the traditional Hertfordshire Mumping or begging days, also called Gooding Day and Doleing Day from the old custom of giving to the poor and unfortunate in the Advent season.

Edwin Grey wrote:

> An old custom observed in my boyhood days [around Harpenden in the mid-nineteenth century] was that of 'going a-Thomasing'. I knew several elderly widows who each year at the feast of St Thomas would go round to some of the principal houses in the neighbourhood 'a-Thomasing'. The women that I knew always called at the same houses and were evidently expected, for they told me they always got a 'something' at each place of call; one gentleman gave a new sixpence each year to every 'Thomaser' calling at his home. I asked what they said or did when calling at the house. Said they: 'All we ses is "Please we've cum a-Thomasin', remember St Thomas's Day".'

In December 1900, the *Hertfordshire Mercury* reported that at Braughing 'The widows of the parish again carried out the ancient custom of goodening on the 21st instant. There are 18 widows, but some were too infirm to perambulate the village, and had to find substitutes. The oldest dame who went round was Mary Dellow, aged 93. . . .'

In some Hertfordshire parishes it was customary for the Thomasers to give gifts in exchange for their alms, usually sprigs of holly, mistletoe, or other greenery gathered from the woods and hedgerows. As reminders of generosity to the less fortunate these were thought to bring luck to the house, and were carefully displayed among the seasonal decorations. In the 1840s the Thomasers at Braughing carried small pyramids of gilt evergreens, hedge-nuts, and apples for their presents. At Tewin it was the tradition to call upon friends with gifts of gilded nuts and apples on St Thomas' Day.

The Feast of St Thomas was a favoured time for distributing parochial charities. At Therfield the rent of lands known as Bateman's Stock – 'including that of the schoolhouse' – was 'distributed to the necessitous'; Thomas Tooke of Hatfield left three pounds per year from his estate of Wormleigh to be divided 'amongst six poor men on St Thomas's Day'. In the eighteenth century the poor of Ware received two bequests: Paul Hogge, 'a musician', left the sum of 20 groats 'to twenty of the poorest, yearly to be paid on St Thomas, out of Hogg's Close in Amwell Parish', and George Mead, 'Doctor in Physick', gave a rent charge of £5 out of the George Inn, for the poor on St Thomas' Day. John Jones of Hertford, by his will made 20 October 1702, gave 'to the poor of Sandon out of a farm called Killogs in this parish, a Rent charge of 40s. yearly for ever, upon the feast of St Thomas the Apostle, to be distributed then by the Churchwardens and Overseers'.

The folk customs of Christmas began, as did those of the church, with the coming of Advent. The four weeks which followed were the time when the wassailers (carol singers), the guisers (Mummers) and hand-bell ringers made the rounds of villages and towns performing as did the Waits in the streets, or by custom and prior arrangements for the upper classes, in the drawing rooms of vicarages and other homes of the well-to-do. In many places carol singers, now often led by the Vicar and making a collection for church or charity, still come round in much the same way, and in Whitwell and other places the parish bell-ringers with their hand-bells.

Carols in Hertfordshire have as long a history as in any County. The first English Carols to appear in print were included in the *Boke of St Albans*, said to have been compiled by Dame Juliana Berners, Prioress of Sopwell, and published by the 'Schoolmaster-printer' at St Albans in 1486. *Christmasse Carolles*, issued by William Caxton's apprentice and successor Wynkyn de Word, in 1521, is the oldest known printed book of English carols. Only one of its pages, the last containing the colophon, has survived, with two carols: 'A Caroll, bringing in the bore's head', and 'A carol of huntynge' – reprinted from the *Boke of St Albans*. One of the earliest surviving manuscript collections of carols, moreover, is in the early sixteenth century Commonplace Book of Richard Hill (Balliol MSS. 354) of Hillend, Langley, in the parish of Hitchin, a member of the Grocers Company and Lord Mayor of London. More than half the 62 carols in Hill's Book relate to the Nativity, Epiphany, the Christmas Saints and the Annunciation.

No carol has yet been identified as of Hertfordshire origin, however, and it appears that Hertfordshire to some degree at least shared the carols of London and the Home Counties north of the Thames.

For singing at Christmas-tide, in the nineteenth if not in centuries before, was the winter counterpart to the 'Mayers Song' – referred to simply as 'The Old Christmas Song'. William Chappell in *Popular Music of the Olden Time* (1855) identifies this as the tune for the traditional carol 'God Rest You, Merry Gentlemen', a version of which was printed as early as 1827 in *Facetiae* by William Hone. At the beginning of this century William Gerrish in Hertfordshire noted that 'The Old Christmas Song' was sung in Sandon parish 'like the May Song' antiphonally, two lines at a time, with the entire company joining in the chorus.

In Hertfordshire – as in other places – there was a sharing of good and well-loved tunes among songs. About 1840 the Hoddesdon Waits used the following variant of 'The Old Christmas Song' tune as their setting for a 12-verse version of 'The Joys of Mary'. It was collected by the eminent folklorist Helen Creighton in Nova Scotia from Norma Smith of Halifax, who wrote of it:

> My grandfather [Saunders] used to sing this every Christmas Day until he passed on. He came to Canada from Hoddesdon, Herts. He would only sing this on Christmas Day, no matter how much we would coax to have it at other times. When he was a tiny boy the Waits used to sing it in the village, and when he was old enough he would steal away from home and sing it with them. He was born in 1833. Because of the demi-semiquavers at the end he said only an Englishman could sing it.

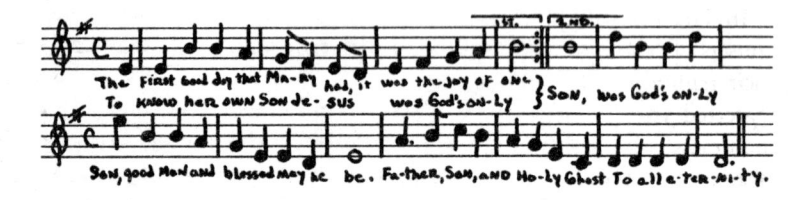

This tune, as sung by the Hoddesdon Waits about 1840, may have been the dominant version used – if not originated – in Hertfordshire. Most widely known today, however, is the so-called 'London' version (*Oxford Book of Carols*, 1928, No. 12) as printed by Dr E. F. Rimbault in *A Little Book of Christmas Carols*, in 1846. 'The

Mayers Song', sometimes called after the beginning of one of the verses 'The Moon Shines Bright', was sung to 'The Old Christmas Song' at Christmas as well as around May Day. In Hertfordshire carol singers, bell-ringers, and other performers still follow the old tradition of performing their entire repertoire before appreciative audiences, regardless of the season.

A number of other carols have been associated with Hertfordshire. Among the earliest must be the secular songs of that master of medieval music and pioneer of new forms, John Dunstable (d.1453) who, it is thought, may have been born in Hertfordshire and whose patron, the Duke of Bedford, was a brother of Humphrey Duke of Gloucester and a friend of John of Wheathampstead, Abbot of St Albans, 1420-40 and 1452-65. Among the carols ascribed to Dunstable, who wrote the noted Motet for St Alban's Day, *Albanus roseo rutilat,* is 'Wonder Tidings', (*Oxford Book of Carols,* 1928, No. 40), which begins:

> What tidings bringest thou, messenger,
> Of Christès birth this jolly day?

A particular favourite in the nineteenth century was 'As I sat on a Sunny Bank'. Lucy Broadwood (d.1929) recorded an eight-verse version sung near King's Langley before the end of the century. Another version, with six verses that she heard as a child in Hertfordshire, is given by Elizabeth Poston in her *Penguin Book of Christmas Carols,* 1965.

In Hertfordshire Christmas Eve was the popular time for the 'guisers, as the mummers were called, to make their rounds giving their traditional plays at the larger houses in the parish. It is to be regretted that no text or detailed description of a Hertfordshire mummers' play has been found. There is evidence, however, that Bishop's Stortford had a play about the legend of St Michael and the Dragon: St Michael was the patron saint, and the Churchwardens' Accounts mention both the 'pley' and the parish dragon, made of hoops with canvas stretched over them, who was not only a popular performer in the town but was rented out to Braughing and other neighbouring parishes for their plays as well. At Hexton plays about Robin Hood were given in Queen Elizabeth's reign, and probably later. The most curious survival of mumming, perhaps, is the graffito of a full-size Hobby Horse, deeply cut in the stone of the church porch at Wallington where the parish Hobby Horse was probably kept. The custom of 'guising at Christmas is now no longer remembered: by the end of the nineteenth century the 'guisers in the neighbourhood of Hitchin and Baldock performed only on Plough Monday in January.

At South Mimms the custom is still kept of distributing a loaf to every person who attends Evensong at the parish church on Christmas Eve. The bread-dole and sermon were endowed in 1698 by John Bradshaw. James Smith, describing the Ware of his childhood in the 1830s, wrote: 'It was among the pretty traditions of the period that, on Christmas Eve, the bees might be heard singing in their hives; that oxen might be seen kneeling in their stalls towards the east; and that if you applied your ear to the ground, you would be sensible of the ringing of peals of subterranean bells'. There could be no doubt about the latter: Christmas Eve in Hertfordshire was one of the great ringing nights, while early morning peals were rung in many churches on Christmas Day. In recent years the custom has been to ring for the 'Midnight Services' which, as at St Paul's Walden and Hitchin, usually begin at 11.30 p.m.

One would wish to have been at Berkhamsted early on Christmas morning in Victorian times when, by custom, after St Peter's Band had lugged their instruments up the hundred winding steps of the church tower, they assembled on top and played 'Christians, awake . . .' and other carols. On Christmas morning there were toys and sweets for the children, in many families left in pillow-case sacks at the foot of the bed, bull's eyes and pink-and-white sugar mice being especial favourites, and family gifts were exchanged. Church-going was the rule. James Smith described Christmas Day at Ware about 1835:

> Not to have gone to church on Christmas Day, of all the good days in the year, would have been an inexcusable social solecism, as well as a breach of religious duty. The building was quite a spectacle. The pillars and arches, the galleries and chandeliers, the brass lectern and the carved pulpit, the antique font, and the very organ itself were masked with holly and ivy, bay, laurel, and other evergreens. The roomy old family pews, in which you could slumber so comfortably on hot drowsy sunday afternoons in the

summer time, were filled with troops of children home for the holidays. The 'gentry' from the Park were accompanied by other 'gentry', from London, whose costumes were the admiration and envy of the less fashionable townsfolk. The services were more musical than usual, and Luppino, the organist, used to regale our ears with a grand 'Voluntary' . . . As to the sermon, it was short and sweet, genial and practical. There was the largest offertory of the year, and Meares, the Sexton, and Mrs. Meares, the pew-opener, used to stand at the entrance of the great porch to receive their annual donation from the worshippers. Outside there were friendly greetings innumerable, family enquiries, invitations 'to come round in the evening', and an interchange of the compliments of the season. The keen frosty air seemed to be pervaded by an odour of roast turkey, and from the bakehouses there soon streamed forth a procession of working-men's wives carrying home the steaming Christmas joint. The afternoon and evening were devoted to social enjoyment, prolonged until far into the night; and next day, if the weather was favourable, every sheet of ice in the neighbourhood was populous with skaters. . . .

In a number of parishes it was the custom to distribute alms to the poor on Christmas Day, usually by the vicar and churchwardens: Cheshunt and Braughing, Bishop's Stortford, Reed, Great Hormead, Widford, Great and Little Gaddesden, Datchworth, Elstree and Rickmansworth. St Ippolyts gave 10s. 'to the poorest of the poor' to be given out by the vicar and churchwardens 'and two or three honest men of the parish'. At Ware the will of Dame Margaret Tufton provided for 20 quartern loaves to be given to the poor, while at Bramfield the vicar gave bread to the poor every Christmas Day after matins. Every other year, at Christmas, each poor widow in the almshouse at Berkhamsted St Peter's received a 'cloth gown' or '20s. value at least' under a bequest of John Sayer in 1681.

December 26th, the feast of St. Stephen, is known as Boxing Day from the custom of giving Christmas Boxes – gifts, often of money – to servants, the employees of tradesmen and others who had served one in the past year. In some parishes it was another begging day, with the children making the rounds of the well-to-do houses asking for Christmas Boxes. At the beginning of this century, when the Queen Mother was a girl, children from Whitwell called regularly at

St Paul's Walden Bury, then the property of her father, the Earl of Strathmore and Kinghorne, the day after Christmas, singing this traditional Hertfordshire Wassail:

We wish you a merry Christmas
    And a happy New Year,
A pocket full of money,
    And a cellar full of beer,
Pray, ma'am, give me a Christmas Box.

Hot mince pasties,
    And cold mince pies,
I can't stand no longer,
    Because I'm dry,
Pray, ma'am, give me a Christmas Box.

Me shoes are very dirty,
    Me stockin's are very clean,
I've got a little pocket,
    To put me coppers in –
Pray, ma'am, give me a Christmas Box.

Boxing Day was – as it still is – a traditional hunting day, and there were always meets of the Hertfordshire Hounds and the Puckeridge Hounds and other County Packs. In centuries past it was the custom for gangs of boys to go Hunting the Wren, and afterward to carry the birds in little boxes from door-to-door asking for treats. In 1896 U. B. Chisenhale-Marsh wrote:

In a part of Epping Forest near our house it was a regular custom on St Stephen's Day, and occasionally on Good Friday, to hunt squirrels, probably a variation from the Wren hunt. I have tried to ascertain if any special song belonged to this occasion, but none is known now, and the hunt is only kept up by a few boys; though when I was a child there were 'droves of them,' as the exasperated keepers complained.

December 28th, Holy Innocents, was thought to be the most unlucky day in all the year, and no project was ever begun upon that day if it could possibly be avoided. Good luck in the coming year, however, could be assured by eating thirteen mince pies between Christmas and Twelfth Night: one for each month and the last for the luck.

On New Year's Eve people took care to observe the direction of the wind as a portent of the weather in the coming year, and rang the church bells to keep the Devil (evil) away while the New Year came in. Customs of ringing varied from parish to parish: at Braughing the bells were rung all evening until 10 o'clock when the ringers adjourned to a supper provided by the vicar. At 11.15 they returned to the belfry and rang a dumb peal until midnight when the muffles were removed and an open peal rung for about an hour. In recent years many churches have held watchnight services to welcome the New Year, as at Bramfield and St Paul's Walden, usually beginning about 11.30 p.m. At Berkhamsted revellers and worshippers from the watchnight service joined together under the churchyard yew for singing to welcome the New Year.

Mummers mask, with stag's horns and bells, graffito, Graveley Church

Ashwell Church Steeple, graffito, Ashwell Church

11 Local Humour

HERTFORDSHIRE, among the smallest of English counties, is referred to protectively as 'our country' by its own people. To the 'furriner' – anyone born elsewhere, particularly in what is called 'the Sheres' – and to the satirist, however, Hertfordshire, still so largely an agricultural county, was always noted for its rustics. These appear at their most grotesque in the antiquary Joseph Strutt's (1748-1802) lampoon of two Hertfordshire farmers in the parish of Bramfield, John Carrington of Bacon's ('Ploughshare') and his friend Thomas Hunsdon of West End Farm, ('Clodpoll'), in his sketch *The Bumpkin's Disaster*.

'Hertfordshire Clubs and Clouted Shoon' were already well known by the beginning of the seventeenth century. Michael Drayton wrote in *Polyolbion* (1622):

So Hertford blazon'd is 'The Club and Clouted Shoon,'
Thereto 'I'll rise betime and sleep again at noon'

Tom Fuller included 'Hertfordshire Clubs, and Clouted Shoon' among the County proverbs in his *Worthies of England* (1662):

Some will wonder how this shire, lying so near London, the staple of English civility, should be guilty of so much rusticalness. But the finest cloth must have a list, and the pure peasants are of as coarse a thread in this County as in any other place. Yet, though some may smile at their clownishness, let none laugh at their industry the rather because the high shoon of the tenants pays for the Spanish leather boots of the landlord.

Hertfordshire people are known as Hertfordshire Hedgehogs (a reference to their alledgedly slow-moving ways); Hertfordshire thick-heads (lacking in wit); and Hertfordshire Hawbucks – loosely, a reference to hay, Hertfordshire's largest crop, hay-seeds – from Huck-me-buck, the local name for the last crop of hay from fields grazed by cattle.

Hertfordshire Hay-abouts were the raw recruits of the Hertfordshire Militia, so-called because they wore a hayband on the right and a straw band on the left leg to distinguish between them. The sergeant ordered: Hay-about and Straw-about instead of right and left. Hertfordshire regiments, however, were known – among other things – as the Swedes – the County was also noted for growing and 'exporting' this vegetable for use as cattle fodder, particularly to London – and the regimental march as 'The Swede Bashers'.

It must be said that Hertfordshire folks gave as good as they got from neighbouring counties, called Cambridgeshire Cranes (or Camels), Essex Calves, Middlesex Clowns, Bedfordshire Bulldogs, and Buckinghamshire Great Fools.

In spite of its comparative wealth among English Counties, Hertfordshire had reputation for parsimony, reflected in the old saying 'Hertfordshire Kindness.' The Rev. Nathaniel Salmon, born at Meppershall Old Rectory in 1675 and Curate at Westmill, describing the tenure of the Lordship of Great Wymondley by the office of Cup-bearer at the Coronation, which was to present the first cup, of silver gilt, to the sovereign, and to receive it back again as the fee of the office, wrote: 'Hence we are told comes the common saying, for it deserves not the name of a Proverb, *Hertfordshire Kindness*. And it is used when a Person drinks to one that hath drank to him before.

It's to be wished, for the Credit of the Proverbmaker, there may be something better found couched under it than is generally understood.'

Hertfordshire people are as boastful as any. From the beginning of the seventeenth century – and probably much earlier – they have claimed that:

> Ware and Wadesmill are Worth all London.

'This, I assure you,' wrote Tom Fuller (*Worthies of England,* 1662) 'is a master-piece of the Vulgar wits in this County, wherewith they endeavour to amuse Travellers, as if Ware, a thoroughfare market, and Wade's Mill (part of a village lying two miles north thereof) were so prodigiously rich as to countervail the wealth of London. ...' But this may not have been an idle boast, as we have seen from the stories of 'Treasures and Tunnels' in an earlier chapter.

Some village boasts were rhymed:

> Ashwell is a pretty place,
> It stands all in a valley;
> There are six good ringing bells
> Besides the bowling alley.
>
> The houses they stand thick and thin,
> Young men there are in plenty;
> Young ladies they can have their choice,
> For their ain't such a place in twenty.

Neighbouring parishes – in Hertfordshire as elsewhere – jeered in reply:

> Ash'ell, po'r people,
> Sot on the church steeple,
> A-crackin' o' meece
> With a five-farden beetle.

Some boasts reflected ancient rivalry – often acute – between adjoining parishes, as in the saying:

> I would rather be hanged in Watford
> Than die a natural death in Bushey.

Most towns and villages had their nicknames, which have passed into folklore, many of them dating back for centuries. There were taunts and witticisms, proverbial sayings – the best with that necessary germ of truth in them which exaggeration turned into humour, satire, and ribaldry. The cleverest were alliterative, and the more elaborate rhymed. Some nicknames, in turn, inspired legends of their own.

Hertford, the County town, has always been 'Poor and Proud'. Pirton is still 'proud', though few remember that in Saxon times – and later – it was a place of some importance. The *Domesday Survey* (1086) noted four mills, and the residents included 'one English Knight' as well as a priest and an estimated 200 people.

The saying still is:

> Tewin for Pride,
> Burnham Green for Money.

Since the eighteenth century, at least, Tewin has been a fashionable village. People in the hamlet of Burnham Green, however, are said to keep their money in their pockets and not upon their backs.

The adjoining parishes of Stevenage and Knebworth from Elizabethan times were notorious for their miserly Overseers of the Poor, who in popular legend are remembered for starving to death more than one family on parish relief. They are still known as Stevenage Starveguts and Knebworth Knawbones.

'Lying Tring', on the western border with Buckinghamshire, was an allusion to the supposed craftiness of the inhabitants of this market town. To others it was 'Dirty Tring':

> Tring, Wing, and Ivinghoe
> Three dirty villages all in a row,
> And never without a rogue or two.
> Would you know the reason why?
> Leighton Buzzard is hard by.

It was a truism that rogues and rascals found in one parish were said to belong to another, and that a county border offered a let-out better still. Tom Fuller traced the proverb 'Here if you beat a bush, it's odds you'll start a thief' to Camden's *Britannia* (1586) and Buckinghamshire. 'No doubt', Fuller wrote in *The Worthies of England* (1662),

> there was just occasion for this proverb at the original thereof, which then contained satirical truth, proportioned to the place before it was reformed: whereof thus our great antiquary [Camden]; 'It [the neighbourhood of Watling Street] was altogether unpassable in times past by reason of trees, until that Leofstane, abbot of St Alban's did cut them down, because they yielded a place of refuge for thieves.'
>
> But this proverb is now antiquated as to the truth thereof, Buckinghamshire affording as many maiden assizes as any county of equal populousness. Yea, hear how she pleadeth for herself that such highwaymen were never her natives, but fled thither for their shelter out of neighbouring counties.

Some Hertfordshire parishes had a reputation for canny people. Foremost among these is Much Hadham, whose large and picturesque village on the road from Ware to Bishop's Stortford has long been a country retreat for the titled and successful at Court or in the City. It is said, moreover, to have been called 'Much-had-'em' for the large number of prosperous lawyers traditionally resident in the parish.

'Cunning Kimpton' is a reminder that among other sharp tricks the villagers here were supposedly given to leaving their cottage doors open when flocks of sheep were driven down the long, winding High Street, as they most often were to escape turnpike tolls, in the hope that some would stray inside. This story is also told of the hamlet of Potten End, on the far side of the Common from Berkhamsted.

There are parts of most counties which by tradition are noted for the slow wit and lack of enterprise of their inhabitants. 'Backward Sarratt' is a small parish on the border with Middlesex, still largely rural and sparsely settled as compared with its neighbours. 'Tyttenhanger Treacle-minds' lived at this village in the parish of Ridge, also on the Middlesex border, but farther east.

The names of some parishes, such as Much Hadham, mentioned above, invited plays upon words, usually when made by people from elsewhere to the disadvantage of the inhabitants. People still say that it is a foolish man who would get 'Well-in', – the local pronounciation of the parish name Welwyn – when he could get 'well-out'. It is still 'Walk-on Walkern' to the people of that district, who say that it was the Devil himself who, passing by, shouted 'Walk-on' and thus named the village by the River Beane.

Some parishes were reputed to be lawless places, to be approached with caution. There was no doubt in the minds of God-fearing country folk that the real Sodham and Gomorrah were those twins of temptation Wheathamstead and Sandridge. At the beginning of the nineteenth century the parish clerk of Welwyn, William Nobbs, reminded parishioners beating the bounds of approaching iniquity when they drew near the boundary with Stevenage:

> Cross the North Road also.
> By Pullen's Lane, then Lumbiss' you take,
> And onwards to Cave Wood your way you stake,
> Where Stevenage Robbers often did conceal
> What to the World they never dare reveal.
> Long noted Stevenage, where the Mothers bawl
> And to the scorpion brood, poor things, they call;
> Turnips and Gate posts they are taught to steal
> Soon as the Pap within their mouths they feel. . . .

People from the parish of Codicote, on the highroad from Welwyn to Hitchin, have long been known as 'Codicote Cutthroats'. There is no doubt that this village, which still makes its living so largely from road traffic, was in times past a haunt of highwaymen and footpads in search of well-to-do travellers. Best known of the Codicote robbers was one William Darvell, called 'the Phaeton Highwayman', from his use of that vehicle, who gleaned information about the plans of travellers worth waylaying when they stopped at the George and Dragon Inn, which still stands in the centre of the village opposite the old green, now paved over.

There was no match in Hertfordshire tradition, however, for the lawlessness of the people of Wigginton, a small and still remote parish in the Chiltern Hills, on the Buckinghamshire border. It remains 'Wicked Wigginton', with one of the oldest and best-known of Hertfordshire's parish nicknames. Matthew Paris, the thirteenth-century chronicler of St Albans Abbey, described the whole of the Chiltern district as an almost impassable forest in which numerous banditti found refuge.

It is an old saying that 'Wigginton people do as they please'. Certainly for centuries there was no resident clergyman, and services in the last two centuries were held infrequently by a curate who rode over from Tring. Wigginton men were notorious for their poaching and for 'bringing their dinners to work in a sack'. Their less troublesome neighbours from Tring 'brought dumplings'. They said, too, that a Wigginton man was never lost so long as he could see a cockpit, a reference to the spinney called The Cockpit along the path from Wigginton to Tring Station, where cock-fighting was held long after it had become illegal. Nor were Wigginton pubs ever said to turn away a customer at any hour, day or night.

'Thirsty Newnam' the benighted parish – one of the smallest in the County – was for more than a century without an inn or beer house, although once there was beer in plenty to be had here.

> But the more noisy fellows *would* quarrel over their pint, and sometimes even 'scrapped in the street, until the Squire, who owned every inch of the soil, declared that no beer should be sold on his property'. 'I dunno as it matters much either', one of the inhabitants explained to Herbert Tomkins when he visited the vollage collecting material for *Highways and Byways in Hertfordshire* (1902). 'Them as warnts beer goes to th' Compasses [at Radwell], an' gets it, an' them as don't warnt none goes without. It don't trouble me – leastways not much. When I gets a pot unner my nose I don't spend no time blowin' no 'ead off, but I drinks no beer to speak on now....

Some town and parish nicknames referred to the occupations of the inhabitants, hence the 'Baldock Brewers' and 'Baldock Bakers'. Men from neighbouring villages who dress up to go to Baldock's famous fairs and market are still said to have their 'Baldock shirts' on. The people of Frithsden – pronounced 'Freezeden' – and Potton End, two hamlets near Ashridge, are called 'Cherry-Pickers'. From the seventeenth century – if not earlier – the district was noted for its fine orchards of the old Hertfordshire Black Cherries. In high-summer, Frithsden held its popular Cherry Fair, and claims to have originated the cordial Cherry Bounce – a field name still – and the

Cherry Turnover. The saying, 'Like Redbourn, all on one side', came from Redbourn January Fair, held the first week in the High Street – but only on the west side where horses were tethered to rings fixed in the walls of Cumberland House Garden.

West Hertfordshire people borrowed the name of a nearby Bedfordshire town to describe any obstinate and ignorant farmer who refused to take on the new and improved methods of husbandry much talked about in the eighteenth century: nobody wanted to be described as a 'Downright Dunstable farmer'. 'Afternoon Farmers', on the other hand, were merely lazy.

The inhabitants of rural villages in Hertfordshire, like those of most isolated communities in past centuries when travel was difficult and hazardous, were much inbred. Some parishes, moreover, were particularly noted for this and for the ancient practice of 'wife stealing' from neighbouring places, such as the mid-Hertfordshire villages of Weston and Graveley. Weston people were known as the 'Weston Partners' for their habit of marrying within the parish – which in any case was so difficult to reach in wet weather that it was called 'God-Forsaken Weston' for most of the year. The 'Graveley Grinders' were so-called because of the way in which they were supposed to drive away swains from other parishes 'comin' a-courtin' Graveley girls. Those unlucky enough to be caught in this activity by the young men of the parish were liable to have the seat of their britches 'ground' on the big stone at the smithy on the Great North Road. It must be remembered that for people in other parts of the County the ultimate in desolation was any parish in east Hertfordshire where it is still said that 'even the ducks do fly backwards'.

Royston, a busy market town on the Cambridgeshire border, and with all the flavour of East Anglia, has been renowned from Medieval times for its enterprise, particularly its malting trade. Queen Elizabeth, it was said, 'being told that the Spaniard would restraine their sacks from us answered "a figge for Spaine so long as Royston Hill afforded such plentie of good Malts".' The zeal of the people at the time of the great movement for Parliamentary reform, which gained success with the Reform Bill of 1832, earned for the town the name 'Radical Royston'. Centuries older is the traditional name Royston Crows, after the grey-and-black Royston, or Hooded Crow (*Corvus Cornix*) that winters on Royston Heath and along the Chiltern Hills.

Quietest of all are what are called in Hertfordshire the 'sleeping villages', shrunken villages and deserted hamlets such as St Paul's Walden and Crow End, the latter for two centuries and more farmland in the medieval manor of Stagenhoe. Such places, now mainly lost to history, are clusters of folk legend, not the least known among gravediggers who say with some justice that they are the last to do there the work of the living.

The decay and growth of towns and villages, particularly those near to each other and whose fortunes are therefore connected in the popular mind, have that element of mystery about them which creates legend. Some legends of this kind have found their way into folk rhymes, and the oldest refer to Roman – or even Belgic – towns. The following was already, as he says, a 'traditional rhyme' when S. G. Shaw, the St Albans scrivener and bookseller published his *History of Verulam and St Albans* in 1815:

> When Verulam stood,
> St Albans was a wood.
> But now Verulam's down,
> St Albans is become a town.

Some miles to the west and near the Bedfordshire border, they had another saying:

> Bulbourne was a city,
> When St Albans was a Wood.
> Tring was a little place,
> And never any good.

When no legend took the fancy of storytellers or rhymesters, they sometimes turned to prominent and well-known landmarks, in towns, especially, to inn-signs. One of the most elaborate is about St Albans, and probably dates from the mid-nineteenth century:

> I'll mention the names of each Pub in the town:
> North Western; the Marlborough; the Anchor and Crown;
> The Maltster; the Postboy; the Trumpet; and then,
> White Hart; Two Brewers; and the famous Peahen.

Cross Keys; Potter's Arms; and the Queen's Hotel;
The Duke; Bat and Ball; the Lamb; and the Bell.
The White Horse; the Wheatsheaf; and the Queen Adelaide;
The Cock, and the Peacock; and the naughty Mermaid.

The Blacksmith's Arms is close by his shop,
Then on to the Sailor Boy and there we stop.
We pass by the Cricketers on our way back,
And find the Beehive behind the Woolpack.

There's the old Garibaldi in his flaming red coat;
The savage White Lion and the tame little Goat;
The Horse and Hound is in Sopwell Lane still,
And the two Fighting Cocks is down by the Silkmill. . . .

In Hertfordshire, as in other counties, tall tales of every kind were welcomed and valued as entertainment, re-told at celebrations and, of course, anytime to fool 'furriners'.

A Hertfordshire man was one of the best of the old English story tellers, and became a legend in his own lifetime: Sir John de Mandeville, author of the collection of fabulous tales called *Travels*, completed in 1366, was, as an inscription set up in the Abbey proclaims, born in St Albans. He recounts such marvels as the diamonds from India which when wetted with May-dew grew larger every year; how he drank at the Well of Youth, whose waters had the odour and taste of all spices; how he went down into the perilous valley which was an entrance to Hell, full of devils and their hoard of gold and silver. John Weever wrote in 1621 (*Ancient Funerall Monuments*) how 'This Towne [St Albans] vaunts her selfe very much of the birth and buriall of Sir Jon Maundeuill, Knight, the famous Trauailer . . . and that you may beleeue the report of the Inhabitants to be true, they have lately pensild a rare piece of poetry, or an Epitaph for him, upon a piller; neere to which they suppose his body to haue been buried . . .'

Most tall tales connected with the County, however, ventured no farther from the parish boundary than the sight of the cottage chimney smoke – nor did they lose anything in the telling. Many stories were attempts to explain natural phenomena. They say that when it rains on the chalk hills in Hertfordshire it rains milk, which can be seen running down them in torrents in bad storms when the ground is saturated. Everyone knew that the best cow in any farmer's herd was the cow with the 'iron' tail – the long handled barn yard pump. According to legend treacle comes from the mines at the hamlet of Wareside in a hollow near the River Ash. Children from other places in East Hertfordshire were 'warned' about the treacle pits and genuinely feared that they might get stuck in them, or fall in. Even today Wareside, low-lying under the hills, is a muddy place in wet weather.

Much of the land in Hertfordshire is chalk-with-flints, and although flints are numerous they were, and are still by many, credited with magical powers. Flints were believed to make the land fertile by holding moisture under them, and each one was supposed to contain within it a 'seed of fire' that kept the ground beneath warm – the secret, according to some, of the supposed greater productivity of flinty lands. Nor was the supply of these stones ever exhausted, even where stone-pickers, under the watchful eye of the parish stone-warden, gathered them by the basketful for road mending and the like. People said that no matter how many flints were taken away from a field in one season there would always be the same number there the next year: 'like 'taters' in Hertfordshire flints were said 'to breed in the ground'.

The Hertfordshire Plum Pudding Stones, rarely found and very heavy for their size, were even more remarkable. The large Plum Pudding Stone in the bank of a lane leading from the village of Thorley to Bishop's Stortford was said to turn round when it heard the town clock at Bishop's Stortford strike midnight. Another large piece by Kingsbury Mill in the parish of St Michael's, St Albans, believed to have been dragged from the River Ver nearby, will continue to grow, people say, as long as it stands.

In the west of the County, particularly, they still spin yarns about that most famous of local dishes, the Hertfordshire Clanger, called also after the places which claim to have originated it: the Boxmoor Barge, and the Tring or Trowley (Bottom) Dumpling. The traditional Hertfordshire Clanger is oval shaped, with meat and vegetables at one end for the first course, and plum (or other) jam at the other for 'afters', with a piece of dough across the middle – called the 'jam jar' – to catch the gravy.

TROWLEY DUMPLINGS

1 lb. chuck steak or shin of beef
1 medium onion

2 lb. suet crust pastry
pepper and salt to taste
plum jam

Have ready a large pan of boiling water, 4 pudding cloths and safety pins. Trim and chop meat into small pieces, finely chop onion. Add seasoning and mix together. Divide suet crust into 8 parts, pat into ovals $\frac{1}{4}$ in. thick. Place meat and onion mixture in centre of 4 ovals and sprinkle with stock or water. Dampen edges and press crust edges lightly together, forming a roll shape. Spread remaining 4 ovals with jam, and roll up. Then, with 4 small reserved bits of dough in-between, join ovals by two's, making 4 dumplings. Roll in floured pudding cloths, leaving space for the dough to rise, pin securely. Drop into boiling water, and boil for 15 minutes, then simmer for two hours. The 'meat ends' were often served at Trowley cottages with thick brown gravy, cabbage and boiled potatoes.

Cottage favourites, Clangers were also much eaten for lunches in the fields by farm labourers, cold, or wrapped in damp newspaper and warmed under a brazier fire. Clangers were said to be so hard that they had to be bounced several times on the ground, or better still, against the side of a barn before they were fit to eat. Clangers were traditionally good keepers, better than Blenheim apples some maintained, and when clamped like potatoes (to keep out the frost) would last the hardest winter. Others were said never to eat their Clangers at all, but to set them with daub to mend cottage or garden walls when no flints were ready-to-hand.

There were many stories about which end of a Clanger to eat first, and, not least, of how to tell a Hertfordshire from a Bedfordshire Clanger. As one man put it:

> Same loike as I said. Trowley Dumplin's is jist loike Bedfordshire Clangers, on'y th' diff'rence is, 'ey orlus 'ave th' meat up th' hoopersite eend. I 'member one ole bloke wot took one o' 'ese 'ere dumplin's wiv'im fer'is dinner an' when 'e went t'eat it, 'e di'n't know which eend was meat an' which was jam. 'E got in a real flommux 'e did an' started creatin' proper unkid, put isself out an' sooar summat shameful.

'E 'ollered at'is ole gal when 'e got 'ome an' dew yew know wot she done? Wal, she was a crafty ole crayter an' when she made th' next dumplin', she got 'old o' some plait wot she 'ad fer sheenin' into 'ats an' she stuffed it into one eend, 'stead o' th' meat an' 'at larnt 'im not tew 'oller at 'er noo mooar. But 'at gon 'er a hidea, ever arter, when she made a dumplin', she orlus put a bit o' plait in an' left it a-stickin' out'n the meat eend, so be good rights 'at done some good arter orl.

Probably the best known of all Hertfordshire's tall tales had to do with the Great Bed of Ware, which people came from far and near to see. Shakespeare alluded to the Great Bed in *Twelfth Night* (Act III, scene 2) when Sir Toby Belch, urging Auguecheek to write a challenge to his supposed rival, tells him to put as many lies in a sheet as will lie in it, '... although the sheet were big enough for the Bed of Ware in England'.

> At Ware was a bed of dimensions so wide,
> Four couples might cosily lie side by side
> And thus without touching each other abide....

According to one tale, the Great Bed was made by Jonas Fosbrooke, a journeyman carpenter of Ware, who presented it to King Edward IV in 1463 for the use of the Royal Family and their guests. Later, however, the bed for several centuries took pride of place in the best inns at Ware – the Crown, the Bull and the Saracen's Head – but with growing notoriety from the strange adventures of those who spent the night in it. Among other things the Great Bed was said to be haunted by old Fosbrooke, who, when he disapproved of any guest, would prevent their sleeping by sharp pinches, nips, and scratches so fierce as finally to make the hapless victims jump out and flee the room.

But, says legend, Fosbrooke did not always prevail. Now it happened that one Harrison Saxby of Lancashire, Master of the Horse to Henry VIII, fell in love with the ravishing daughter of a rich miller and maltster living at Chalk Island, near Ware – Ware was noted for its prosperous maltsters – and swore that he would do anything to gain her hand. The King, hearing the story as he was riding through Ware on the way to his royal residence at Hertford

Castle, determined to settle the question. He ordered the girl and her many suitors to appear before him, and promised her in marriage to the man who would spend that night in the Great Bed of Ware. All declined except Saxby, who endured the worst of the ghost's torment – and claimed his bride at daybreak.

Apart from exaggeration and satire, Hertfordshire humour was noted for its hoaxes, some of them quite elaborate and demanding performing ability. The best hoaxes were done over and over when opportunity came, and copied from place to place, becoming in their turn part of parish and County folk legend. Some hoaxes even found their way into print.

The largest collection of Hertfordshire hoaxes and tall tales of every description, oddly enough, is to be found among the many anecdotes and stories scattered through the works of William Ellis, the eighteenth-century London brewer turned Hertfordshire farmer, at Little Gaddesden, writer of books on the new and 'scientific' methods of farming, which included *The Practical Farmer, or the Hertfordshire Husbandman, containing many new experiments in husbandry*. Ellis was one of those writers, scholarly or no, who trouble to make didactic works interesting to readers, nor could he resist a good story, wherever he found it, and the urge to pass it on. Ellis' somewhat curious but very English mixture of fact with tale and fantasy, however, has never been to the taste of the pedant or the purist. The Swedish economist Peter Kalm, who visited Little Gaddesden in 1748, recorded that Ellis 'had taken as true, what false and made up stories his mischievous neighbours amused themselves by telling him'. Whatever their source, Ellis' anecdotes are well suited to his lively, racy style and undoubted abilities as a story teller. Well grounded in local legend they illustrate the folk memory and popular imagination in the Hertfordshire of their time.

Ellis describes a number of hoaxes – which he calls by their country names for tricks: 'bites' and 'skits' – traditionally least benevolent – if later butts of village humour – when done by strangers and particularly gypsies.

'In former days', said Ellis,

> there were greater Numbers of Gypsies than now, as, the Boswell Company, the Herne Company, and others.
>
> Herne had Cloaths of silver Lace, kept a couple of Race-horses,

was always full of Money, and acted as a Chieftan; this Herne got so much into the good Graces of the Owner of a Brick-kiln, near Berkhamsted Common, that he had Leave to take Possession of the Brick-kiln-house; and here it was that he resided near half a Year together with near thirty Gypsy-Men and Women, who stroled about the Country, and lived their by wicked Wits.

Now, it happened while Herne was here, that Races were run at Wards-combe, just by, and here it was that Herne won a great deal of Money by a particular Bite.

He run a little black Horse against a Gentleman's large grey one, and suffered himself to be beat, to draw in a greater Bet, in the following Manner. At the Nick of Time a Man rides by the Place on a Market-pannel with a Hempen Halter on a Bay-horse's Head in a most slouching careless Posture; and to make him appear a mere Market-horse, he thumped him now and then with a Broom-stick.

This accidental Horse, says Herne, shall run with the grey Horse for so much Money; accordingly great Bets were laid against this Horse and then the Pannel was taken off, and a little Saddle and a rider put on; but, as soon as the Drum beat, this Bay horse discovered himself trained up for the Purpose; for he immediately put himself into another Posture, and run so swift as to give the grey Horse no Share of the Prize.

Most often the hoaxers relied for effect upon the force of a local ghost story or legend. Around Whitwell they still tell of the phantom woodman who chops through eternity in the now vanished woods along Old Bendish Lane, where followers of John Bunyan made their way secretly to hear forbidden sermons in the Bendish Puritan Preaching Shed, and of how hoaxers playing-the-ghost once gave two old soot-spreaders working in the fields nearby the fright of their lives.

The great Hertfordshire wains and farm waggons that carried hay and other fodder up to London brought back profitable loads of refuse, which was used to improve the fertility of the land: mostly bags of chimney soot, and old rags. The rags were commonly ploughed in, but the soot was 'broadcast' by hand in the ancient way of sowing seed. Soot-spreading was an extra job taken on by the more enterprising farm labourers, and was done when regular tasks were finished, preferably on moonlight nights.

Spreaders bound for the fields near Bendish Lane made a point of stopping at the little thatched pub that stood, until this decade, near the bottom of Horn Hill called the Woodman – according to legend after the spectre – for a quick one, and to have their gallon beer jugs filled, for soot-spreading was thirsty work. 'Chippy' Wood and Arthur Seabrook were drinking in the parlour of the Woodman one night when two soot-spreaders, 'Tiddly' Day and 'Wacky' Saunders came in, and 'had a mind to take them down a peg or two' by playing the ghost of the phantom woodchopper. Collecting an old white sheet and a chain, 'Chippy' and Arthur made their way up Horn Hill and along behind the hedgerow by Chime Dells Field where 'Wacky' and 'Tiddly' were working – and settled down to wait. At 'beaver time' when the workmen came to the edge of the field to have their sandwiches and beer, out jumped the hoaxers, white sheet, rattling chains, and all. The poor soot-spreaders stood rooted to the ground for a second or two, then 'hollerin' mightily took to their heels, not stopping until they reached the safety of Whitwell Village. The hoaxers had their intended feast of the abandoned sandwiches and beer, nor were they disappointed in the next evening's telling of the tale to the regulars in the parlour of the Woodman. Another village story was thus created, with the hoaxers – as usual – triumphant, and, more than this, a traditional parish ghost was once more given new life.

Other hoaxes were inspired mainly by devilment, and again, if clever enough, were told in years to come as village legend. Such a one was the 'Great Buntingford Mail Robbery'. Stephen Jordan, blacksmith, cutler, and landlord of the Crown at Buntingford, was long remembered as a great organizer of pranks, and the driver of the mail coach which called at the Crown for refreshment invited trouble by boasting about his courage. One day Jordan and three or four friends waylaid the mail coach, armed only with cudgels and iron candlesticks, slotted to allow the candle or rushlight to move up or down. Seeing so many 'pistols' and hearing their 'clicks', the driver cried for mercy – which by a miracle seemed answered when the thieves left the driver and the mail and made away only with his blunderbuss, money, and watch. When the driver called as usual at the Crown that night the hoaxers were all waiting, and heard his tale with great compassion – which turned to laughter when they finally produced the things they had taken. Tradition says that they all made a night of it.

Medieval jug, graffito, Anstey Church

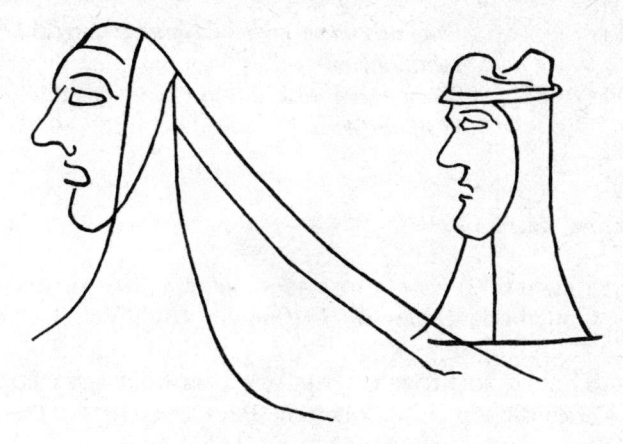

Knight and Lady, graffito, Hatfield Church

Notes

ABBREVIATIONS

E.H.A.S.	*East Hertfordshire Archaeological Society Transactions*
F.L.J.	*Folk-Lore Journal**
H.A.N.Q.	'Hertfordshire Archaeological Notes and Queries', *Hertfordshire Mercury*
H.C.	*Hertfordshire Countryside*
H.C.R.O.	Hertfordshire County Record Office
H.I.R.	*Hertfordshire Illustrated Review*
(H) N. & Q.	'Notes and Queries', *Hertfordshire Advertiser*
J.E.F.D.S.	*Journal of the English Folk Dance and Song Society*
J.F.S.S.	*Journal of the Folk Song Society*
M.H.N.Q.	*Middlesex and Hertfordshire Notes and Queries*
S.A.H.A.S.	*St Albans and Hertfordshire Architectural and Archaeological Society, Transactions*

* The Journal of the Folklore Society was called, successively, *The Folk-Lore Record* (1872-1882), *The Folk-Lore Journal* (1883-1889), *Folk-Lore* (1890-1957) and, finally, *Folklore*.

V.C.H.   *Victoria History of the Counties of England. Hertfordshire*
W.H.N.Q.   'West Hertfordshire Notes and Queries', *Watford Observer*

Introduction, pages 13-20

REV. NATHANIEL SALMON AND THE SUBJECT OF LOCAL HISTORY: Robert Clutterbuck, *History of Hertfordshire,* 1815, Vol. 1, Preface, p. 1.
FIRST SURVEY OF FOLKLORE ON THE HERTFORDSHIRE-ESSEX BORDER: U. B. Chisenhale-Marsh, 'Folk-Lore in Essex and Herts.', *The Essex Review,* Vol. V, 1896, pp. 142-162.

1   *Churches and Bells,* pages 21-30

LEGEND OF ST ALBAN: Bede, *Historia Ecclesiastica Gentis Anglorum.* S. G. Shaw, *History of Verulam and St Albans,* 1815, pp. 5-6. Dr Elsie Toms, *The Story of St Albans,* 1962, pp. 10-11.
ST ALBANS ABBEY: Rev. Peter Newcombe, *The Abbey of St Albans,* 1795, pp. 24-7.
ST MARY DE PRÉ: Shaw, *History of Verulam and St Albans,* 1815, pp. 219-20. Herbert Tomkins, *Highways and Byways in Hertfordshire,* 1902, pp. 54-6. John Cussans, MSS., H.C.R.O.
ST PAUL'S WALDEN: A. Cotton to author, 1964; M. Valentine to author, 1964. John Carrington, Diary. MSS., H.C.R.O.
STANSTEAD ABBOTS: William Gerish MSS., H.C.R.O.
PIRTON: John Cussans, *History of Hertfordshire,* Vol. II, 1874, Half Hundred of Hitchin, pp. 15-16; Ellen Pollard, 'Some Points of Interest In and Around Hitchin', H.I.R., Vol. 2, 1893, p. 290. E.H.A.S., *Transactions,* Vol. IV, Part I. 1908-9. Geoffrey Lucas, 'St Mary's Church, Pirton', pp. 5-18.
WALKERN: Recollections of James Bunce, b. at Buntingford in 1838, Guy Ewing, *Westmill,* p. 251; Walkern W.I. to author, 1971.
CHURCHES FACING EAST; POSITION OF CHANCEL: A. Whitford Anderson, 'Some Hertfordshire Churches', William Andrews, ed. *Bygone Hertfordshire,* 1898, p. 154.

ANSTEY: R. T. Andrews, 'Anstey Castle', E.H.A.S. *Transactions*, Vol. II, Part II, 1903, pp. 114-19; Rev. Frank Williams, *Anstey, a Hertfordshire Parish*, 1929, pp. 27-41.

HEMEL HEMPSTEAD: John Cussans MSS., H.C.R.O.

GRAVELEY: Rev. and Mrs Aubrey Marshall-Taylor of Graveley to author, 1967; Jones-Baker, *Old Hertfordshire Calendar*, 1974, pp. 239-40.

BALDOCK CHURCH TOWER LEGEND: E. V. Scott, 'The Pryors of Weston', H.C. Oct., 1971 pp. 48-9; Gerald Curtis, *A Chronicle of Small Beer*, 1973, based on the diaries of John Izzard Pryor of Clay Hall, Walkern, and brewer of Baldock (1827-61), p. 3; It was the sovereign's custom to reward the bearer of good news, and it is a matter of record that Priour was granted an annual pension of 40 marks, later commuted to a grant of land at Baldock. *Calendar of Patent Rolls, 1330-34* (1893), p. 74.

HERTFORDSHIRE CHURCH BELLS: Jones-Baker, *Old Hertfordshire Calendar*, 1974, pp 14, 47, 150; the standard work is still Thomas North, *The Church Bells of Hertfordshire*, 1886.

CHURCH BELL INSCRIPTIONS: Jones-Baker, *Old Hertfordshire Calendar*, 1974, 226.

ALBURY BELL: W. B. Gerish, 'Albury Church', E.H.A.S. *Transactions*, Vol. II, Part III, 1904, p. 235.

HITCHIN BELL: Reginald Hine, *History of Hitchin*, Vol. I, 1927, p. 241; John Cussans, *History of Hertfordshire*, Half Hundred of Hitchin, 1874, p. 75.

STOCKING PELHAM BELL: William Gerish and John Cussans MSS., H.C.R.O.

HARPENDEN RHYME: Mary Coburn of Harpenden to author, 1968; *Harpenden, A Picture History*, Harpenden W.E.A. 1973, p. 24.

WELWYN RHYME: William Gerish MSS., H.C.R.O. For Welwyn Church, see W. Branch Johnson, *Welwyn Briefly*, 1960, pp. 31-2.

HODDESDON RHYME: H. F. Hayllar, *The Chronicles of Hoddesdon*, 1948, p. 35.

SALE OF BELLS UNLUCKY: William Gerish MSS., H.C.R.O.

SUNDON AND TODDINGTON BELLS: Sundon W.I. to author, 1970; Thomas North, *Church Bells of Bedfordshire*, pp. 197, 201; Joseph Blundell, *Toddington: Its Annals and People*, 1925, pp. 86-8.

LOST BELLS OF HEXTON: Ralph J. Whiteman, *Hexton: A Parish Survey*, 1936, p. 125.

LOST BELL OF ST PAUL'S WALDEN: A. Cotton to author, 1964.
LOST BELL OF ALBURY: W. B. Gerish, 'Albury Church', E.H.A.S. *Transactions,* Vol. II, Part III, 1904, pp. 235-6.
LOST BELL OF SOUTH MIMMS: Herbert Tomkins, *Highways and Byways in Hertfordshire,* 1902, pp. 338-9.
SILVER BELLS: North, *The Church Bells of Hertfordshire,* 1886, p. 189.
DULL BELLS OF BUSHEY: North, *The Church Bells of Hertfordshire,* 1886, p. 164.
BELL RHYME OF WARE: Tom Ingram, *Bells in England,* 1954, pp. 168-9.
GHOST BELLS OF MINSDEN: Reginald Hine, *History of Hitchin,* Vol. II, 1929, pp. 36-7; A Cotton to author, 1966.
GHOST BELLS OF LAYSTON: William Gerish MSS., H.C.R.O.
TRING RHYME: The earliest mention known is in the reply made by the Rev. John Yale, Rector of Great Hampden, to Brown Willis' circular of interrogations in 1712. MSS. in Bodleian Library, Oxford.

2   *Treasures and Tunnels,* pages 31-45

LEGEND OF ROSE'S HOLE: William Gerish MSS., H.C.R.O.; Percy Birtchnell, *A Short History of Berkhamsted,* 2nd edn. 1972, p. 120.
LEGENDS OF SOUTH MIMMS CASTLE: For archaeological excavations and research at South Mimms Castle since 1960, see: Dr J. P. C. Kent, *The Story of Potters Bar and South Mimms,* 1966, 29-34; Sir Walter Scott used the neighbourhood of the Castle with its (still) sinister atmosphere as the setting for the murder of Lord Dalgarno in the penultimate chapter of *The Fortunes of Nigel.* 'The Place', he wrote, 'was at that time little more than a mound, partly surrounded by a ditch, from which it derived the name of Camlet Moat. A few stones there were, which had escaped the fate of many others that had been used in building different lodges in the forest for the royal keepers. These vestiges, just sufficient to show that here in former times the hand of man had been, marked the ruins of the abode of a once illustrious but long-forgotten family, the Mandevilles, Earls of Essex, to whom Enfield Chase and the extensive domains adjacent had belonged in elder days. A wild woodland prospect led the eye at various points through broad and seemingly interminable alleys, which, meeting at this point as at a common centre, diverged from each other as they receded.'

WAYSIDE CROSSES: J. L. Glasscock, 'The Ancient Crosses of Stortford', *Hertfordshire Mercury*, 7 Feb 1906; G. Aylott, 'The Ancient Crosses of Stortford', *Hertfordshire Mercury*, 7 April 1906; W. F. Andrews, 'The Crosses of Hertfordshire', *Hertfordshire Mercury*, 7 April 1906.

PLACE NAMES SUGGESTIVE OF TREASURE: Fortune Gate and Common – John Seller, *Hertfordshire Surveyed*, 1676, quoted in Gower, Mawer and Stenton, *The Place Names of Hertfordshire*, 1938, p. 83; Money Hill, Rickmansworth, Salmon, *History of Hertfordshire*, 1728, pp 109-111; Money Hill, Oxhey – Watford Tithe Award, c. 1840; Lady Brownlow and the children at Moneybury Hill – Money Barr Hill, Sess. Rolls, 1672; Sheila Richards of Tring to author, 1975; Hordweill at Orwell Bury – Gover, Mawer and Stenton, *The Place Names of Hertfordshire*, p. 160; nearby fields (in 1797) were called Great Horwell, Mead Horwell, and Horwell Pightle. *V.C.H.* Vol. III, 1912, p. 243.

PIRTON POND TREASURE: William Gerish MSS., H.C.R.O.

LEGEND OF KNOCKING KNOLL: Ellen Pollard, 'Some Points of Interest in and around Hitchin', H.I.R., Vol. II, 1894, pp. 289-291.

LOST TREASURE CITY OF WATLING STREET: These rhymes are similar to the old Hertfordshire saying about the scarlet pimpernel, known as the 'ploughman's weather glass' and the 'shepherd's clock' because in fair weather it opened a little past seven in the morning and closed at a little past two:

> Pimpernel, Pimpernel, tell me true,
> Whether the weather be fine or no;
> No ear hath heard, no tongue can tell,
> The virtues of the Pimpernel.

Jones-Baker, *Old Hertfordshire Calendar*, 1974, p. 113; Middlesex Rhyme – Walter Jerrold, *Highways and Byways in Middlesex*, 1909, p. 267; Salmon, *History of Hertfordshire*, 1728, for parishes of Elstree and Shenley, pp. 59-61; H. Braun, 'Some Earthworks of North-West Middlesex', *Trans. of the London and Middlesex Arch. Soc.*, Vol. 7 (1937) p. 686; K. M. Richardson, 'Report on the Excavations at Brockley Hill, Middlesex, August and September, 1947', *Trans. of the London and Middlesex Arch. Soc.*, Vol. 10, 1951, p. 1; S. H. Applebaum, 'Sulloniacae – 1950', *Ibid.*, p. 201.

LOST TREASURE LEGENDS OF VERULAMIUM: This is described as a 'traditionary rhyme' by G. Shaw in his *History of Verulam and St Albans,* 1815, p. 182n and pp. 10-11.

LEGEND OF WARE AND WADESMILL: For notes on recent excavations in this area made by the East Herts. Archaeological Society, see *Hertfordshire Archaeology,* Vols. 1 (1968), 2 (1970), and 3 – to date – (1973). It is not known when the Roman bridge at Ware was destroyed. Once the bridge went, traffic to and from London along the Roman road would veer left at Hertford Heath and follow the 'modern' road to the ford at Hertford and then up Port Hill to Wadesmill, or up the Watton road to link up with Ermine Street again. This path of trade is thought to have been the basis of Hertford's growth and importance. See: Robert Kiln, *The Dawn of History in East Hertfordshire,* 1974, p. 19.

LEGENDS OF TEMPLE DINSLEY: Wentworth Huyshe, *The Royal Manor of Hitchin,* 1906, pp. 76-9; Reginald Hine, 'The Early History of Temple Dinsley', a paper read to the E.H.A.S. and published in their *Transactions,* Vol. X, Part III, 1939, pp. 284-291.

LEGENDARY TREASURE AT ST ALBANS AND THE ABBEY: John Shrimpton (1591-1636), 'Antiquities of Verulamium and St Albans', MSS at H.C.R.O. and the Bodleian Library, Oxford; Letter of Sir Gerard Herbert to Carleton, 12 Jan., 1618. (*Calendar of State Papers Domestic James I,* 1611-1618., p. 512) and *Ibid.,* 1623-5, p. 516; Sir Walter Scott described Davey Ramsay as 'an ingenious, but whimsical and self-opinionated mechanic, much devoted to abstract studies', in Notes to *The Fortunes of Nigel* (published in 1831).

TREASURE AT ST IPPOLLITTS: Reginald Hine, *History of Hitchin,* 1929, Vol. 2, p. 244.

THE LOST TREASURE OF MARKYATE CELL: Cussans MSS., H.C.R.O.; *The Gentleman's Magazine,* November 1846, pp. 467-70; A version of the tale of the 'Wicked Lady Ferrers' told to Augustus Hare on a visit to Lord Brownlow's estate at Ashridge in November, 1894, has several 'late' embellishments. In his *Diary,* 19 Nov. 1894, Hare wrote.. '... Breakfast was at small tables. Lord Brownlow, at ours, talked of a neighbouring house where a Lady Ferrers, a freebooter, used to steal out at night and rob the pilgrims coming from St Albans. She had a passage from her room to the stables. In the morning one of the horses was often found tired out and covered with foam: no one could tell why. At last the poor lady was found dead on her doorstep in her suit of Lincoln Green.' *In My Solitary Life*, 1900, Vol. II, p. 67.

LEGEND OF DUN THE ROBBER: Worthington G. Smith, *Dunstable, Its History and Surroundings*, 1904, pp. 157-8.

HIGHWAYMEN'S TREASURE PLACES: William Nobbs MSS. in the Welwyn Parish Chest – the original MSS directions for beating the parish bounds can no longer be found. Local legends of Dick Turpin and other highwaymen were used by William Harrison Ainsworth in writing his novel *Rookwood*, published in 1834.

LEGEND OF ROYSTON CAVE: Alfred Kingston, *Fragments of Two Centuries*, 1893, pp. 36-7.

THE TALE OF THE LOST FIDDLER OF ANSTEY: William Gerish MSS., H.C.R.O. This appears to be a more elaborate version of the tale of 'The Lost Fiddler of Grantchester', as told by Enid Porter in *Cambridgeshire Customs and Folklore* (1969) p. 183, and *The Folklore of East Anglia* (1974) pp. 106-7. Grantchester is not far north of the Hertfordshire parish of Anstey. For Anstey, see Rev Frank Williams (Rector of the parish 1907-28) *Anstey, a Hertfordshire Parish*, 1929, pp. 21-6.

THE HEMEL HEMPSTEAD TUNNEL: F. S. Brereton, *Hemel Hempstead Through The Ages*, 1945, p. 46.

TUNNELS AT VERULAMIUM: Shaw, *History of Verulam and St Albans*, 1815, p. 11.

TUNNELS AT ST ALBANS, CALLED 'MONK'S HOLES': Shaw, *History of Verulam and St Albans*, 1815, pp. 131-2; Dr Joshua Webster, 'Gleanings of Antiquity from Verulam and St. Albans', in W.H.N.Q., 24 July 1915, p 3.

TUNNEL FROM ST ALBANS ABBEY TO KING'S LANGLEY AND KING'S LANGLEY TO ABBOT'S LANGLEY: Rev J. P. Haythornthwaite, *King's Langley*, 1924, p. 197.

TUNNEL FROM HATFIELD HOUSE TO QUEEN HOO HALL: This legend is very well known in mid-Hertfordshire today – Tewin W.I. to author, 1974. For Queen Hoo Hall, see Sir Walter Scott's Preface to the *Waverley Novels*.

WIDFORD TUNNEL LEGEND: William Gerish, 'Widford Church', E.H.A.S. *Transactions*, Vol. II, Part 2, 1903, pp. 124-9.

SECRET TUNNEL AT THE RED LION INN, MUCH HADHAM: Author shown the entrance by publican of the Red Lion who gave a version of the tale, 1967. See also: G. Tyrell to H.C., Oct. 1971, p. 21.

TUNNEL FROM THE BULL INN, WHITWELL, TO ST PAUL'S WALDEN BURY AND PARISH CHURCH: Miss Dorothy Bailey-Hawkins (late of Stagenhoe Park) to author, 1962; A. Cotton of Bendish to author, 1963; there are a number of references to the Bull Inn at Whitwell in the 'Diary' of John Carrington, High Constable of the Liberty of St Albans, at the H.C.R.O.

3 *Giants and Bogeymen*, pages 46-53

GIANTS AS FIRST INHABITANTS: Bohn, tr. Geoffrey of Monmouth, *Historia Britonum;* Matthew Paris, *Henrici De Blaneforde Chronica,* p. 132 (MSS. Cotton. Claudius D.).
WALLINGTON AND THE WANDLEBURY GIANTS: Gover, Mawer and Stenton, *The Place Names of Hertfordshire,* 1938, p 168; V.C.H. *Hertfordshire,* Wallington, 1912, Vol. III, p. 284; Enid Porter, *Cambridgeshire Customs and Folklore,* 1969, p. 187; Enid Porter, *The Folklore of East Anglia,* 1974, pp. 93-5; T. C. Lethbridge, *Gogmagog and the Buried Gods,* 1957, pp. 7-9.
HICCATHRIFT THE GIANT: Tales using his ancient name have survived in the Fen districts around the Wash. See: Enid Porter, *Cambridgeshire Customs and Folklore,* 1969, pp. 188-92; Enid Porter, *The Folklore of East Anglia,* 1974, pp. 96-101.
THE GIANT AND THE SIX HILLS AND GRAVELEY CHURCH: Jones-Baker, *Old Hertfordshire Calendar,* 1974, pp. 239-40.
JACK O'LEGS, THE WESTON GIANT: Rev. Nathaniel Salmon, *History of Hertfordshire,* 1728, p. 184. Jack's thigh-bone, however, was not identified in the first catalogue of the *Musaeum Tradescantianum,* printed in 1656.
PIERS SHONKS, THE PELHAM GIANT: John Weever, *Funeral Monuments,* 1621. Remains of Shonks' 'castle': British Museum – ADD.MSS. 5806, *f.*18; 5806, *f.*19. Nathaniel Salmon, *History of Hertfordshire,* 1728, pp. 289-90.
CADMUS, THE BARKWAY GIANT: V.C.H., Edwinstree Hundred, Barkway, pp. 27, 31. Nathaniel Salmon, *History of Hertfordshire,* 1728, p. 290.
HISTORICAL BOGEYMEN: Alfred Kingston, *Fragments of Two Centuries,* 1893, 'The Dark Night of the Eighteenth Century – the Shadow of Napoleon', pp. 56-73; Mary Coburn of Harpenden to author, 1966; A. Cotton, Bendish, to author, 1964; J. P. Sansom to author, 1962.

MILES'S BOY: William Gerish MSS., H.C.R.O.; Carbery and Grey, *Hertfordshire Heritage*, 1948, p. 111.
SPRING-HEELED JACK: at Bushey: 'Mr Renton's Recollections of Bushey' (c. 1840) MSS. of the Rev. Montagu Hall, author of *A History of Bushey*, 1938. Grant Longman to author, 1966; at Hitchin: the hoax of Henry Hawkins: Reginald Hine, *Hitchin Worthies*, 1932, pp. 290-300, and Richard Harris, ed. *The Reminiscences of Sir Henry Hawkins*, 1904.
BOB ARCHER OF BENDISH: A. Cotton of Bendish, to author, 1962.
SIMON HARCOURT: Ruth, Lady Craufurd, 'Tales of Aldbury', H.C., September 1971; Sheila Richards of Tring to author, 1975.
JACK O'LANTERNS: 'Mr Renton's Recollections of Bushey' (c. 1840) MSS of the Rev. Montagu Hall, Grant Longman to author, 1966.

4 Dragons and Monsters, pages 54-61

ST PAUL AT BERKHAMSTED: John Cobb, *Two Lectures on the History and Antiquities of Berkhamsted*, 1855, p. 5; Percy Birtchnell, *A Short History of Berkhamsted*, 2nd edn. 1972, p. 118.
BELIEFS ABOUT SNAKES: Rev. Nathaniel Salmon, *History of Hertfordshire*, 1728, p. 318; John E. Cussans, MSS., H.C.R.O.; William G. Gerish MSS., H.C.R.O.
DRAGON OF WORMENHERT: Matthew Paris, *Gesta Abbatum Monasterii Sancti Albani*, Henry T. Riley, ed. London, Longmans, 1867, Vol. 1, pp. 24-25; V.C.H., *Hertfordshire*, 1912, Vol. IV. 'Religious Houses', p. 371.
DRAGONS AND MONSTERS AS GRAFFITI: V. Pritchard, *English Medieval Graffiti*, 1967, pp. 101, 110, 165-7; Reginald L. Hine, MSS collection of graffiti, The Society of Antiquaries Library, Burlington House; D. W. Jones-Baker, MSS., collection of rubbings of Hertfordshire graffiti.
DRAGONS IN CHURCHES: *Inventory of the Historical Monuments in Hertfordshire*, Royal Commission on Historical Monuments, 1910, pp. 62-3; John Cussans, MSS., H.C.R.O.
OLD DOG OF CODICOTE: W. Branch Johnson, *The Codicote Story*, p. 16; William B. Gerish MSS., H.C.R.O. Beliefs about the 'Old Dog' are still current in the parish. The 'Old Dog' himself is now part of a book trough for large prayer and hymn books.

DRAGONS AS PROTECTIVE FIGURES: on barge-boards in Hitchin: *Inventory of the Historical Monuments in Hertfordshire*, Hitchin, pp. 122-3; Reginald L. Hine, *History of Hitchin*, Vol. 2., 1929, p. 263; John Cussans, MSS., H.C.R.O.

THE DRAGON AND FOLK PLAYS: Alfred Kingston, *A History of Royston*, 1906, pp. 44-5, which quotes the Bassingbourn Churchwardens' Accounts; Enid Porter, *Cambridgeshire Customs and Folklore*, 1969 p. 244 gives a very brief note on 'The Holy Martyr St George' performed at Bassingbourn in 1511; J. L. Glasscock, *Records of St Michael's, Bishop's Stortford*, 1882, pp. 21, 27, 29, 31, 39-40, 43, 90-1, 126-131; Francis Taverner, MSS., 'History of Hexton', British Museum (Add. MSS. 6223).

PIERS SHONKS AND THE PELHAM DRAGON: See also: U. B. Chisenhale-Marsh, 'Folk-Lore in Essex and Hertfordshire', *The Essex Review*, July-October, 1896, pp. 147, 156; William B. Gerish MSS., H.C.R.O.

5 *From the Cradle to the Grave*, pages 62-76

BIRTH: predicted by gathering of magpies: William Gerish MSS., H.C.R.O.; sex predicted by four crows: to author, St Paul's Walden, 1962; commemorated at Bayfordbury: 'County Notes', H.I.R., Vol. 2, 1894, p. 245; gifts for; William Gerish MSS., H.C.R.O., O. May to author, 1962.

CHURCHING WOMEN: author's observation, 1960s, 1970s, John Cussans MSS., H.C.R.O.

BAPTISM: letting the Devil out: William Gerish MSS., H.C.R.O.; christening dinner at Little Munden: the diary of John Pryor in Gerald Curtis, ed. *A Chronicle of Small Beer*, 1970, p. 80.

COURTSHIP: divination for name of true love: Doris Jones-Baker, *Old Hertfordshire Calendar*, 1974, pp. 13, 77, 87, 105, 126-8, 226; Ashwell rhyme: Rev. Canon J. Catterick, Rector, to author, 1973; there is an old copy in the Ashwell Village Museum; 'Weston Partners' and 'Graveley Grinders': the Rev. and Mrs. Aubrey Marshall-Taylor, Graveley Rectory, to author, 1967: Sneezing Rhyme: printed in Edith Rinder, 'Twilight in Hertfordshire . . .', H.I.R., Vol. 2, 1894, p. 69.

MARRYING TIMES: Unlucky: William Gerish MSS., H.C.R.O.; ignored in practice: John Cussans, *History of Hertfordshire*, Cashio Hundred, Vol. III 1881, p. 108.

WEDDING RINGING: William Gerish MSS., H.C.R.O.

REFRESHMENT AT THE CHURCHYARD GATE: 'Dick Taylor' at Baldock: E. V. Methold, 'The Inns at Baldock', William Gerish MSS., H.C.R.O.

WEDDING FESTIVITIES: Gerald Curtis, Ed. *A Chronicle of Small Beer*, 1970, p. 65; Edwin Grey, *Cottage Life in a Hertfordshire Village*, 1935, pp. 153-7.

MARRIAGE: legend of the rosemary: Percy Standing, ed. *Memorials of Old Hertfordshire*, 1905, p. 167; straw warning: O. May, Whitwell, to author, 1963; William Gerish MSS., H.C.R.O.; Rough Music: Edwin Grey, *Cottage Life in a Hertfordshire Village*, 1935, pp 160-3; diary of John Pryor: Gerald Curtis, Ed. *A Chronicle of Small Beer*, 1970, p. 107; St Uncumber (Wilgefortis) cult at Bovingdon and Hemel Hempstead: Susan Yaxley, ed. *History of Hemel Hempstead*, 1973, pp. 49-50. quotation from an un-named newspaper of 31 May, 1775, in Reginald Hine, *Confessions of an Un-Common Attorney*, 1945, pp. 7-8.

WIFE-SWAPPING RHYME: traditional, William Gerish MSS., H.C.R.O; and printed in Tom Ingram, *Bells in England*, 1954, pp. 168-9.

'APERN-STRING-'OLD': Carbery and Grey, *Hertfordshire Heritage*, 1948, p. 57.

MEETING A FUNERAL: The beliefs in bad luck and even death to follow meeting a funeral are still current in rural parts of Hertfordshire. A number of people have told me about it in different parts of the County: pins to avert bad consequences: Edith Rinder, 'Twilight in Hertfordshire', H.I.R., Vol. II, 1894, pp. 69-70.

DEATH OMENS: William Gerish MSS., H.C.R.O.; Edith Rinder, 'Twilight in Hertfordshire . . .', H.I.R., Vol. II, 1894, pp. 69-70; U.B. Chisenhale Marsh, 'Folk Lore in Essex and Herts', *The Essex Review*, 1896, pp. 158-9; the 'Black Hearse of St Paul's Walden', told to author by A. Cotton of Whitwell, 1963, then over 80: the 'warning' of the Lyttons of Knebworth: H. Mortimer, 'Ghosts of Famous Castles,' *Hertfordshire Mercury*, 26 Dec. 1899; Lytton, *The Life, Letters, and Literary Remains of Edward Bulwer, Lord Lytton*, 1883. Vol. I, pp. 32-8.

WALLINGTON PEOPLE LIVE AS LONG AS THEY CHOOSE: Herbert Tompkins, *Highways and Byways in Hertfordshire*, 1902, p. 252.

PASSING BELL: various customs in Hertfordshire parishes: see Thomas North, *The Church Bells of Hertfordshire*, 1886, p. 79. Edwin Grey, *Cotttage Life in a Hertfordshire Village*, 1935, p. 165.
RUSTIC EUPHEMISMS FOR DEATH: Carbery and Grey, *Hertfordshire Heritage*, 1948, pp. 89, 134.
WALKING FUNERALS: Tradesmen in 'full dress': *The Buckinghamshire Gazette Bedford Chronicle & Hertfordshire, Oxfordshire, Berkshire, Huntingtonshire & Northamptonshire Advertiser*, 27 Sep 1834, p. 4; around Harpenden: Edwin Grey, *Cottage Life in a Hertfordshire Village*, 1935, pp. 165-9.
CARRIAGE FUNERALS: John Carrington MSS., H.C.R.O.
FUNERAL GARLAND: Carbery and Grey, *Hertfordshire Heritage*, 1948, p. 87.
TELLING THE CREATURES: U. B. Chisenhale Marsh, 'Folk Lore in Essex and Hertfordshire', *The Essex Review*, Vol. V, 1896, pp. 158-9; Edith Rinder, 'Twilight in Hertfordshire . . .', H.I.R., Vol. II, 1894, p. 68.
THE SUNDAY AFTER BURIAL: MOURNERS PROCESSION TO CHURCH: Edwin Grey, *Cottage Life in a Hertfordshire Village*, 1935, pp. 168-9.

6 *Graves and Ghosts,* pages 77-90

RESURRECTION MEN: Herbert Tompkins, *Highways and Byways in Hertfordshire*, 1902, pp. 166-7. Tompkins' father was a Non-conformist Minister at Whitwell, and Herbert grew up in the village hearing many old tales about the parish of St. Paul's Walden and other places in Hertfordshire which he later put into this book, one of the best in the *Highways and Byways* series.
JOHN GOOTHERIDGE: This story is still remembered in Codicote where it was told to me by several people; his wooden grave rail, too, is always carefully painted and repaired, the idea being that, Gootheridge having been 'disturbed', it is just as well to give him no reason 'to come out again'.
THE OPEN TOMB AT ESSENDON: (H) N.&Q., 13 Feb. 1909, p. 3.
RESURRECTION GAMES: at Aston: Aston W.I. to author 1971: at St Nicholas' churchyard tomb, Stevenage: Stevenage Townswomen's Guild to author 1970; Snooks' grave at Boxmoor: oral tradition dating from the 1830s, in Francis Tompkins to H.C., June-July 1965, p. 46.

RESURRECTION BELIEF: trees from grave at Tewin: Tewin W.I. to author, 1974, a belief still current in the parish; Fig tree tomb at Watford: W. R. Saunders, *A History of Watford*, 1931, p. 57.
HENRY TRIGG'S COFFIN: the best known of Stevenage tales; Stevenage Townswomen's Guild to author 1970; E. V. Methold, *Notes on Stevenage*, 1902, pp. 22-3; the appearance of Henry Trigg's ghost during alterations to the former Castle Inn in 1964 caused quite a stir in the town. See *Hertfordshire Express and Stevenage Gazette*, 18 Dec. 1964, p. 3.
GHOSTS AS CHURCHYARD GUARDIANS: William Gerish MSS., H.C.R.O.
MOTHER SHIPTON AT TRING: Sheila Richards of Tring to author, 1975.
TOMB LEGENDS: at Eastwick: as told to author by a lifelong resident, 1964; William Gerish MSS., H.C.R.O.
BURIAL IN CONSECRATED GROUND ENDS HAUNTING: The headless pedlar of Bygrave: William Gerish MSS., H.C.R.O.; the Bull Inn ghost, Whitwell: Dr. T. Probyn to author, 1963.
MURDERER IDENTIFIED BY EXHUMED VICTIM: an old belief still remembered; Edith Rinder, 'Twilight in Hertfordshire . . .' H.I.R., Vol. II, 1894, pp. 70-1.
SIR JOHN JOCELYN'S GHOST: John Cussans MSS., H.C.R.O.; William Gerish MSS., H.C.R.O.
THE WICKED GHOST OF CODICOTE: H. C. Andrews and E. E. Squires, 'Codicote Past and Present', E.H.A.S., Vol. V, Part I, 1912, pp. 58-9; John Cussans MSS., H.C.R.O.; William Nobbs' verses were used at the last beating of the bounds of Welwyn Parish in 1904. According to the historian of Welwyn, W. Branch Johnson (1972), the whereabouts of Nobbs' MSS are unknown. For a sketch of Nobbs based upon the account of another Welwyn man, John Batten, see W. Branch Johnson, *Welwyn, By and Large*, (1967) pp. 48-9.
BENEVOLENT BURIAL AT CROSSROADS: William Gerish MSS., H.C.R.O.; at Bishop's Stortford: U. B. Chisenhale Marsh, 'Folk Lore in Essex and Herts.', *The Essex Review*, Vol. V, 1896, p. 158; Local History Society, *Bishop's Stortford, A Short History*, pp. 22-3; Tommy Deacon's grave: W. R. Saunders, *A History of Watford*, 1931, p 16.
BODIES STAKED TO PREVENT THEIR BECOMING GHOSTS: TALE OF CLIBBORN'S POST: the best account of Clibborn the footpad is in the MSS. Diary of John Carrington, of Bacon's Farm, Bramfield,

H.C.R.O. See also: D. Jones-Baker, *Old Hertfordshire Calendar*, 1974, pp. 281-2.

BELIEF IN GHOSTS: Henry Nash, *Reminiscences of Berkhamsted*, 1890, pp. 30-1; at Royston in the latter part of the 18th century: Alfred Kingston, *Fragments of Two Centuries*, 1893, pp. 26-7, 30.

HISTORIC FIGURES AS GHOSTS IN HERTFORDSHIRE: Nell Gwynne at Salisbury Hall: a number of people have seen her in recent years, though she is a venerable ghost. See A. F. N. Joyner, 'An Old Hertfordshire Manor House, Salisbury Hall', H.I.R., Vol. II, 1894, pp. 189-95; Churchill's step-father George Cornwallis-West saw Nell when he lived at Salisbury Hall: G. Cornwallis-West, *Edwardian Hey-Days*. 1930, pp 254-5. Lord Capel's ghost at Cassiobury Park: William Gerish MSS., H.C.R.O.; S. Elfering, 'Historic Hadham Hall', H.C., spring, 1951, pp 164-5; Sir Henry Blount at Tyttenhanger: a descendant of Sir Henry's who lived in the house, Lady Jane van Koughnet, *A History of Tyttenhanger*, 1895, p. 54; Lord Anson at Moor Park: Hilary Armitage, *A History of Moor Park*, 1964, pp. 20-1: ghosts at bowls: Reginald Hine, *The Story of the Sun Hotel, Hitchin, 1575-1945*. 2nd. edn. 1946, p. 14. For Mark Hildesley, see Reginald Hine, *Hitchin Worthies*, 1932, pp. 143-64.

GHOSTS OF ROMAN SOLDIERS AT TRING: Sheila Richards, *A History of Tring*, 1974, p. 9.

GHOST OF THE HEADLESS WHITE HORSE: A pub at Burnham Green is called the White Horse after the legendary ghost, and is one of a very few pubs in Hertfordshire to show a ghost upon its sign. The haunted White Horse Lane runs from the Green along one side of the pub and on down the hill. Rabley Heath Over Sixties Club to author, 1968; Wynn Hughes to author, 1967.

GHOST BATTLE OF ST. ALBANS: William Gerish MSS., H.C.R.O.; F. G. Kitton, 'The Old Inns of St. Albans', S.A.H.A.S. Vol. I, part III, new series, 1900, p 249; Christina Hole, *Haunted England*, p. 74.

GHOST MIST OF BARNET: William Gerish MSS., H.C.R.O.

GHOSTS OF CAVALIERS AND ROUNDHEADS: Watton-at Stone: William Gerish MSS., H.C.R.O.; Graveley: The Rev. and Mrs. Aubrey Marshall-Taylor to author, 1968; at Soldiers' Bottom, Berkhamsted: Henry Nash, *Reminiscences of Berkhamsted*, 1890, pp. 47-8; Percy Birtchnell, *A Short History of Berkhamsted*, 2nd. edn. 1972, p. 120; Goring the Cavalier: Clive Holmes, *The Eastern Association in the English Civil War*, 1974, pp. 162-3; Reginald Hine, *History of Hitchin*,

Vol. I, 1927, pp. 205-7; Ellen Polland, 'High Down, Pirton', (her family home) E.H.A.S., Vol IV, Part 3, 1911, pp. 233-4.
WHITE HART GHOST: William Gerish MSS., H.C.R.O.
GHOST TANK OF KNEBWORTH: a local tale. I have seen this ghost myself in broad daylight, on a mid-afternoon sunny day in the autumn.
GHOST MONKS OF ST ALBANS ABBEY: These are very well known today, and quite often seen. Rev. Timothy Lewis Lloyd, a former Precentor at the Abbey, to author, 1972.
GHOST MONKS OF BRAUGHING: William Gerish MSS., H.C.R.O.; for a recent account, see *Hertfordshire Mercury*, 22 December, 1967, p. 3.
SCREAMING GHOST OF HINXWORTH PLACE: Geoffrey Lucas, 'Hinxworth Place,' E.H.A.S. *Transactions*, Vol. IV, part 2, 1911, p. 159; and Letchworth paper *The Citizen*, 27 Oct. 1939. p. 4.
GHOST CHOIR OF ST ALBAN'S ABBEY: William Gerish MSS. H.C.R.O.; for the late Canon Glossop's experiences with the ghost music of the Abbey see Frank Drakard to H.C., April, 1968, p. 42.
GHOST PRIOR OF WYMONDLEY PRIORY: Anne Sworder, 'Some Traditions of the Wymondleys', H. C. Spring, 1947, p. 115.
SIR GEOFFREY DE MANDEVILLE OF SOUTH MYMMS: William Gerish MSS., H.C.R.O. Doris Jones-Baker, *Old Hertfordshire Calendar*, 1974, p. 270.
THE GHOST TRAIN DRIVER: *Hertfordshire Express* (a Hitchin paper) 14 March, 1974. p. 3, reprinted from the *Hertfordshire Express* of 17 March, 1894.

7   *Cures, Charms and Healers*, pages 91-103

THE POST BOY'S SONG: 'A Man o' Ware', *Hertfordshire Mercury*, Aug. 30, 1935.
CANUTE'S EDICT: Benjamin Thorpe, *Monumenta Ecclesiastica*, 1846. Vol. I, p. 379.
LEGEND OF UTHER PENDRAGON: Rev. Peter Newcome, *The History of the Abbey of St Albans*, 1795, p. 11; 'Copy of MSS kept in the Watch Tower at St Albans', Appendix No. IV, Shaw, *History of Verulam and St Albans*, 1815. pp. 7, 222.
HOLY WELLS AT CADWELL AND CHAD'S WELL: Cussans MSS., H.C.R.O.

HOLY WELL AT BISHOP'S STORTFORD: Annie Berlyn, *Bishop's Stortford and its Story* 1930, p. 60; Bishop's Stortford Local History Society, *Bishop's Stortford, A Short History,* 1969, p. 26.
HOLY WELL AT BERKHAMSTED: Percy Birtchnell, *A Short History of Berkhamsted,* 2nd. edn. 1972, p. 118.
HOLY WELL AT HEXTON: Francis Taverner, 'History of Hexton', MSS, British Museum, Add. MSS., 6223.
PAGAN WORSHIP AT ST. JOHN'S WELL: Dora Fry, 'St John's Well', H.C., Winter, 1953-4, pp. 106-7. By a lifelong resident of Berkhamsted: Percy Birtchnell, *A Short History of Berkhamsted,* 2nd. edn. 1972, p. 118.
MEDICINAL WATERS: Sir Henry Chauncy, *The Historical Antiquities of Hertfordshire,* 2d. edn., 1826, Vol. I, introduction, pp. 11-12.
LEGENDS OF GUARDIAN STONES: Alfred Kingston, *History of Royston,* 1906, pp. 2-10; Dixie's Stone: William Gerish MSS., H.C.R.O.
LEGENDS OF PLUM-PUDDING STONES AND FLINTS: William Gerish MSS., H.C.R.O.
GOD STONES: Hine, *History of Hitchin,* Vol. II (1929) p. 39n.; Carbery and Grey, *Hertfordshire Heritage,* 1948, p. 88; Grey, *Cottage Life in a Hertfordshire Village,* 1935, p. 180. Grey wrote: 'I've seen some [potato charms] that the men have shown me which they had carried in their pocket for years; they had become as dry and as hard as rock.'
CURATIVE TREES: William Gerish MSS., H.C.R.O.; *Chambers' Journal,* No. 504, 23 Aug. 1873, p. 7.
JOHN OF GADDESDEN: Vicars Bell, *Little Gaddesden,* 1949, pp. 22-4; Fuller, *The Worthies of England,* 1662. (J. Freeman, ed., London, Allen & Unwin, 1952, p. 233.)
HILL'S COMMONPLACE BOOK: Balliol MSS. 354.
CURES FROM A HANGED MAN: William Gerish MSS., H.C.R.O.
WARTS: U. B. Chisenhale-Marsh, 'Folk Lore in Essex and Herts', *The Essex Review,* July-Oct. 1896, Vol. V, pp. 159-60. Grey, *Cottage Life in a Hertfordshire Village,* 1935, pp. 180-93.
TOOTHACHE: Mary Coburn, 'Cottage Cures', H.C., Sept. 1967, p. 12; William Ellis, *The Country Housewife's Family Companion,* 1750, p. 78.
HICCUP CHARM: K. W. to author, 1967, and see Jones-Baker, *Old Hertfordshire Calendar,* 1974, p. 243. Jacob's Vision is in Genesis, XXVIII, 12.
CONSUMPTION: Carbery and Grey, *Hertfordshire Heritage,* 1948, p. 135.

RINGS AS CURES: Sheila Richards of Tring to author, 1975; William Gerish MSS., H.C.R.O.
JAUNDICE, SHINGLES, AND SORE THROAT: William Gerish MSS., H.C.R.O; Ellis, *The Country Hosewife's Family Companion*, 1750, pp. 63, 86; Coburn, 'Cottage Cures', H.C., Sept. 1967, p. 12.
WHOOPING COUGH: *Hertfordshire Mercury*, Aug. 3, 1912; Grey, *Cottage Life in a Hertfordshire Village*, 1935, pp. 176-77.
'YARBS': Grey, *Cottage Life in a Hertfordshire Village*, 1935, pp. 177-8.
PIRTON MEDICINE WOMAN: K. W. to author. See also: Ellen Pollard, 'Some Points of Interest in and Around Hitchin', H.I.R., Vol. II, 1894, p. 289.
QUACKS AT HARPENDEN RACES: Lady Mary Carbery, *Happy World*, 1941, p. 19.
CUNNING MAN OF ICKLEFORD: Hertfordshire County Records, H.C.R.O.

8 *The Devil*, pages 104-109

THE DEVIL'S 'WAYS': Lady Mary Carbery and Edwin Grey, *Hertfordshire Heritage*, 1948, p. 151.
THE DEVIL'S WEEDS: *Ibid.*, p. 152.
THE DEVIL'S FOSSILS: William Gerish MSS., H.C.R.O.; Wyn Hughes to author, 1970.
GRIME'S BROOK: Gover, Mawer and Stenton, *The Place Names of Hertfordshire*, 1938, pp. 2-3; Percy Birtchnell, *A Short History of Berkhamsted*, 2nd. edn. 1972, p. 119.
DEVIL'S HOPSCOTCH: Kingston, *A History of Royston*, 1906, pp. 193-4.
THE SIX HILLS AND THE GRAVELEY CHURCH SPIRE: Tomkins, *Highways and Byways in Hertfordshire*, 1902, pp. 179-80.
DEVIL'S DITCH, DEVIL'S DYKE, and GRIM'S DYKE: V.C.H. Hertfordshire, 'Ancient Earthworks', pp. 124-6; V.C.H. Dacorum Hundred, Wigginton, p 314.
MARFORD JOHN: Tomkins, *Highways and Byways in Hertfordshire*, 1902, pp. 41-2.
DEVIL AT TRING: Sheila Richards, *A History of Tring*, 1974, pp. 12-13, and to author, 1975.
DEVIL AT BERKHAMSTED: Percy Birtchnell, *A Short History of Berkhamsted*, 2nd. edn. 1972, p. 119.

DEVIL AT BUSHEY: MSS. of the Rev. Montagu Hall, Rector of Bushey 1898-1934, and author of *A History of Bushey,* 1938. In possession of Grant Longman, of Bushey.
DEVIL AT ASTON: Mrs K. Carter to H.C., September, 1972. G. W. Partridge to H.C., November, 1972.
DEVIL AT TEWIN: Tewin W.I. to author, April 1974. See Gover, Mawer and Stenton, *The Place Names of Hertfordshire,* 1938, p. 232. For tales of the supernatural – based upon the local knowledge of Joseph Strutt who lived at Tewin for some four years – in the vicinity of Tewin, see the romance by Joseph Strutt completed by Sir Walter Scott, *Queen Hoo Hall,* published in 1808.
TRING PARK WOOD: Percy Birtchnell, 'Berkhamsted's Old Wives Tales', H.C., No. 17, summer, 1950. p. 38.
DEVIL AT WALKERN AND GADDEDSEN: William Gerish MSS., H.C.R.O.
DEVIL'S HEAD AT ROYSTON: Larwood and Hotten, *The History of Signboards,* (first edition, 1866) 2nd. edn. 1898, p. 295.
LEGEND OF SIR JOHN SHORNE AND THE BOOT: Rev. W. H. Kelke, 'Master John Shorne', *Records of Buckinghamshire,* 1870, Vol. II, pp. 60-70; James Sheahan, *History and Topography of Buckinghamshire,* 1862, pp. 28-9. John Cussans MSS., H.C.R.O.
ST DUNSTAN AND HUNSDON CHURCH: Jones-Baker, *Old Hertfordshire Calendar,* p. 103.
LEGEND OF THE MERRY DEVIL OF EDMONTON: See John Norden, *Survey of Hertfordshire,* 1598 and *Survey of Middlesex,* 1593; and John Weever, *Ancient Funerall Monuments,* 1621, quoted in Michael Robbins, *Middlesex,* 1953, pp. 243, 245; Rev. Thomas Fuller, *Worthies of England,* 1662, Middlesex. (J. Freeman, ed., London, Allen & Unwin, 1952, p. 391).
DEVIL AT ST ALBANS: Only the title page of this quarto pamphlet is preserved in the British Museum.
DEEV'L-DOGERS: Carbery and Grey, *Hertfordshire Heritage,* 1948, p. 75.

9 *Witches and Wizards,* pages 110-118

FRIAR BUNGAY'S PROPHECY: Percy Standing, 'The Battles of St Albans and Barnet', in Percy Standing, Ed., *Memorials of Old Hertfordshire,* 1905, pp. 87-91.

MOTHER HAGGY: William Gerish MSS., H.C.R.O.
WITCH POWERS TO TRANSFORM THEMSELVES: Carbery and Grey, *Hertfordshire Heritage,* 1948, pp. 154-6.
ROSINA MASSEY: Vicars Bell, *Little Gaddesden,* 1949, pp. 132-4.
WITCHES AND HURDLES: People used to say in the parish of St Paul's Walden that the local witch, Betty Deacon, would be seen riding on a hurdle round and round Dove House Close, near the Bury, at sunset. Anon. to author, 1966.
LEGEND OF THE DATCHWORTH WITCHES: Frank Ballin of Welwyn to Author, 1965; William Nobbs, 'The Parish Bounds of Welwyn', MSS., c. 1820. W. Branch Johnson, *Welwyn, By and Large,* 1967, pp. 48-52, gives a sketch of Nobbs based on the account of another Welwyn man, John Batten.
DAME SAD: Joseph Strutt, *Queen Hoo Hall,* 1808. Sir Walter Scott wrote the last chapter and edited this book after Strutt's death, in 1802. See Scott's 'Preface' to the *Waverley* novels, dated London, April 1, 1808, quoted in Sir Walter Scott, ed., *Queen Hoo Hall,* by Joseph Strutt, London, John Cunningham, 1840, pp. 3-4.
FEAR OF WITCHES TODAY: Carbery and Grey, *Hertfordshire Heritage,* 1948. p. 156. Anon. to author, 1962.
SALLY RAINBOW: William Gerish MSS., H.C.R.O.; *Hertfordshire Mercury,* 7 July, 1939.
THE WITCH-FINDER GENERAL: C. L'Estrange Ewen, *Witchcraft and Demonianism* edn. 1971, pp. 254-61. Enid Porter, *The Folklore of East Anglia,* 1974, Chapter 7: 'Witch Hunting: East Anglia's Black Record'.
JANE WENHAM: William Gerish, *A Tour Through Hertfordshire recording its Legends, Traditions and Ghostly Tales* (1914) MSS. in possession of the author.
WITCHES AT TRING: William Hone, *The Every-Day Book,* Vol. I, 1824, pp. 1045-8. A good summary of the case and trial. Colley's Ghost: W.H.N.Q., 2 Dec. 1911, p. 3.
KENSWORTH WITCH: Jones-Baker, *Old Hertfordshire Calendar,* 1974, p. 93.
THE AGDELL GHOST: Grey, *Cottage Life in a Hertfordshire Village,* 1935, pp. 184-5.
SIR GUY DE GRAVADE: William Gerish MSS., H.C.R.O.
BEWITCHED PERSONS AT GREAT GADDESDEN: Robert Cropwell, Vicar, to Archdeacon of Huntingdon. Acta. 29 March, 1614. Urwick,

Nonconformity in Hertfordshire, 1884 p. 409.
WITCH BURNING AT AYOT ST LAWRENCE: E.H.A.S., Vol. V, part II, 1913. p. 213.

10   *The Turning Year,* pages 119-179

JANUARY

NEW YEAR: Jones-Baker, *Old Hertfordshire Calendar,* 1974, pp. 1-3.
NEW YEAR CAROL: Commonplace Book of Richard Hill, of Hillend, Langley, Hitchin. Balliol MSS. 354.
POPE LADY BUNS: William Gerish MSS., H.C.R.O.; M.H.N.Q., Vol. 1, 1895, pp. 77, 130-1, 180.
WASSAILING: Household Account Book of James Forrester of Broadfield Hall, 1689-1696. Reginald Hine MSS., H.C.R.O.; Ashwell Wassail: Rev. Canon John Catterick to author, Ashwell, 1975.
PLOUGH SUNDAY: Jones-Baker, *Old Hertfordshire Calendar,* 1974, pp. 8-9,
PLOUGH MONDAY: William Gerish MSS., H.C.R.O.
WEATHER LORE: Edith Rinder, 'Twilight in Hertfordshire. Some Gleanings of Folk-Lore', H.I.R., Vol. II, 1894, p. 69; A. Cotton of Bendish to author, 1965.

FEBRUARY

WEATHER LORE: William Gerish MSS., H.C.R.O.
ST BLAIZE: Reginald Hine, *The History of Hitchin,* Vol. I, 1927, pp. 85-6; John Cussans MSS., H.C.R.O.
ST VALENTINE'S DAY: Legend of the Moat Lady: Percy Ilott of Hertford used the traditional tale of the Moat Lady as the basis for his one-act play, 'The Moat Lady of Much Hadham', which is set in the bar parlour of the old Red Lion Inn on the night of Feb. 13, 1851. Percy Ilott, *Hertfordshire Stories, Plays, and Poems,* 1938, pp. 36-45. Valentines: Edwin Grey, *Cottage Life in a Hertfordshire Village,* 1935, p. 147: Breachwood Green Customs: Olive Folds, 'Childhood Memories of Sixty Five Years Ago', H.C., autumn, 1962, p. 253. This variant of the rhyme was found in east Hertfordshire:

Good morrow to you, Valentine,
Curl your hair as I curl mine,
One before and two behind,
Good morrow to you, Valentine.

U.B. Chisenhale Marsh, 'Folk Lore in Essex and Herts'., *The Essex Review.* Vol. x, 1896, p. 148; Cambridge tune: Enid Porter, *Cambridgeshire Customs and Folklore,* 1969, p. 105; A. Cotton of Whitwell to author, 1963.
SHROVE TUESDAY: at Hoddesdon: William Hone, *The Every-Day Book,* 1826, p. 242; at Hatfield: Jocelyn Antrobus, *Hatfield: Some Memories of its Past* 1912, p. 89n.; Pancake Witch: Toddington Womens Institute to author, 1974; Baldock rhyme: Edith Rinder, 'Twilight in Hertfordshire . . .', H.I.R., Vol. 2, 1894, p. 70; Breachwood Green rhyme: Olive Folds, 'Childhood Memories of Sixty Five Years Ago', *H.C.,* autumn, 1962, p. 253; thrashing the hen and cockfighting: Alfred Kingston, *Fragments of Two Centuries,* 1893, p. 23; Frank Harrowell to *H.C.* Jan., 1975, p. 42; E.H.A.S. *Transactions,* Vol. IV, Part III, 1911, p. 319.
ASH WEDNESDAY: William Gerish MSS., H.C.R.O.

MARCH

PRIM-E-ROSE TIME: William Gerish MSS., H.C.R.O.
DAFF-A-DOWN DILLY RHYME: H.A.N.Q., March, 1908.
CURFEW BELLS: William Gerish MSS., H.C.R.O.; John Cussans MSS., H.C.R.O.
MOTHERING SUNDAY: Carbery and Grey, *Hertfordshire Heritage,* 1948, p. 113.
MID-LENT SUNDAY FISH DOLES: Salmon, *History of Hertfordshire,* 1728, pp. 292, 233.
PALM OR FIG SUNDAY: Dorothy Bailey-Hawkins, late of Stagenhoe Park, to author, 1962; O. May of Whitwell to author, 1963; William Hone, *The Year Book,* 1832, p. 1593.

APRIL

GOOD FRIDAY: a ringing day: Thomas North, *The Church Bells of Hertfordshire,* 1886, pp. 76-7.

HOT CROSS BUNS: William Gerish MSS., H.C.R.O.
GOOD FRIDAY FAIRS: Stevenage: E. V. Methold, *Notes on Stevenage*, 1902, pp. 25-6; Robert Trow-Smith, *The History of Stevenage*, 1958, p. 79; Hexton: Page Woodcock, 'Tales from a Hexton Taproom', *H.C.*, Autumn, 1950, p. 62.
HEXTON ORANGE ROLLING: Woodcock, 'Tales from a Hexton Taproom', *H.C.*, Autumn, 1950, pp. 62-3.
EASTER EVE: Legend of the Pasque Flower: Alfred Kingston, *The Heath and its Wild Flowers*, 1904, pp. 17-18; William Gerish, MSS., H.C.R.O.
EASTER SUNDAY: ringing: North, *The Church Bells of Hertfordshire*, 1886, p. 76; new clothes: O. May, Whitwell, to author, 1964; G. Rhodes to author, 1963; easter dishes: *ibid.*, and D. Bailey-Hawkins, late of Stagenhoe Park, to author, 1963.
EASTER WEATHER: Percy Standing, *Memorials of Old Hertfordshire*, 1905, p. 167.
EASTER WEEK: Jones-Baker, *Old Hertfordshire Calendar*, pp. 66-67.
CUCKOO DAY: For other versions of the Cuckoo Song, see: Jones-Baker, *Old Hertfordshire Calendar*, 1974, pp. 68-9; Rinder, 'Twilight in Hertfordshire...', H.I.R., Vol. 2, 1894, p. 67.
HOCK DAY: Francis Taverner (lord of Hexton, d. 1657) manuscript history of Hexton, British Museum, Add. MSS. 6223.

MAY

MAY DAY AT HITCHIN: Louisa Hinde was the daughter of Capt. Robert Hinde, of Preston Castle, who wrote *Discipline of the Light Horse* (1778). Miss Hinde died in 1855. Her sketch of May Day at Hitchin was printed by William Hone, *Every-Day Book,* Vol. I, 1826, pp. 565-6. See: Reginald Hine, *Hitchin Worthies*, 1932 pp. 182-4.
MAY DAY AT BALDOCK: William Hone, *The Year Book* (1832) pp. 1593-5.
HERTFORDSHIRE MAYERS SONG: The earliest known version is in the 'Commonplace Book' of Richard Hill of Langley, Hitchin, Balliol MSS. 354. The text of the Hitchin version is in William Hone, *The Every-Day Book*, Vol. I, 1826, pp. 567-8; and the 'Old Christmas Song' see: William Chappell, *Popular Music of the Olden Time...* Vol. 2, 1859, pp. 752-3. King's Langley and Weston Mayers Songs: Lucy Broadwood and J. A. F. Maitland, *English County Songs*, 1893, pp.

108-9; the largest printed collection of the texts (only) of the Hertfordshire Mayers Song, with 9 variants, is still William Gerish, *The Mayers and their Song, or Some Account of the First of May and its Observance in Hertfordshire*, 15 pp., Hertford, 1904; Words of the Letchworth Mayers Song: *F.L.J.*, Vol. III, 1883, pp. 185-6; Mayers Songs from the south-west parishes of Hertfordshire: MSS. presented to Vaughan Williams Library of the English Folk Dance and Song Society by Ruth Lady Craufurd of Aldbury, author of 'Hertfordshire May Songs', *H.C.*, Winter, 1961, pp. 114-5, and contributed to the collection of May Songs in *J.E.F.D.S.*, Vol. IX, No. 2, December 1961, pp. 86-88. May songs from several nearby parishes are a feature of the modern Aldbury Women's Institute May Festival held on Whit-Saturday.

SONG OF THE TRING SWEEPS: Sheila Richards, *A History of Tring*, 1974, p. 44. The song of the Marsworth (a few miles into Bucks.) Mayers makes reference to visits of the Tring sweeps:

> Sweeps come a-dancing all May-Day,
> Maypole, Maypole, Maypole day.

'Some Additional May Songs from the East Midlands', by Ruth Lady Craufurd of Aldbury, *J.E.F.D.S.*, Vol. IX, No. 2., Dec. 1961, pp. 87-8.

JACKS-IN-THE-GREEN: at Ware: James Smith, 'Ware as it was Forty-Five Years Ago', contributed to the Melbourne (Australia) *Argus* in 1880 and quoted by Edith Hunt, *The History of Ware*, 1949, p. 14.

GARLAND DAY: at Hatfield: Harold Sheehan to *H.C.*, Summer, 1962, p. 216; Watford and south Hertfordshire: Percy Standing, 'Folk Lore and Legend', *Memorials of Old Hertfordshire*, 1905, pp. 164-6; at King's Langley: Reginald Fisher (who also remembered seeing the last Jack-in-the-Green in the neighbourhood of King's Langley in the early 1890s to *H.C.*, Summer, 1962, p. 216.

TRING CHILDREN'S MAY POLE: Sheila Richards to author, March 1975.

MAYPOLES: Jones-Baker, *Old Hertfordshire Calendar*, 1974, p. 85; at Hoddesdon: J. A. Tregelles, *History of Hoddesdon*, 1908, p. 87; at Hitchin: Reginald Hine, *History of Hitchin*, Vol. 2, 1929, p. 361 – the maypole was in Bridge Street.

MAY WEATHER: O. May, Whitwell, to author, 1962; G. Rhodes, Whitwell, to author, 1961; Carbery and Grey, *Hertfordshire Heritage*, 1948, p. 84.

'PROCESSIONING': the legend of Parson's Field: Sir Henry Chauncy, *The Historical Antiquities of Hertfordshire*, 2nd edn. 1826, Vol. II, p. 124.
WHITSUNDAY: Jones-Baker, *Old Hertfordshire Calendar*, 1974, pp. 98-100.
LEGEND OF THE FAITHFUL SHEPHERD: and rhyme: Sheila Richards, *A History of Tring*, 1974, p. 43, and to author, 1975; James Sheahan, *History and Topography of Buckinghamshire*, 1862, p. 87; *Records of Buckinghamshire*, Vol. I, 1858, p. 124.
EMPIRE DAY RHYME: William Gerish MSS., H.C.R.O.
OAK-APPLE DAY: Doris Jones-Baker, 'Oak-Apple Day', *H.C.*, May, 1966; Mary Coburn to *H.C.*, Sept., 1966, p. 56; William Gerish, MSS., H.C.R.O.

JUNE

DOG ROSE AND HARVEST: A. Cotton, S. Todd, G. Rhodes to author, 1961-3.
KIMPTON MERRYMAKING: Robert Clutterbuck, *The History and Antiquities of the County of Hertford*, Vol. III, 1827, p. 78.
CORPUS CHRISTI: at Ware: Edith Hunt, *The History of Ware*, 1949, pp. 63-5; at St Albans: Elsie Toms, *The Story of St Albans*, 1962, pp. 71, 74, 84.
HERTFORDSHIRE MORRIS MEN DANCE TO LONDON: described in Clerkenwell by a correspondent – J.R.P. of Islington – of William Hone, *The Every-Day Book*, Vol. II, 1827, pp. 792-4.
HAY-HARVEST: Carbery and Grey, *Hertfordshire Heritage*, 1948, pp. 93-5; Great Longman, 'Our Village', *Bushey Then and Now*, Dec. 1967.
HAY-WAGGON LUCK: A. Cotton; D. Sansom of Whitwell to author, 1964.
SHEEP SHEARING: drovers' stops: W. Branch Johnson, *Hertfordshire Inns*, 1963, Vol. II, p. 110; Lady Robertson Nicoll, *Bells of Memory* (n.d., but 1934), p. 26, formerly Ellen Pollard whose family owned the High Down estate at Pirton; Arthur Young, *General View of the Agriculture of the County of Hertfordshire*, 1804, pp. 182-3.
SHEEP SHEARING SONG: E. K. Vowell to *H.C.*, Autumn, 1949, p. 64.
ST ALBANS FEAST DAY: S. G. Shaw, *History of Verulam and St Albans*, 1815, Addenda.

TURNIP PLANTING DAY: William Gerish, MSS., H.C.R.O.
MIDSUMMER'S EVE: Jones-Baker, *Old Hertfordshire Calendar,* 1974, pp. 126-8.
MIDSUMMER BONFIRES: along the Chiltern Hills: Worthington Smith, *Dunstable: Its History and Surroundings,* 1904, p. 167; at Bishop's Stortford: J. L. Glasscock, ed., *The Records of St Michael's Parish Church, Bishop's Stortford,* 1882, pp. 36, 92, 93.

JULY

GOOSEBERRY PIE SUNDAY: William Gerish, MSS., H.C.R.O.
FRITHSDEN CHERRY FAIR: Percy Birtchnell, *A Short History of Berkhamsted,* 2nd. edn. 1972, p. 119.
BECKET FAIR: Rev Edward Conybeare, *Highways and Byways in Cambridge and Ely,* 1923, p. 246.
BENNINGTON FAIR DAY: John Cussans, *History of Hertfordshire,* Vol. II, 1878, Broadwater Hundred, pp. 125-6.
ST SWITHIN'S WEATHER: William Gerish, MSS., H.C.R.O.; A. Cotton to author, 1963.
ST SWITHIN'S STEVENAGE FAIR: E. V. Methold, *Notes on Stevenage,* 1902, p. 26.
GROTTO DAY: William Gerish, MSS., H.C.R.O.
HERTFORD RINGING FEAST: John Carrington of Bacon's Farm, Bramfield, Diary, July 27, 1809. MSS., H.C.R.O.

AUGUST

'CRYING THE NECK' and 'CRYING THE MARE': Carbery and Grey, *Hertfordshire Heritage,* 1948, pp. 91-2. In 1912 Mrs Sale of Hinxworth Place told Reginald Hine of Hitchin that these customs were still being observed in her parish. Upon every farm it was believed there was a corn spirit, which at harvest was driven from field to field until it was cut down with the final swathe of the scythe. The labourer attired in the last sheaf, or carting it to the stack, was regarded for the time being as the embodiment of the spirit of fertility, and, in order to ensure a good crop for the following year, it was essential that he should be watered. Reginald Hine, *The History of Hitchin,* Vol. II, 1929, p. 260n. See also William Gerish and John Cussans, MSS., H.C.R.O.

There is evidence that the horse was a prominent folk figure, particularly in north Hertfordshire: at the beginning of the 19th century it was still said at Welwyn 'that the recent dead rode a white horse without a head' – see above, Chapter 6; a life-size graffito of a Hobby Horse is cut into the porch of Wallington Church; the customs of 'crying the neck' and 'crying the mare' were kept within living memory in Hinxworth parish; while in the neighbouring parish of Caldecote archaeologists in 1975 found ritual horse burials under buildings in a deserted medieval village. For horses in folklore, see Venetia Newall, *Discovering the Folklore of Birds and Beasts,* 1971, pp. 37-8.

WATERING THE HOCKEY LOAD: near Royston: Alfred Kingston, *Fragments of Two Centuries,* 1893, pp. 99-100.

HARVESTMEN'S BEANO: A Cotton to Author, Whitwell, 1963.

DRINKING DAY IN THE PELHAMS: William Hone, *The Year Book,* 1832, pp. 1068-9; *Memoirs of Woolmore Wigram,* by his wife, 1908, p. 130.

THE 'HOCKEY' OR 'HARVEST HOME' SUPPER: at The Hoo, St Paul's Walden: A. Cotton to author, Whitwell, 1964.

'HOCKEY' SUPPER TOAST: Reginald Hine MSS., H.C.R.O.

GLEANING CUSTOMS: Jones-Baker, *Old Hertfordshire Calendar,* 1974, p. 168; William Nobbs, 'The Parish Bounds of Welwyn', c. 1820, *Ibid.,* p. 159.

SEPTEMBER

GORSE AND FERN HARVEST AT BERKHAMSTED: Percy Birtchnell, *A Short History of Berkhamsted,* 2nd. edn. 1972, p. 117.

BARNET FAIR DROVERS RACE: A. G. Bradley, *Highways and Byways in North Wales,* 1909, pp. 100-2.

'STATTY FAIRS': Edwin Grey, *Cottage Life in a Hertfordshire Village,* 1935, pp. 209-13.

OLD BALDOCK FAIR: William Gerish, MSS., H.C.R.O.; for the stallholders' celebration with 'Dick Taylor' on the eve of Old Baldock Fair, see E. V. Methold, 'The Inns at Baldock', William Gerish, MSS., H.C.R.O.

'MAYOR-MAKING': at Hertford: Lewis Turner, *History of . . . Hertford,* 1830, pp. 101-2; at St Albans: Elsie Toms, *The Story of St Albans,* 1962, p. 129.

MICHAELMAS 'STUBBLE GOOSE': William Gerish, MSS., H.C.R.O.; John Carrington, Bacon's Farm, Bramfield, 'Diary', MSS., H.C.R.O.

TENANTS' MICHAELMAS GIFTS: at Hitchin: Reginald Hine, *History of Hitchin,* Vol. II, 1929, p. 252n.

OCTOBER

'OLD MAN'S DAY' at Braughing: John Cussans, *History of Hertfordshire,* Vol. I, 1870, Braughing Hundred, p. 200. Cussans observed that Wall had since 1595 been 'thus gratifying thirty-seven persons every year for the trifling sum of one pound sterling'.

'GANGING DAY' at Bishop's Stortford: William Hone, *The Every-Day Book,* Vol. I, 1826, p. 1340. From 'a London Newspaper' dated 18 October 1787.

ALL HALLOW'S EVE, OR 'NUTCRACK NIGHT': William Gerish and John Cussans, MSS., H.R.C.O.; O. May and A. Cotton, Whitwell, to author, 1965; U. B. Chisenhale-Marsh, 'Folk Lore in Essex and Herts', *The Essex Review,* Vol. V, 1896, pp. 148-9.

NOVEMBER

ALL SAINT'S EVE STRAW BURNING: Reginald Hine, *History of Hitchin,* Vol. II, 1929, p. 365.

GUY FAWKES DAY: fireballs: still within living memory. A. Cotton, Bendish, to author, 1963; rhyme as chanted at Ware about 1900: W. T. Hills, to *H.C.,* April, 1969, p. 16; bonfires: the accounts of John Plomer of Blakesware are quoted in Reginald Hine, *Charles Lamb & His Hertfordshire,* 1949, p. 175.

ST CLEMENT'S DAY: William Gerish MSS., H.C.R.O.

'KEEPING KATTERN': William Gerish, MSS., H.C.R.O.; D. Jones-Baker, 'Keeping Kattern in Old Hertfordshire', *H.C.* Dec. 1974, pp. 44-5; women in-mates of the workhouses were put to lace-making by the Overseers to ease the burden on the rates, and thus the Vestry records of Tring in the 1750s show that money was given to the workhouse women 'to keep Cattern'. Quoted in Sheila Richards, *A History of Tring,* 1974, p. 45.

ST ANDREW'S DAY: Bailiff's election and feast at Hemel Hempstead: Susan Yaxley, ed. *History of Hemel Hempstead*, 1973, pp. 163-4; Chapman's Charity: John Cussans, *History of Hertfordshire*, Vol. II, Broadwater Hundred, 1874, pp. 100-1.

DECEMBER

ST NICHOLAS DAY: ghost of St Nicholas: Stevenage Townswomen's Guild to author, 1971; D. Jones-Baker, *Old Hertfordshire Calendar*, 1974, pp. 255-6.
BALDOCK BLACK PUDDING FAIR: William Gerish, MSS., H.C.R.O.
SCHOLARS REVEL AT BERKHAMSTED: Percy Birtchnell of Berkhamsted to author, 1970.
THOMASING DAY: around Harpenden: Edwin Grey, *Cottage Life in a Hertfordshire Village*, 1935, pp. 194-5; at Braughing: *Hertfordshire Mercury*, 24 Dec. 1900; at Tewin,: Tewin Women's Institute to author, 1971.
'THE OLD CHRISTMAS SONG': William Chappell, *Popular Music of the Olden Time*, Vol. II, 1859, pp. 752-3.
HODDESDON WAITS CAROL: Helen Creighton and Doreen H. Senior, *Traditional Songs from Nova Scotia*, 1950, p. 275. In this version the demi-semiquavers do not appear: probably they were not put in by the granddaughter of the Hoddesdon emigrant when giving the song to the collectors.
'THE MOON SHINES BRIGHT' AND 'THE OLD CHRISTMAS SONG' TUNE SHARED: Lucy Broadwood, J.E.F.D.S., Vol. I 1902, p. 177.
FOLK PERFORMER'S DISREGARD OF SEASONS: Author's observations, 1961-76.
JOHN DUNSTABLE and Hertfordshire; D. R. Howlett, 'A Possible Date for a Dunstable Motet', *The Music Review*, Vol. 36, May 1975, pp. 81-4.
'AS I SAT ON A SUNNY BANK': Collected by Lucy Broadwood near King's Langley: L. E. Broadwood and J. A. F. Maitland, *English County Songs*, 1893, p. 111; Carbery and Grey, *Hertfordshire Heritage*, 1948. p. 48; Elizabeth Poston, *Penguin Book of Christmas Carols*, 1965, No. 8, pp. 22, 48-9.
'GUIZERS' OR MUMMERS: Carbery and Grey, *Hertfordshire Heritage*, 1948, p. 89; Hexton plays: Francis Taverner, MSS., history of Hexton, British Museum, Add. MSS. 6223; at Hitchin: Reginald Hine, MSS., H.C.R.O.

CHRISTMAS EVE: South Mimms Dole: Dr F. Brittain, 'Looking at South Mimms', *H.C.*, Dec. 1966, p. 450; legend of bees, oxen and bells: at Ware: James Smith in Melbourne (Australia) *Argus*, 1880, reprinted in Edith Hunt, *The History of Ware*, 1949, p. 14; ringing: D. Jones-Baker, *Old Hertfordshire Calendar*, 1974, pp. 273-4.
CHRISTMAS DAY: William Gerish, MSS., H.C.R.O.; carols at Berkhamsted: Percy Birtchnell, *A Short History of Berkhamsted*, 1972, p. 117.
WASSAILING ON BOXING DAY: Gladys Rhodes to author, words and music of the Wassail used at the beginning of this century in St Paul's Walden parish, 1969.
HUNTING THE WREN AND HUNTING SQUIRRELS: U. B. Chisenhale Marsh, 'Folk-Lore in Essex and Herts', *The Essex Review*, Vol. V, 1896, p. 153.
HOLY INNOCENTS AND LUCK: William Gerish, MSS., H.C.R.O.; A. Cotton, O. May, to author, 1963, Whitwell.
NEW YEAR'S EVE: ringing: Thomas North, *The Church Bells of Hertfordshire*, 1886, p. 77; Berkhamsted revels: Percy Birtchnell, *A Short History of Berkhamsted*, 1972, p. 117.

11 *Local Humour*, pages 180-196

HERTFORDSHIRE, OUR COUNTRY: Carbery and Grey, *Hertfordshire Heritage*, 1948, p. 7.
THE BUMPKIN'S DISASTER: copies in the British Library and H.C.R.O., see also William Strutt, *A Memoir of the Life of Joseph Strutt*, London, pp., 1896, p. 27.
HERTFORDSHIRE COUNTY NICKNAMES; NICKNAMES OF NEIGHBOURING COUNTIES: Jones-Baker, *Old Hertfordshire Calendar*, 1974, p. 158.
COUNTY REGIMENT NICKNAMES: 'An Old Soldier' to author, Hitchin, 1975.
ASHWELL VILLAGE BOASTING RHYME: The Rev. Canon J. Catterick, Rector of Ashwell, to author, 1973; Jones-Baker, *Old Hertfordshire Calendar*, pp. 203-4.
ASHWELL JEERING RHYME: Carbery and Grey, *Hertfordshire Heritage*, 1948, p. 113.
WATFORD BOAST: William Gerish, MSS., H.C.R.O.
HERTFORD POOR AND PROUD; PROUD PIRTON: William Gerish, MSS., H.C.R.O.

TEWIN AND BURNHAM GREEN RHYME: Tewin Women's Institute to author, 1974.
STEVENAGE AND KNEBWORTH NICKNAMES: A. Cotton to author, 1964.
TRING NICKNAMES AND RHYME: Sheila Richards of Tring to author, 1975; William Gerish, MSS., H.C.R.O.
MUCH HADHAM NICKNAME: Gover, Mawer and Stenton, *The Place Names of Hertfordshire*, 1938, p. 177.
CUNNING KIMPTON: Miss Dorothy Bailey-Hawkins, late of Stagenhoe Park, to author, 1966.
POTTEN END STORY: Birtchnell, *A Short History of Berkhamsted*, 2nd. edn. 1972, p. 119.
BACKWARD SARRATT, TYTTENHANGER TREACLE-MINDS: Jones-Baker, *Old Hertfordshire Calendar*, 1974, p. 147.
WELWYN SAYING: Frank Ballin of Welwyn to author, 1967.
WALK-ON WALKERN: Walkern Women's Institute to author, 1971; William Gerish, MSS., H.C.R.O. for the story of the Devil naming Walkern; a different version of the 'Traveller' naming the village was put into verse by the Quaker poet of Hemel Hempstead, John Henry Salter (1810-1900) in 'Walkern, commonly Called Walkon a Village in Hertfordshire'. See the (now rare) collection of his poems: John Henry Salter, *Heaven's Golden Key*, published by Joshua Brackett, High Street, Hemel Hempstead (n.d.) and sketch of Salter, 'The Quaker Poet of West Hertfordshire A Brief Memoir of John Henry Salter' (no author), *H.C.*, Winter, 1961, p. 119.
WHEATHAMPSTEAD AND SANDRIDGE NICKNAMES: Mary Coburn of Harpenden to author, 1972.
PARISH BOUNDS OF WELWYN: last used in the parochial 'perambulation' of 1904. Rhyme by William Nobbs, Parish Clerk, c. 1820. W. Branch Johnson of Welwyn to author, 1965. Nobb's MSS. are now lost, though there is a copy of his Parish Bounds Rhyme at H.C.R.O., and several are in private hands. Excerpts of Nobb's rhyme are printed in Jones-Baker, *Old Hertfordshire Calendar*, 1974, pp. 24-5, 60, 92, 94, 152, 232.
CODICOTE CUTTHROATS: Jessie Peacock Sansom of Whitwell to author, 1962; for story of the 'Phaeton Highwayman' see William Gerish, MSS., H.C.R.O.
WICKED WIGGINTON: Salmon, *History of Hertfordshire*, 1728, p. 128; Cussans, *History of Hertfordshire*, Vol. III, Dacorum Hundred, pp.

46-7; Frank Harrowell – who lived more than half a century at Wigginton – to *H.C.*, January, 1975, p 42.
THIRSTY NEWNHAM: William Gerish, MSS., H.C.R.O.; Tomkins, *Highways and Byways in Hertfordshire,* 1902, p. 245.
BALDOCK NICKNAMES: Rev. and Mrs Aubrey Marshall-Taylor, Graveley Rectory, to author, 1967.
FRITHSDEN AND POTTON END 'CHERRY-PICKERS': Percy Birtchnell, 'Home of the Cherry Turnover', *H.C.*, summer 1950, p. 28; and Percy Birtchnell, *A Short History of Berkhamsted,* 2nd. edn., 1972, p. 119.
REDBOURN SAYING: John Cussans, MSS., H.C.R.O.
DOWNRIGHT DUNSTABLE: Jones-Baker, *Old Hertfordshire Calendar,* 1974, p. 147; Sir Walter Scott used this expression in *Redgauntlett* (chapter XVII) 'If this is not plain speaking there is no such place as downright Dunstable'; Worthington Smith, *Dunstable* ... 1904, p. 160; An old saying at Tring is 'as plain as Dunstable road', Richards, *A History of Tring,* 1974, p. 16.
WESTON PARTNERS AND GRAVELEY GRINDERS: Rev. and Mrs Aubrey Marshall-Taylor, Graveley Rectory, to author, 1967.
SAYING OF DUCKS FLYING BACKWARDS: An 'old resident' of Thundridge to author, 1974.
RADICAL ROYSTON AND ROYSTON CROWS: Kingston, *A History of Royston,* 1906, pp. 194-5; Kingston, *Fragments of Two Centuries,* 1893, pp. 126-7; the story of Queen Elizabeth and the saying of the malts: John Layer (1586-1640) author of *The Duty of Constables* (1641) in Harl. MSS. 6768, f.1. British Library.
SLEEPING VILLAGES: A. Cotton of Bendish to author, 1968; two Hertfordshire grave diggers to author, 1970.
BULBOURNE RHYME: Richards, *A History of Tring,* 1974, p. 13.
ST ALBANS PUB RHYME: W. E. Frost of St Albans (who went there as a boy in 1906 when his father took over as keeper of the *Beehive*) to *H.C.*, Winter, 1961, p. 103.
MILK RAIN ON CHALK HILLS: Baldock Townswomen's Guild to author, 1973.
WARESIDE TREACLE MINES: An 'old resident' of Thundridge to author, 1974.
TALL TALES OF FLINTS AND PUDDING STONES: Chauncy, *The Historical Antiquities of Hertfordshire,* 1700 (2nd. edn. 1826, Vol. II, p. 515); Carbery and Grey, *Hertfordshire Heritage,* 1948, p. 84.
HERTFORDSHIRE CLANGER: Rev. Rex E. Merry, of Boxmoor, to *H.C.*,

November, 1975, p. 43; recipe for a traditional Clanger by Hilda Flitton in *The House and Home Cook Book*, compiled by the High Street, Flamstead, Methodist Circuit to raise funds for a new manse, 1969, p. 9, reprinted by permission in Jones-Baker, *Old Hertfordshire Calendar*, 1974, pp. 210-11; tale of which end of the clanger to eat first: Reg. A. Nelsey to *H.C.*, September, 1975, p. 25.
TALE OF THE GREAT BED OF WARE: William Gerish, MSS., H.C.R.O.; see also Edith Hunt, *The History of Ware*, 1946, pp. 164-5.
LARGEST COLLECTION OF HERTFORDSHIRE HOAXES: works of William Ellis, including *The Practical Farmer, or the Hertfordshire Husbandman, containing many new experiments in husbandry*, London, 1732.
HERNE THE GYPSY'S HOAX: recorded by William Ellis, and quoted in Vicars Bell, *To Meet Mr. Ellis, Little Gaddesden in the Eighteenth Century*, 1956, pp. 76-7.
PHANTOM WOODMAN HOAX: Sam Todd of Whitwell, retired gamekeeper at King's Walden, to author, 1964; Bert Cotton of Whitwell, retired keeper of *The Lamb* at Whitwell, to author, 1964; legend of the Phantom Woodman: Tomkins, *Highways and Byways in Hertfordshire*, 1902, pp. 165-6.
BUNTINGFORD MAIL COACH ROBBERY HOAX: Guy Ewing, *Westmill, The Story of a Hertfordshire Parish*, 1925, pp. 250-1.

MUSEUMS

Folk exhibits and displays of traditional crafts in Hertfordshire may be seen at the Ashwell Village Museum, Barnet Museum, Hertford Museum, Hitchin Museum, Stevenage Museum, and St Albans City Museum (which includes the noted Salaman Collection of craft tools, model saw-pit, and other exhibits). The Royston Museum, opened in 1976, includes displays of folk material.

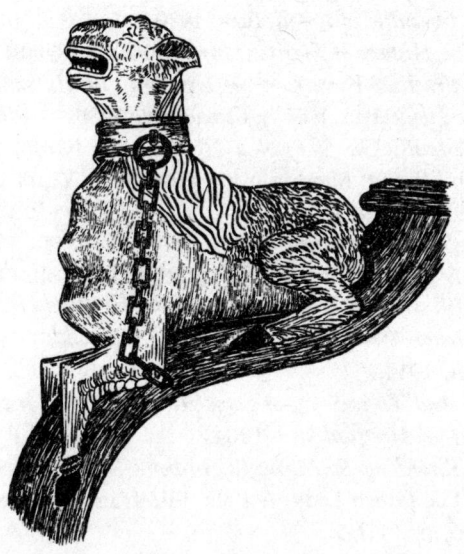

The Old Dog of Codicote, medieval woodcarving, Codicote Church, 1976

Select Bibliography

Andrews, W., *Bygone Hertfordshire*, 1898.
Antrobus, J., *Hatfield, Some Memories of its Past*, 1912.
Bagshawe, T., 'A Stable Charm', *F.L.*, Vol. 66, 1955, pp. 416-7.
Bell, V., *Little Gaddesden*, 1949.
Birtchnell, P., 'Berkhamsted's Old Wives Tales', *H.C.* Summer, 1950, pp. 38-9.
   A Short History of Berkhamsted, 2nd. edn. 1972.
Carbery, Lady M., *Happy World*, 1941.
   with Edwin Grey, *Hertfordshire Heritage*, 1948.
Chauncy, Sir H., *The Historical Antiquities of Hertfordshire*, 1700.
Chisenhale-Marsh, U. B., 'Folk Lore in Essex and Herts', *The Essex Review*, Vol. v., 1896, pp. 142-162.
Coburn, M., 'Cottage Cures', *H.C.*, September, 1967, pp. 16-8.
Craufurd, Lady R., 'Hertfordshire May Songs', *H.C.*, Winter, 1961, pp. 114-5.

SELECT BIBLIOGRAPHY

Curtis, G., *A Chronicle of Small Beer*, 1970.
Cussans, J., *The History of Hertfordshire*, 3 Vols., 1870-81.
Ellis, W., *The Practical Farmer, or the Hertfordshire Husbandman*, 1732.
   The Country Housewife's Family Companion, 1750.
Ewing, G., *Westmill, The Story of a Hertfordshire Parish*, 1925.
Folds, O., 'Childhood Memories of Sixty-Five Years Ago', *H.C.*, Autumn, 1962, pp. 252-3.
Fuller, T., *The Worthies of England*, 1662.
Gerish, W., 'A Hertfordshire St George', F.L., Vol. 12, 1901, pp. 303-7.
   A Tour Through Hertfordshire Recording its Legends, Traditions, and Ghostly Tales, 1914.
   The Mayers And Their Song, or Some Account of the First of May and its Observance in Hertfordshire, 1904.
Glasscock, J., *Records of St Michael's, Bishop's Stortford*, 1882.
Gomme, A., 'The Green Lady. A Folk Tale from Hertfordshire', *F.J.*, Vol. 7, 1896, pp. 414-5.
Grey, E., *Cottage Life in a Hertfordshire Village*, 1935.
   and with Lady Mary Carbery, *Hertfordshire Heritage*, 1948.
Hall, M., *A History of Bushey*, 1938.
Haythornthwaite, Rev. J., *King's Langley*, 1924.
Hine, R., *History of Hitchin*, 2 vols., 1927, 1929.
   Hitchin Worthies, 1932.
Hone, W., *The Every-Day Book*, 2 vols., 1826, 1827.
   The Table Book, 1827.
   The Year Book, 1832.
Hunt, E., *The History of Ware*, 1949.
Ilott, P., *Hertfordshire Stories, Plays and Poems*, 1938.
Johnson, W., ed. *'Memorandums For . . .' The Carrington Diary*, 1973.
Jones-Baker, D., *Old Hertfordshire Calendar*, 1974.
   'A-Thomasing in Hertfordshire', *H.C.*, December 1966, pp. 454-5.
   'Candlemas in Old Hertfordshire', *H.C.*, March 1968, pp. 12-13.
   'The Hoddesdon Christmas Ghost', *H.C.*, Jan. 1968, pp. 22-3.
   'Keeping Kattern in Old Hertfordshire', *H.C.*, Dec. 1974, pp. 44-5.
   'The Mystery of the Witch of Datchworth', *H.C.*, April/May 1965, pp. 222-3.
   'Oak-Apple Day', *H.C.*, May, 1966, pp. 420-1.
   'Old Hertfordshire Carols for Christmas', *H.C.*, Jan. 1975, pp. 20-1.
   'Old Hertfordshire Harvest Fare', *H.C.*, Sept. 1967, pp. 26-7.

'Old Hertfordshire's Man in the Moon', *H.C.* Dec. 1969, pp. 46-7.
'Old Hertfordshire Parish Churches and their Founding Legends', *H.C.,* April 1975, pp. 24-5.
'Some Old Hertfordshire Yuletide Customs', *H.C.,* Dec. 1963, pp. 104-5.
'The Tale of the Red-Cloaked Knight', *H.C.,* Jan. 1969, pp. 45-7.
'Tales of Hertfordshire Tunnels and Secret Passages', *H.C.,* May 1967, pp. 818-20.
Kingston, A., *Fragments of Two Centuries,* 1893.
A History of Royston, 1906.
Methold, E., *Notes on Stevenage,* 1902.
Nicoll, Lady R., *Bells of Memory,* 1934.
(as Ellen Pollard) 'Some Points of Interest in and Around Hitchin', *H.I.R.,* Vol. 2, 1894, pp. 286-92.
Norden, J., *Speculi Britaniae Pars; A Description of Hartfordshire,* 1598.
North, T., *The Church Bells of Hertfordshire,* 1886.
Paddick, E., *Hoddesdon, Tales of a Hertfordshire Town,* 1971.
Paris, M., *Gesta Abbatum Monasterii Sancti Albani,* H. Riley, ed., 1867.
Richards, S., *A History of Tring,* 1974.
Rinder, E., 'Twilight in Hertfordshire. Some Gleanings of Folk-Lore', *H.I.R.,* Vol. 2., 1894, pp. 65-71.
Salmon, N., *History of Hertfordshire,* 1728.
Saunders, W., *A History of Watford,* 1931.
Shaw, G., *History of Verulam and St Albans,* 1815.
Standing, P., 'Folk Lore and Legend', *Memorials of Old Hertfordshire,* 1905, pp.164-70.
Strutt, J., *Sports and Pastimes of the People of England,* 1801.
Sworder, A., 'Some Traditions of the Wymondleys', *H.C.,* Spring 1947, pp. 115-6.
Tompkins, H., *Highways and Byways in Hertfordshire,* 1902.
Weever, J., *Ancient Funerall Monuments,* 1621.
Woodcock, P., 'Tales from a Hexton Taproom', *H.C.,* Autumn, 1950, pp. 62-5.
Yaxley, S., ed. *History of Hemel Hempstead,* 1973.

Index of Tale Types

Folktales are named and classified on an international system based on their plots, devised by Antti Aarne and Stith Thompson in *The Types of the Folktale*, 1961; numbers from this system are preceded by the letters AT. Local legends have been partly classified by R. Th. Christiansen in *The Migratory Legends*, 1958; his system was further developed by K. M. Briggs in *A Dictionary of British Folktales*, 1970-1. These numbers are preceded by ML, and the latter are also followed by an asterisk.

AT 300 The Dragon Slayer	59-61
AT 1419 The Husband Hoodwinked	191-2
ML 3020 Inexperienced Use of Black Book	118
ML 3055* The Witch that was Hurt	111
ML 4021* A Troublesome Ghost Laid	81-2
ML 5020 Giants Make a Causeway	104
ML 7060 A Disputed Site for a Church	23-4
ML 7065 Building a Church	24-5
ML 7070 Legends about Church Bells	26-30
ML 8000 The Wars of Former Times	86-8
ML 8010 Hidden Treasures	32-41
ML 8025 Robbers Tales	39-41, 47-8

Motif Index

A motif is an element occurring within the plot of one or several folktales (e.g. 'cruel stepmother', found in 'Snow White', 'Cinderella', and elsewhere). They have been classified thematically in Stith Thompson's *Motif Index of Folk Literature*, 1966; the numbers below are taken from this, together with E. Baughman's *Type and Motif Index of the Folktales of England and North America*, 1966.

A 941.5 Spring breaks forth through power of saint	22, 92
A 969.9 Hills formed from acts of devil	104-5
A 972.5.2 Leaps of giants, heroes, etc.	104
A 977.3 Devil drops stones	22-4
B 11 Dragons	54-61
B 11.2.11 Fire-breathing dragon	54
B 11.3.3 Dragon lives on hill	55
B 11.11 Fight with dragon	54-5, 59-61
B 15.1.1 Headless animals	87-8, 90
B 143.0.2 Magpie as prophet	62, 73
B 143.0.8 Crow as prophet	63
B 147 Animals furnish omens	73
B 251.1.2.3 Cattle kneel on Old Christmas Eve	122-3, 176
B 733.2 Dogs howling omens of death	73
B 752.2 Snake cannot die before sunset	55
C 401.3 Tabu: speaking while seeking treasure	32
C 430 Tabus on names and words	51, 64, 106, 108
C 631 Tabu: breaking the Sabbath	51, 106
C 726 Tabu: trimming fingernails	106
D 272.13 Holed stone protects against witches	108-9
D 670 Magic flight	111-12, 118
D 671 Transformation flight: transformation to escape pursuer	111

MOTIF INDEX

D 672 Obstacle flight: obstacles thrown behind stop pursuer	73
D 927.1 Spring made by magic	22
D 931 Magic stone	95-6
D 950 Magic tree	96
D 965 Magic plants	64-5, 96-8, 109, 174
D 1273.1.1 Three as a magic number	79
D 1273.1.3 Seven as a magic number	63, 79, 99, 100, 105-6
D 1273.1.5 Nine as a magic number	100
D 1318.5 Blood indicates guilt or innocence	82
D 1355.3 Love charm	64-5
D 1385.5.1 Metal protects against evil spirits	109
D 1385.9 Horseshoe keeps off devil and witches	108-9
D 1500.1.1.2 Well with curative powers	16, 92-4
D 1500.1.2 Sacred healing stones	95-6
D 1500.1.3 Magic tree heals	96
D 1500.1.4 Magic healing plants	96-8
D 1500.1.6 Ghoulish objects cure disease	98
D 1500.1.6.1 Corpse's hand as remedy	98
D 1500.1.15 Magic healing ring	99-100
D 1500.1.23 Magic healing charm	102
D 1502.2.2 Charm for toothache	98
D 1567.6 Stroke of Saint's staff brings water	22
D 1641.2.4 Stone moves at midnight	190
D 1685 Interred body of saint performs signs and miracles	22
D 1786 Magic power at crossroads	83
D 1791 Magic power by circumnambulation	79
D 1812.3.3 Future revealed in dream	22, 64
D 1812.5 Future learned through omens	62-3, 64-5, 73-4, 95
D 1812.5.1.5 Moon furnishes omen	64
D 1812.5.2.5.1 Hearing cuckoo call a good omen	136-7
D 1825.1.2 Magic view of future lover	64
D 2141.1.1 Church bells rung as protection against storm	26
D 2143.3 Mist produced by magician	87, 110-11
D 2161.4.1 Disease transferred to animal	100-1
D 2161.4.2.4 Disease transferred to tree	96
D 2161.4.5 Cure by passing patient through cleft tree	96
D 2188.2 Person vanishes	118
D 2192.1 Church moved at night by supernatural forces	22-4
E 235.3 Ghost chases those who raise him	79
E 265 Meeting ghost causes misfortune	73-4
E 272 Ghost haunts road	81, 87, 89, 118
E 274 Ghost haunts gallows	117
E 281 Ghost haunts house	74, 85-6, 88
E 332.3.3.1 The vanishing hitchhiker	89
E 334.1 Ghost haunts scene of former crime	40, 88
E 334.2 Ghost haunts burial spot	83-4
E 334.5 Ghost of soldier haunts battlefield	86, 88
E 337.2 Re-enactment of tragedy seen	86
E 338.2 Non-malevolent ghost haunts church	29-30
E 338.5 Ghosts of monks haunt former cloister	89
E 363.3 Ghost warns the living	89-90
E 386.4 Running around grave raises ghost	79

E 402.1.1.8 Sound of ghosts quarreling	86
E 402.1.1.4 Ghosts sing	89
E 402.1.3 Invisible ghost plays musical instrument	29-30
E 411.1 Murderer cannot rest in grave	84
E 411.0.3 Horse unable to draw evil dead man	83
E 411.10 Person who died by violence cannot rest in grave	40, 82-3
E 413 Murdered person cannot rest in grave	83, 88-9, 117
E 421.3.6 Ghosts as dogs with glowing tongues and eyes	32, 80-1, 117-8
E 422.1.1 Headless revenant	88, 118
E 422.4.4 (b) Female ghost in grey	85
E 423.1.1.1 (b) Ghostly black dog	89
E 531 (a) Building seen as it had been many years before	30, 118
E 581.2 Ghost rides horse	40, 82, 87-8
E 585.4 Revenant visits earth yearly	85, 88, 118
F 361.4 (c) Fairies throw down church built on their land	24
F 420.5.2 Water spirit lures mortal into water	125-6
F 491.1 Will-o'-the-wisp leads people astray	53
F 531 Giants	46-50, 81, 119
F 531.3.2 Giant throws great rocks	47
F 531.4 Gigantic possessions of giant	47
F 531.4.5 Giant with enormous weapon	47
F 531.5.1 Giant friendly to man	47
F 531.6.2.1 Giant lives on hill top	46, 48-9
F 531.6.8.3 Enmity between giants	47, 49-50
F 531.6.12.6 Giant slain by man	47
F 531.6.13 Giant's grave	47-8
F 713.2 Bottomless pool	28
F 721.1 Underground passages	31, 41-5
F 933.1 Miraculous spring bursts forth for holy person	22
F 993 Sunken bell sounds	174
F 1068.1 Advice and information given in dream	32
G 211.1.7 Witch in form of a cat	111
G 211.2.7 Witch in form of a hare	111
G 220.0.1 Black and white witches	110, 112
G 225 Witch's familiar spirit	111, 115
G 225.0.3 Familiars do work for witch	111
G 225.7 Animal as witch's familiar	115
G 242.1 Witch flies on broomstick	111
G 242.5 Witch flies through the air on household object	111-2
G 271.6 Countercharm worked by white witch	116-7
G 272.19 Holed stone protects against witches	95
G 275.12 Witch in form of animal killed	111
G 263.4 Witches cause sickness	115
G 265.3 Witch rides horse by night	95
G 265.4 Witches cause death or disease in animals	114
G 269.4 Curse by offended witch	114-5
G 303.3.3.1.7 Devil in form of a ram	108
G 303.3.3.3.1.2 Devil in form of a cat	117
G 303.6.1.2 Man raises Devil	96, 105-6, 108
G 303.6.2.14 Devil appears to Sabbath-breakers	51, 106
G 303.8.13 Devil in the woods	104
G 303.9.1 Devil as a builder	21-6, 104-5

MOTIF INDEX

G 303.9.1.7 Devil builds a road	103
G 303.9.1.8 Devil builds a ditch	105
G 303.9.4.4 Devil tempts cleric	108
G 303.9.5.8 Devil takes violinist when he needs a good one	41-2
G 303.14.1.2 Devil shifts building materials	22-4
G 303.16.2 Devil's power over one avoided by prayer	99
G 303.16.12 Ringing of churchbell causes Devil to lose power	105
G 303.16.19.18 Devil caught with tongs	108
G 303.24.4 Devil destroys church steeple	104
H 222.5 Ordeal by water for suspected witch	116-7
H 1584.2 Land measured by area encompassed under conditions	25
J 1495.1 Person runs from real or supposed ghost	190-1
J 1545 Wife outwits her husband	189-90
J 1700 Fools	188
M 211 Man sells soul to Devil	118
M 341.2 Prophecy: death by particular instrument	112-3
M 411.22 (a) Abbot curses land taken from church	39
M 411.23 Wronged man's curse	32-3
M 419.12 Witch's curse	114-5
M 470 Curse on objects or animals	32, 104, 106-7
N 511 Treasure in ground	31-40
N 511.1.8 Treasure buried in chest	32-4
N 511.1.9 Treasure buried under tree	40
N 512 Treasure in cave	40-1
N 513 Treasure hidden under water	34
N 550.1 Continual failure to find treasure	38-9
N 553 Tabus while seeking treasure	32
N 557 Treasure disappears after being uncovered	32-3
N 571 Devil as guardian of treasure	32
N 571.2 Ghostly animal as guardian of treasure	32
Q 223.6.1.1 Sunday stick-gatherers put on moon	51, 106
Q 223.6.5 Sunday nut-pickers taken by Devil	51, 106
Q 565 Man admitted neither to Heaven nor to Hell	61, 107
V 61.8 Burial in grave mound	34
V 67.1 Man buried with possessions	34
V 111.1 Stones for church miraculously shifted	22-5
V 111.3 Site of church miraculously indicated	21-2
V 115 Church bells	26-30
V 115.4 What church bells say	29
V 134 Sacred wells	92-5, 108
V 134.2 Offerings to holy wells	93-4
V 140 Sacred relics	22
V 221.0.1 Relics of saint cure disease	22
V 223 Saint has miraculous knowledge	22
V 229.4 Saint kills dragon	58-9
V 331.1 Conversion to Christianity	21-2
V 510 Religious vision	22, 25-6
X 410 Jokes on parsons	29
X 680 Jokes about towns and villages	180-6
X 685 Jokes about small, quiet villages and towns	186
X 687 (a) Jokes about villages with wet climate	185
X 1088 Remarkable mine supplies food	188

General Index

Abbot's Langley 66, 131
Advent 173-5
Albury 26, 28
alchemists 105, 118-20
Aldbury 33, 105, 118, 124, 140
Aldenham 35
Alfred the Great 37
All Saints' Day 166
All Souls' Day 166
Anglo-Saxon Chronicle 15-6, 31, 37
Animals 73-6
Anstey 23, 25, 41-2, 154
Ardeley 16
Arthurian legends, 16, 92
Ashridge 43
Ash Wednesday 127-9
Ashwell 65, 95, 123, 129, 154-5, 182
Aspenden 24, 55
Aston, 79 105
Ayot St. Lawrence 120, 132

babies 38 62-4
Bacon, Sir Francis, 43
Baldock 18, 25, 47-8, 66-7, 116, 128, 129, 132, 137-8, 162, 171, 186
baptism 23, 62-4
Barkway 49-50 60
Barnet 87, 89 94, 108, 110-1, 161
barrows (burial mounds) 31, 34, 35, 47, 128, 167
Bassingbourn 58
battles 87, 110-1, 112-3, 133
beating the parish bounds 143-4
bees 76, 111, 123, 176
begging chants 126-7, 128, 132, 142-3, 146, 155, 166, 167-8, 178
begging days 123, 126-7 128, 142-3, 155, 166, 167-8, 171-2, 176
bells, church 26-30, 74, 105, 106, 121, 127-8, 130, 132, 144, 156, 160, 176, 179, 180
bells, hand 173, 175
bells, subterranean 174
Bendish 52
Bennington 154
Berkhamsted 54-5, 56, 84-5, 87, 93, 94, 95, 96, 104, 116, 144-5, 161, 171, 176

birds 62-3, 73, 136-7, 177-8
birth 62-3
Bishop's Stortford 33, 57, 58-9, 83, 93, 98, 125, 153, 164-5, 175
blackberries 104, 164
Blackthorn Winter 143
Blakesware 44
body-snatching 77-8
bogeymen 38, 50-3
bonfires 153, 166-8
bottomless pool 28
Bovington, 71, 81
Boxbury 24
Boxing Day 177-8
Boxmoor 79
Bramfield 18, 44, 114
Braughing 14, 58, 88, 131, 134, 144, 164, 172
Breachwood Green 126-7, 128
Brent Pelham 16, 24, 49-50, 59-61, 81, 107, 158-9
Broxbourne 27, 85
Buntingford 14, 29, 195-6
Burnham Green 77, 87, 90 (illus.), 114, 183
Bushey, 29 51, 53, 104, 105, 131, 182
Bygrave 81

Candlemas 125
carols: New Year 121-3; May 138-43; Christmas 173-5
Camlet Moat, South Mimms 32-3
Cadmus (a giant) 49-50, 60
Castles, 18 23, 25, 32-3, 34, 38, 41-2, 49, 105, 118
cats 100-1, 116-7
cattle 123, 176
caves 40-1, 48, 55, 60
Chad's Well 93
charities, 130, 131, 134-5, 147, 164, 170, 172-3, 176-8
Charles II 146
charms 95-6, 98, 99-100, 102 (illus.), 108-9, 151
Chesfield 144
Cheshunt 44-5
children's beliefs 34, 50-2, 64, 79, 99, 114, 190
children's customs 105, 108, 126-8, 133-4, 141-3, 146, 162, 165-9, 171, 177-8

GENERAL INDEX 237

chimney sweeps 18, 140-1
Christmas 122-3, 175-8
Christmas Eve 175-6
churches 21-29
Civil War, the 14-5, 28, 50, 87-8
Clangers, Hertfordshire, 190-1
'Clibborn's Post' 77 (illus.), 84
Clothall 124
cock-throwing 129
Codicote 33, 57, 78, 83, 134, 160, 185
Collop Monday 127
Corpus Christi 147-8
Cottered 123-4
courting 64-5
cross-roads 33, 83, 96
crows 63
cuckoos 121, 134-5
Cuffley 94
cunning man/woman 108, 110-12
cures, magical 92-102
curses 39, 89, 114, 131, 164

Danes, Danelaw 14, 47, 56, 86-7, 93, 133
Datchworth 74, 87, 112, 113-4
death and burial 73-6, 78-84
Deev'l-Dodgers 109
DeMandeville, earls 18, 32-3, 89
DeMandeville, Sir John 16, 55-6, 189
Devil, the 21, 23-5, 26, 28, 30, 32, 41-2, 47,
    51, 60-1, 64, 79, 81, 96, 99, 103-9, 116-7,
    118, 133
Devil, Mowing 103 (illus.), 107
Devil's Chains 105
Devil's Door 25, 64
Devil's Dyke 104
Devil's Hills 104
Devil's Hopscotch 104
Devil's Plants 103
Devil's Roads 103
Devil's Thunderbolts 104
Devil's Toenails 104
divinations 64-5, 112-3, 125, 147, 152-3, 165
Dough-nut Day 127-9
dragons 16, 50, 54-61, 81, 107, 175
drinking customs 66-7, 158-60, 169, 181-2
Drinking Day 158-9
Dunstable 40
Dunstable, John 175

Easter 87, 110, 133-4
East India College (Haileybury) 8-9
Eastwick 81

Edward II 38
Edward III 25, 38
egg-rolling 133
Elstree 35
Empire Day 146
Enfield Chase 32, 108, 161
Epiphany 123
Epping Forest 178
Ermine Street 14, 37
Essendon 73, 78-9
Essex 14-5, 181
evil spirits, protection from 26-7, 73, 95-8,
    116, 151

fairies 24
fairs 130, 132-3, 144-7, 152, 154-5, 161-2,
    165-6, 171, 187
farm customs 123-4, 132, 147-53, 156-64, 168
Ferrers, the 'Wicked' Lady 40
Fiddler of Anstey, the 41-2
Fig Sunday 131
fireballs 167
fish 88, 131
Flamstead 123-4
flowers 65, 69, 73, 129, 133, 143, 156
folk medicine 92, 101
folk rhymes 27, 29-30, 34-7, 40, 62-6, 72, 79,
    91, 99, 123, 125-8, 130, 132, 134-5, 140-3,
    145-6, 149-53, 155, 157, 159-60, 166-71,
    180-1, 186
folk songs 123, 139-40, 145, 152, 157, 159-60,
    166, 169, 170
foods, seasonal 122, 127-9, 131-4, 144, 152-4,
    156, 158-9, 162-3, 166-7, 169, 172, 177
fools 191-6
Frithsden 32, 153-4, 186
funerals 73-6

Gaddesden, Great and Little 17, 107, 111,
    120
Ganging Day 164-5
Garland Day 141-2
ghosts 32-3, 40, 44, 52, 61, 73-4, 79-90, 117-8,
    125-6, 144, 153, 165, 194
giants 46-50, 59, 61, 81, 119
Gilston 117
Good Friday 103, 132-3
Gooding Day 172-3
Gooseberry Pudding Sunday 153
Gosmore 166
Graveley 25, 30 (illus.), 47-8, 56, 65, 87, 104,
    144, 187

GENERAL INDEX

graves 77-87
Great Hormead 29
Great Offley 33
Grotto Day 155
Gubblecote 117
'Guisers' – see Mummers
Gustard Wood 40
Guy Fawkes Day 166-8
Gwynne, Nell 44, 85

hag-riding 95, 102 (illus.)
Haileybury 9
Hallowe'en 26, 165-6
hares 73, 111, 120
Harpenden 15, 19, 27, 67-70, 74-5, 98, 101-2, 126, 162, 172
harvest 156-61; late 161, 163
Hatching Green 118
Hatfield 14-5, 39, 44, 49, 56, 72, 89, 91, 96, 128, 141, 154, 161, 165
Hatfield House 9
hay-making 150-1
Hemel Hempstead 25, 42, 88, 170
Hertford 38, 74-5, 154, 156, 162, 171, 183
'Hertfordshire kindness' 181-2
Hertfordshire proverbs 180-2
Hertingfordbury 75, 117
Hexton 16, 28, 34, 93-4, 135, 153, 175
Hiccafrith (giant god) 47
highwaymen 40-1, 79, 84, 114, 185
hill figures 46-7
Hinxworth 88, 157
Hitchin 18-9, 26, 49, 51-2, 57, 71-2, 86, 88, 90, 115-6, 125, 134, 136-7, 144, 156, 160, 163
hoaxes 51-2, 193-6
hobby horses 59, 175-6
Hock-tide 16, 135
Hoddesdon 27, 44, 127-8, 143, 174
Holy Cross Day 162, 164
horseshoes 109
hot cross buns 132

'Ice Saints' 143
Iceni (Hiccas) 47, 86
Ickleford 93, 102
Icknield Way 34, 49, 86
illness, caused by magic 110, 114-5; cured by magic 92-102
inn sign, ghost horse 87, 90 (illus.)
iron 108-9

Jack-in-the-box 108
Jack-in-the-green 124, 140-1
Jack o'Lanterns 53, 84
Jack o'Legs, the Weston giant 47-9
James I 38-9, 91, 132, 161
John of Gaddesden 97

'Keeping Kattern' 169-70
'Keeping Warsel' 131
Kelshall 34
Kensworth 23, 118
Kimpton 95, 131, 147, 184
King's Langley 43, 134, 141-2, 175
Knebworth 28, 74, 183
Knights Templar 38, 48

Layston 24, 29
Lent customs 127-9, 130-3
Letchworth 15
Lilley 118-20
Little Munden 64, 67
London 13-14, 15, 26
London Colney 36
Long Marston 108

Magpies 62, 73
Malthus, Thomas 8-10, 12
Man-in-the-Moon 51, 53 (illus.), 106
Markyate 40, 43-4
marriage 65-73
Martineau, Harriet 9
Martinmas 168
May Day 18, 64, 136-43
Mayers' songs 138-43
Meesden 131
Meppershall 181
Mercia 14, 56
Michaelmas 104, 164-5
Middlesex 13, 14, 35, 181
Midsummer Eve 26, 64-5, 152-3
Miles's Boy 51
Minsden 29
Miracle Plays 59, 175
Moat Lady's Night 125-6
Monks' Holes 42-4
Monsters 56-7
Moon 64, 103-5
Moor Park 85-6
Morris Men 123-4, 140, 148-9
Mother Haggy 118
Mother Shipton 81
Mothering Sunday 130-1

GENERAL INDEX

Much Hadham 45, 125-6, 184
Mummers 59, 124, 173, 175-6, 179 (illus.)
Mystery Plays 58-9, 124, 148

Newnham 186
New Year's Day 122
New Year's Eve 106, 121-2, 179
nicknames: county 102, 181
    town and village 65, 182-7
Nomansland 129
Northaw 94, 104
Norton 115-6
nutting 164

Oak Apple Day 146
Old Man's Day 164
omens 26, 62-3, 73-4, 88, 95, 151
oxen 176
Oxhey 33

Palm Sunday 131
Paris, Matthew 13 (illus.), 16, 25-6, 36, 42, 46, 55-6
Pendley 52
Piers Shonks 60-1
Pirton 18, 23, 34, 88, 101, 183
plants 69, 73, 96-8, 109, 174
Plough Sunday, Monday 123-4
plum-pudding stones 31, 95, 190
ponds 28, 34, 35, 38
Pope Lady Buns 122
Potten End 105, 184, 186
Pryor family 25, 64, 67, 70-1
Puckeridge 38

Queen Hoo Hall 17-8, 44, 84, 113

Rabley Heath 111
Rainbow, Sally 114
Redbourn 22, 95, 130, 144, 187
Rhodes, Cecil 11
Rickmansworth 33, 73
Ridge 85
robbers 39-41
Robin Hood 175
Romans 34-5, 36, 37, 86
rosemary 69, 123
'rough music' 69-70
Royston 14, 39, 41, 58, 85, 91, 95, 104, 107, 129, 144, 154, 163, 187
Rye House (Hoddesdon) 44, 85

Sabbath-breaking 51, 106
St. Alban 16, 21-2, 92
St. Alban's Abbey 16, 21, 28, 38-9, 43-4, 56, 76, 88-9, 92
St. Albans (city) 16, 25-6, 36, 55, 87, 92-3, 104, 108, 111-13, 116, 118, 122, 132, 146-7, 152, 188-90
St. Amphibalus 16, 21-2
St. Andrew's Day 170
St. Blase 125
St Catherine's Day 168-70
St. Chad 93
St. Clement's Day 168
St. Dunstan 108
St. Etheldreda (Audrey) 165
St. Faith 93-4
St. George 56-9
St. Ippolytts 39
St. James's Day 155
St. John the Evangelist 93
St. Michael 163
St. Nicholas 171
St. Osyth 93
St. Paul 54
St. Paul's Walden 23, 28, 45, 74, 106, 159, 188
St. Peter's Day 129
St. Swithin's Day 154-5
St. Thomas's Day 171-2
St. Uncumber 71
St Valentine's Day 126-7
Salisbury Hall 44, 85
Sarratt 184
Sawbridgeworth 58, 82
Scott, Sir Walter 18, 44
Shaw, George Bernard 11-2
sheep-shearing 151-2
Shenley 35-6, 44
Shonks, Piers 16, 49-50, 54, 59-61, 81, 107
Shrove Tuesday 127-8
'Six Hills' 47, 104
skipping 170
'Sleeping Villages' 188
snakes 54-6
Sopwell Nunnery 44, 76, 95
souling 166
South Mimms 18, 28, 32-3, 89, 146, 176
Spinner, Jenny 74
Spring-Heeled Jack 51
springs 22, 34, 92-5
squirrels 178
Stanstead Abbots 23

GENERAL INDEX

Stevenage 15, 32, 40, 47, 79, 80-1, 104, 132-3, 154-5, 161, 170, 183
Stocking Pelham 26-7, 160
'God Stones' 95-6
stones, grow and multiply 190
stones, holed 95, 102 (illus.), 109
stones, plum-pudding 31, 95, 190
Strutt, Joseph 17-8, 44, 113-4, 180
Studham 111
Sundon 28

taboos 32, 51, 64, 106, 108, 151
tall stories 187-191
Temple Dinsley 38
Tewin 21 (illus.), 79, 84, 105-6, 113, 154, 172, 183
Theobalds 39, 91
Therfield 58, 138-9, 172-3
Thomasing 171-2
Toddington 28, 128
Totteridge 108
Tradescant, John 49
treacle mine 190
treasure, hidden 31-45, 47
trees 96
Tring 14, 52, 56-7, 81, 86, 104-6, 115, 117, 143, 145, 183, 188
Tring Station 105, 118
tunnels 31, 41-5
Turpin, Dick 40, 114
Twelfth Night 122-3
Tyttenhanger 85, 184

Uther Pendragon 16, 92

Ver, River 21-2, 42, 44, 55, 95, 111, 118
Verulamium 21-2, 34, 35-6, 42, 55, 95

Wadesmill 14, 36-8
Walkern 23-4, 106-7, 116-7, 166, 185
Wallington 46-7, 59, 74, 82, 176
Walpole, Horace 35
Walsingham, Our Lady of 92
Waltham Abbey 13-4, 23, 37
Ware 14, 16, 29, 36-7, 43, 86, 140-1, 147-8, 169, 176-7, 192-3
Wars of the Roses 87, 110-1, 112-3
wassailing 123, 131, 178
Watford 79, 80, 83, 85, 131, 141, 182
Watling Street 35
Watton-at-Stone 25, 37, 87, 144-5
weather lore 124-5, 134, 143, 149, 151, 154, 168, 171, 179
weddings 66-9
wells 16, 34, 92-4, 108
Welwyn 27, 40-1, 83, 86-7, 185
Welwyn Garden City 15
Westmill 16, 49, 181
Weston 25, 47-9, 65, 187
Wheathampstead 23, 27, 104-5, 146, 185
Whit Monday 144-5
Whitsun 144
Whitwell 19, 45, 69, 78, 82, 131, 159, 165-6, 194-5
Widford 44
wife-selling 72-3
Wigginton 87, 104, 112, 129, 151, 169, 185-6
witches 50, 64, 95, 110-20, 128, 153, 165
wizards 43, 87, 105, 110-20
woe-waters 95
wrens 178
Wymondley, Great and Little 43, 89, 181